THE ANCIENT PROBLEM WITH MEN

The prehistoric origins of patriarchy and social oppression

Bruce G

Glastonbury, Somerset

THE ANCIENT PROBLEM WITH MEN

The prehistoric origins of patriarchy and social oppression

Copyright © Bruce Garrard 2011

Published July 2011 by
Unique Publications
10 St Johns Square, Glastonbury, Somerset BA6 9LJ

Design Consultant: Finks Publishing, Aberdeenshire
www.finkspublishing.com

ISBN 978-0-9568546-0-5

All rights reserved. Except for brief quotations in critical articles or reviews, no part of this book may be reproduced in any manner without prior written permission from the publishers.

Printed in the UK by imprintdigital, Devon

Contents

Maps & Plans

Thanks are due to:
The Glastonbury men's discussion group, including Sig Lonegren, Palden Jenkins and John Cousins.
Serena Roney-Dougal, Sarah Clay, Dawn Raven Kline, John Martineau and Suzi Steer, Ramona Belcher, Gareth Mills.
Particular thanks to Miranda Montgomery for the image of the horseman used on the cover, and for the outline map which has been used in several contexts; and to Fiona Hill of Finks Publishing for the cover design and for assistance with the nuts and bolts of the publishing process.

Spelling and Dating Conventions

Published work on almost any subject concerning prehistory produces a number of anomolies regarding spelling and dating conventions, which require a brief note of explanation. The most common is the word 'artefact/artifact', either of which can be regarded as acceptable. There are also differences between English and American spelling. I have used standard English spelling throughout, though where I have quoted other writers from works published in the United States I have followed the spelling as used in the original texts.

For dating I have used 'BCE' (Before Common Era) and 'CE' (Common Era), given the partriarchal associations with the traditional 'BC' and 'AD'. Where the sense of the narrative demands it I have sometimes used so many 'years ago' (which is approximately equivalent to 'BC plus 2,000 years'). Some writers prefer to use 'BP' (Before Present) in either case. I would add that in the context of deep prehistory all dates are inevitably approximate, often rounded to the nearest 1,000 or even 10,000 years.

Introduction

Nearly 30 years ago I was destined to go to Cambridge University to read history. This would have involved returning to school for an extra term after the summer in order to sit the entrance exam - but by then I had visited Glastonbury, spent a week at the first Glastonbury festival, and my life had changed direction. I did not go to Cambridge or become an academic. I did go to a red brick University but I didn't last the course, finishing up in a caravan beside the road back in Glastonbury, then moving to south west Ireland.

Returning to England after a while, I spent ten years as a gardener, as a would-be poet and novelist, and as a political activist, before arriving in Glastonbury once again to make it my home. For the next ten years I was proprietor of the local photocopy shop, publishing booklets and pamphlets that still appear in the bibliographies of books which document the counter-culture of the 1980s, whilst also playing an active role in running the community arts centre across the road. Life was very full, and I wouldn't have had it any other way.

Nevertheless there was sometimes a thought in the back of my mind that I had missed out, that my piecemeal alternative lifestyle had cost me the security, the salary, and maybe the satisfaction of an academic career. Having written this book, I no longer feel such things; in fact, besides being glad at the way things have worked out, I am confident that my writing on a subject involving palaeo-anthropology, and the psychological effects of events in prehistory, has benefited from a life spent delving into - for instance - the hidden aspects of contem-porary life and the psychological effects of events in childhood.

Also, whilst most of my reference material has been the work of archaeologists and anthropologists, I have also looked for insights in the publications of several far less mainstream thinkers, Goddess worshippers and writers on Earth Mysteries; the sideways light which they cast on the scientifically accepted body of knowledge sometimes reveals things that are well worth seeing. The professional world, if it takes any notice at all, may be alarmed, or it may scoff at some enormous blunder I have made through lack of application to accepted conventional practice. No matter. This book contains the statement I wish to make.

The statement is that the human race and human life are not what I had been led to imagine through my twentieth century middle class upbringing. Primarily, 'cave men' were not macho brutes, more like animals than people, who needed 'civilisation' before they could learn to respect each other and their surroundings. We are still living with the myth, left over from nineteenth century imperialist pre-conceptions, that 'primitive man' was brutish, sexist and lacking in culture. The truth is quite the opposite.

Our birthright is for all of us to feel glad and proud to be human beings. And human beings go back a long way; human consciousness and human culture, in a profound sense, evolved out of the dream time, and are integral to our relationship with our ancestral heritage and with the environment. Nevertheless, the distorted and dissatisfied lives we live today - with potentially disastrous consequences for each other and for the planet - are the result of things that did not happen so very long ago, which certainly are not inevitable or irreversible. There is hope, as well as an ancient problem.

The destruction of the Goddess culture of early neolithic Europe was carried out by fiercely armed men who swept violently in from the East, on horseback, from about 4,000 BCE onwards. This is the contention of Riane Eisler, Marija Gimbutas, and the many feminists who have read their books and yearned for a world in which men do not behave in such ways. Their ideas are steadily gaining credence, although archaeologists and historians have by no means been unanimous in supporting them. What is certain is that the history of civilisation, since 4,000 BCE, is predominantly the story of violent men and their armies, power politics, imperial control and, increasingly, destruction of the environment. The yearning for something different is more than justified.

It is also true - and the evidence of archaeologists largely supports this - that before about 4,000 BCE things were generally diffferent. Not only this, but the change had much to do with a profound shift in the balance of power between women and men. There does appear to be an ancient problem with men: but not so ancient that we could describe it in any way as 'natural', or absolve individual men from dealing with their stuff. This shift was not one from rule by women to rule by men, as some have characterised it, but from a form of governance which maintained the balance between men and women to one which was out of balance. Something had happened, or some series of events had taken place, which resulted in an enormous and fundamental change in the way people behave.

For modern men, there is a tendency either to deny all this outright, or else to partake in some form of collective guilt. Neither is helpful. It needs to be said right from the outset that this change has affected everyone, both male and female, in negative and harmful ways. The problem is not entirely with men, but with people. Men may have gained some apparent advantages by way of political control, property rights and so on, but to imagine that this has made them intrinsically happier than women would be to entertain a complete illusion. Sexism - like any other oppressive attitude - harms everyone on both sides of the equation, since we all end up being (and being treated as) less than human.

This book is an investigation into where, when and how all this began. Not just sexism, but a whole range of oppressive attitudes and behaviour, arrived more or less at the same time - at least on a scale that affects the whole of society. Disruption of the balance between male and female coincided with the first real warfare in the human story, which in turn led to slavery and the beginnings of class society. I have used the term 'patriarchy' to describe the whole package. Once there was a time, which we all may yearn for, when it did not exist.

My initiation into the ancient world was reading Jean Auel's novel of neanderthal life, *The Clan of the Cave Bear.* It sparked my imagination and led me to realise that human beings have a very long and interesting prehistory. Then one day a customer in my shop started bringing in catalogues and price lists for me to photocopy, from his small book distribition business. Through him I came across a book by the strangely paradoxical writer Stan Gooch, entitled *Cities of Dreams - When Women Ruled the Earth.*

I say paradoxical because, once I had become fairly well read on the subjects he deals with, I realised that his book, though stimulating, is way off the mark in many respects (indeed, really it is as fictional as Jean Auel's work). Nevertheless, unlike so many writers, he does ask the right questions: Why have there been such huge taboos about all aspects of women's power and reproductive lives? What do we mean by 'humanity' anyway? And what did the neanderthals have to do with all this?

Gooch sets out to show that the neanderthals had a highly developed, matriarchal culture that bequeathed its religion - though not its matriarchy - to the succeeding modern human beings. There is some reason to imagine, as he asserts, that neanderthal religion may have focussed on the earth, the moon, the goddess and sex. Less plausible is his notion that the coming of the new people turned all this on its head, stole the goddess's magic and gave it to the men.

Taboos against women's power and sexuality do not date from this time: people in Europe were remarkably free from such ideas for a further 25,000 years or more. He is also wrong to imagine that neanderthal people once ruled the world, since they never inhabited the world - only Europe and western Asia. And yet, before his work is written off, another curiosity arises: it is in fact just the area of the world that the neanderthals *did* inhabit where people first developed a predisposition for art, culture, and mysticism; and that later became the home of the goddess religion, and of neolithic advances in agri-cultural techniques, which together created the first suggestion of a European 'civilisation'.

Serious exploration of these subjects began when I came across Riane Eisler's *The Chalice and the Blade*. This is the book that gave widespread currency to the idea of an ancient European 'Goddess culture', eventually brought down by invasions from sword-wielding, horse-riding warrior hordes from the east. It is a book written by a feminist and primarily intended for women; reading it as a man was what raised for me the Great Question: Why did this all happen? Where and when did it all begin? If human life was once quite different, what exactly happened to cause the change?

Eisler's book is exciting, but for me it left important questions unanswered. In describing the Old Europeans' demise, she does not explain why this came about nor what caused such a warrior culture to come into being in Asia. But by now I was on the trail, looking for clues to a greater understanding.

By chance an old copy of Friedrich Engels' *The Origins of the Family, Private Property and the State* came into my hands. I was astonished by its clarity and readability - not at all what I imagined 'Marxist' texts to be like - and by its freshness and relevance after well over a hundred years. It was a stark contrast to much of the 'official' history I had read. In particular, it helped me to the concept that herding and farming were, respectively, neolithic developments from hunting and from gathering; that humanity's ancient way of life had effectively split two ways, in Asia and Europe.

With these pegs to hang my ideas on, I started devouring whatever I could find concerning these and related subjects, on friends' bookshelves and in the local second-hand bookshop. Around the same time I took part in a course in Co-counselling (described briefly in chapter 4), which rekindled my interest in the early development of human beings in a slightly different way. If, as co-counsellors believe, humans are born potentially perfect, and only as they grow up do they learn patterns of negative and destructive behaviour, then is it not likely that this was true also for the human race as a whole?

Certainly, I noted (and this is of course still true), the world is in a mess; so full of negative and destructive patterns that the balance of life on the planet itself is threatened. Ecological destruction continues on a frightening scale. Warfare remains endemic, whilst battlefields are becoming toxic wastelands likely to be lethal for all participants. Our political and economic systems seem to have lost touch with common sense - and are quite unable to deal adequately with these problems. There seems to be something wrong with humanity itself. We are all oppressed: women, and men; workers, and all social classes, races, religions ... all the victims of internalised and inherited oppression, unconscious reactions and patterns of behaviour, which conspire together to keep us all enslaved to a system that continues the global destruction.

By whom? Or what? Where did it come from? And how did it manage to get us? Or was it always there? Is that how humans naturally are? The answer to this last question is definitely no. For several million years, hominids and early humans lived as part of a balanced eco-system, first on the sub-tropical plains of Africa, later - perhaps a million years ago - occupying a similar ecological niche on the sub-glacial plains of Asia and Europe.

My earlier interest had focussed on the origins of 'patriarchy'. I was no longer sure that this was the right word, though the problem certainly involved a shift from female-defined to male-defined society. It also involved a shift in attitude toward the natural world. It led to deforestation, territorial disputes, slavery, the Roman Empire, religious wars, the near destruction of the old pagan religions, land enclosure, the Inquisition, industrialisation, imperial conquests of America, Africa, Asia and Australia, the near destruction of traditional tribal lifestyles, the first world war, the second world war, nuclear war ... That is what I wanted to talk about - or rather, the form of consciousness that has led people down this ultimately hazardous road. If it needs a name, 'patriarchy' will do as well as any.

A few years before, my marriage had ended when my wife had left to go to Greenham Common (the Women's Peace Camp, which became an inspiration for the whole peace and anti-nuclear movement, simultaneously presenting a huge challenge to many assumptions and attitudes of traditional left-wing politics). All my own assumptions about how life was lived had been called into question. Up until then, for all my radical outlook on life, when it came to my family and close relationships I hadn't thought to question how it had been done by my parents and their generation.

That had begun to change, though my marriage hadn't survived; now I was in Glastonbury, in and out of relationships with self-empowered women, and I was still confused as to what men's place in the grand scheme of things might be. I needed to find out. Co-counselling precipitated a series of important changes in my personal life which took several years to work through. Meanwhile my thoughts on the prehistoric origins of patriarchy sat on the shelf; my research so far had produced a small booklet which hardly anyone read. Eventually, perhaps with my personal confusion better resolved, I started work on it again.

By now I had given up my High Street shop and I was working in a small office, with low overheads and time whilst 'at work' to devote to my own projects. The inspiration to return to this one came when a friend lent me a copy of Bruce Chatwin's *Songlines*, which I had somehow neglected to read ever before. Life for humans in their original 'natural habitat' became once again vibrant and real for me.

During the past ten years there have been a number of books published, all from the fringes of mainstream psychology or palaeoanthropology, each dealing with a different aspect of this subject. Together they make it clear that patriarchy (and the endless list of injustices and cruelties that have come with it), far from being natural to human beings, constitute an aberration which has only been a significant force in human society since about 4,000 BCE.

Such thinking promises to be the most significant strand of discussion in the coming years, regarding humanity's early beginnings on the African savannah, and our subsequent evolution as creatures who have the ability to destroy our own environment. This is an area in which an understanding of prehistory has an urgent relevance to the most pressing of contemporary issues.

I was invited to join a Men's Discussion Group, a bunch of us Glastonbury types dedicated to exploring ideas and theories. I discovered all sorts of new books - most importantly James DeMeo's *Saharasia* and Steve Taylor's *The Fall.* I was also introduced to Julian Jaynes' *The Origin of Consciousness in the Breakdown of the Bicameral Mind.*

With *Saharasia*, for the first time, here was a book about prehistory that both agreed with what I had read from Riane Eisler and others - and also addressed the psychological issues in a way which made sense from the Co-counselling point of view.

Julian Jaynes, though I sometimes disagreed with him profoundly, described human consciousness and its development through the growth of analog and metaphor, in a way that was revelatory. As I remember being said on one occasion, "There are two types of human being - those who can read Julian Jaynes and those who can't".

The Fall was more of a disappointment. I first thought that here was the book I wanted to write myself, already done. But this was not so. I had now looked at the question from an array of perspectives - the feminist, the Marxist, the Reichian and so on - and here was what I expected to be the closest to my own. But I found it limp and unconvincing in its 'new age' diagnosis of the need to 'transcend the ego' .

All the same, I was building up a rich library of relevant work: Richard Leakey, Marija Gimbutas, Colin Tudge, Geoffrey Ashe, Hugh Brody. I can recommend all the books in my bibliography. I hope I have done them justice in my attempt to synthesise their thinking around the core issue in the story of humankind's past: co-operation and mutual respect between men and women - and latterly, over the past few thousand years, the breakdown of their ancient balance in society. Out of this came patriarchy, along with oppressive social structures and, before long, warfare.

How and why this came about is a question which excites many people, yet academic historians and prehistorians have given it virtually no attention. This book seeks to carry the discussion forward with an exploration of human origins that looks not only at our physical evolution, but also at the economic, cultural and psychological aspects of our development. The results are both intriguing and hopeful. The world deserves better than civilised man has given it. The potential, if we succeed in turning this around, is incalculably wonderful.

Bruce Garrard, June 2011

THE ANCIENT PROBLEM WITH MEN

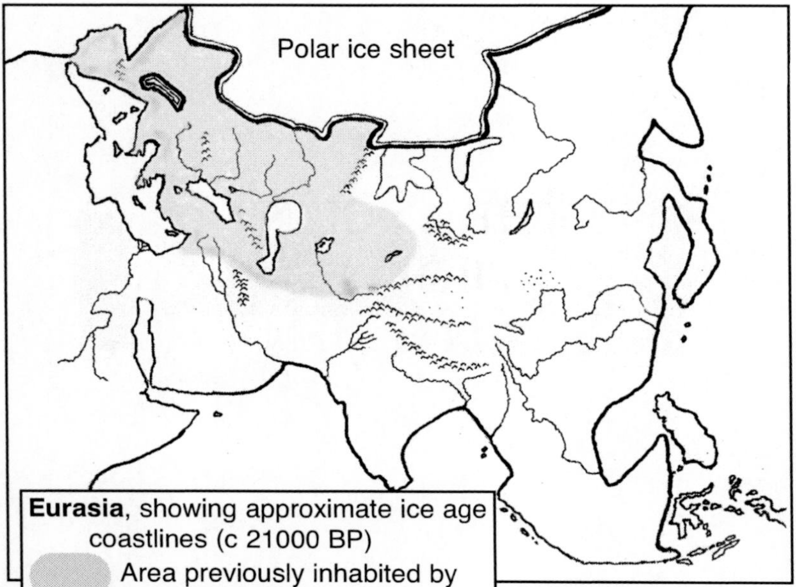

Polar ice sheet

Eurasia, showing approximate ice age coastlines (c 21000 BP)

Area previously inhabited by Neanderthals

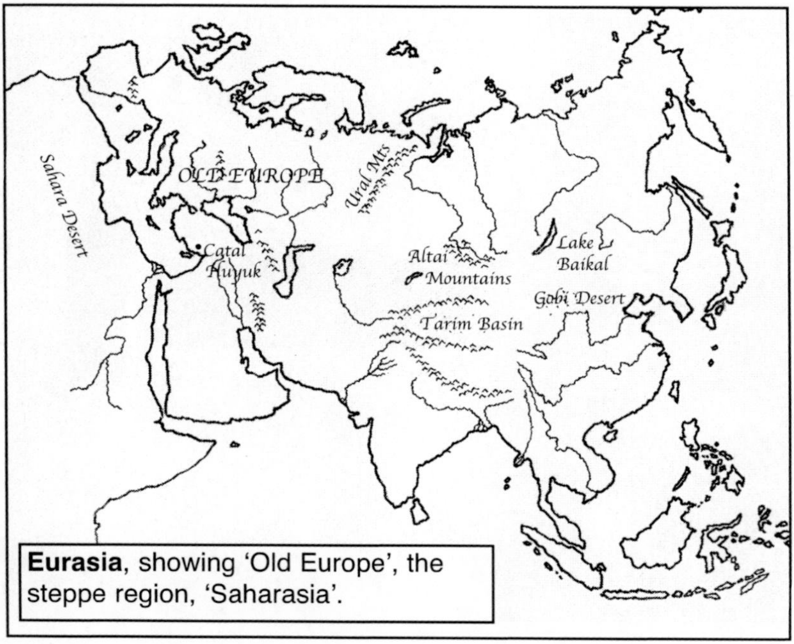

Sahara Desert

OLD EUROPE

Ural Mts

Catal Huyuk

Altai Mountains

Lake Baikal

Gobi Desert

Tarim Basin

Eurasia, showing 'Old Europe', the steppe region, 'Saharasia'.

1 'The World Defeat of the Female Sex'

Through two million years or so of human evolution, our species was defined and sustained by values which were essentially co-operative. Male and female were of equal importance and status. Violence on a scale and with the intent that could be called 'warfare' was unknown. The environment was sacred. As and when human spirituality took form as religion, that religion primarily honoured the Goddess, She who gives birth.

If these statements are controversial, then I shall provide support for them in due course; but this is my starting point. Broadly speaking, this describes human life up until 6,000 years ago.

Clearly, it is not the general condition of humanity today. History, as we have now received it, could well be described as the story of power politics and warfare. This is a very sad reflection on the behavi-our of the most intelligent creature ever to appear on Earth, but it was not always so and need not continue to be so. War is neither natural nor inevitable, but since neolithic times it has certainly been endemic. Along with slavery, territorial aggrandisement, and a cata-logue of oppressive social forms that I shall set out in more detail, warfare came as part of a package with its roots in a particular mind-set.

The Chalice and the Blade

Something had happened to cause this state of affairs, to create this oppressive mind-set; it is not the way that humans would otherwise naturally behave. This chapter's heading, 'The World Defeat of the Female Sex', comes from the nineteenth-century writer and thinker Friedrich Engels, and refers to an event that took place - or at least began - somewhere in Asia during neolithic times or earlier.

There are many ways in which male-defined values have made essential and positive contributions to human development; but first and foremost

I believe that through the defeat of the female, human life lost an essential quality and has suffered profoundly as a result ever since.

The stereotypical image of primitive man as a macho brute is far from the truth. It is certainly quite different from most hunter-gatherer societies still existing today.[101] However, until quite recently it was assumed that this aggressive approach to the planet and its inhabitants is how it always was, that life (in Thomas Hobbes' much quoted words) was for early humans 'nasty, brutish and short', and that this uncomfortable reality has only been ameliorated by the relatively recent development of 'civilisation'.

Gradually, it is now becoming clear that the truth is not just different but more or less the opposite: early humans, however hard their lives, enjoyed a high degree of co-operation with each other and harmony with their environment. This is how the human race evolved; and ironically it has only changed with the recent high degree of cultural sophistication.

As the renowned palaeontologist Richard Leakey has said, "The notion that *homo sapiens* is driven to violent conflict by biological imperative is itself a cultural manifestation." People do not like to feel responsible for the violence and destruction that the human race has visited upon the world, and "to suggest that warfare is common in human history because of our genetic heritage absolves us from guilt."[102] However, as several recent writers have pointed out, before the neolithic - and particularly prior to about 4000 BCE - "the lack of evidence for warfare is striking":

> Overviews of the archaeological evidence in different parts of the world ... [show] no evidence of war during all of the Upper Palaeoloithic period (40,000 to 10,000 BCE). There are no signs of violent death, no signs of damage or disruption by warfare, and although many other artefacts have been found, including massive numbers of tools and pots, there is a complete absence of weapons. As [R.B.] Ferguson points out, 'it is difficult to understand how war could have been common earlier in each area and remain so invisible'. Archaeologists have discovered over 300 cave 'art galleries' dating from the Palaeolithic era, not one of which contains depictions of warfare, weapons or warriors.[103]

The state of mind that has produced aggression as a way of life, mass warfare, slavery and, as time has gone by, imperialism, environmental degradation and even the possibility of planetary destruction, appears to have arrived along with civilisation. Not as the automatic result of civilisation, nor as the inevitable outcome of developing technologies such as iron smelting; but all the same as a relatively recent phenomenon and one that is in fact dramatically at variance with 'human nature'.

Human behaviour, as evidenced during the long millennia of our species' evolution in its natural environment, has since been through a radical change. By the time that the classical cultures of the Mediterranean and the Middle East became established, something had happened which profoundly affected the course of their development.

Civilisation is in any case hard to define. Technically, it means a culture based on living in cities, whilst cities are supposedly conurbations that include cathedrals. So-called 'civilised' attitudes and values, however, clearly do not depend on any such strict definition. What we call 'civil' behaviour is as likely to be found amongst naked tropical islanders as  anywhere else; and the assumption that 'civilised' equals 'advanced' and therefore 'good' is now (not before time) being seriously challenged.

Richard Rudgley, author of *Lost Civilisations of the Stone Age*, also challenges the related assumption that civilisation 'sprang out of nowhere' 5,000 years ago. He documents the gradual development of writing, science and medicine, pottery and metallurgy, indeed every aspect of technology and culture that together make up what we call civilised life. He traces their origins back to the early neolithic, and in some cases further still:

> I believe that civilisations existed before the historical era and that our current view of what is and is not civilisation needs to be radically revised. The growing realisation that our current understanding of the meaning of civilisation is deficient may be perceived as a sign of progress.[104]

We are certainly happy to accept that civilisation began well before the first cathedrals, and that the level of technological achievement that might qualify as civilised is a subjective quality rather than objectively quantifiable.

So, when writers and archaeologists such as Riane Eisler and Marija Gimbutas present the culture of neolithic south-east Europe as the early beginnings of civilisation, we do at least know what they mean. And it is this, specifically Riane Eisler's *The Chalice and the Blade*, which is the beginning of my particular exploration. Looking at life on the cusp between pre-history and history, she presents a picture which is at once radical, hopeful, and undeniably plausible:

> The Goddess-centred art we have been examining, with its strik-ing absence of images of male domination or warfare, seems to have reflected a social order in which women, first as heads of clans and priestesses and later on in other important roles, played a central part, and in which both men and women worked together in equal partnership for the common good. If there was here no glorification of wrathful male deities or rulers carrying thunderbolts or arms, or of great conquerors dragging abject slaves about in chains, it is not unreasonable to infer it was because there were no counterparts for those images in real life. And if the central religious image was a woman giving birth and not, as in our time, a man dying on a cross, it would not be unreasonable to infer that life and the love of life - rather than death and the fear of death - were dominant in society as well as art.[105]

Riane Eisler's work is, however, both an inspiration and a conundrum. 'The Chalice' is the goddess-worshipping, matrifocal culture of Old Europe. Based largely on the research of Marija Gimbutas, she offers a view that is rapidly changing the way we think about the origins of civilisation: it does not depend on kings, armies, or the concentration of power and wealth.

A sophisticated level of culture, including the first known towns, was created by people with a religion centred on the Goddess and an understanding of human genesis based on the lineage from mother to daughter; people whose society did not promote or idealise the role of the warrior, and whose social structure appears to have been remarkably egalitarian. This way of life had its roots in Ice Age Europe, tens of thousands of years ago. It found its final and most impressive expression in Minoan Crete, between about 3000 and 1500 BCE.

'The Blade' is the god-worshipping, patriarchal culture that emerged from the Asian steppes, waged war on the goddess-worshippers of old Europe, and ultimately led to the emergence and growth in importance of the warrior class of Greece and Rome. Apart from ancient Crete, the development of the classical world essentially came to be based on male rather than female values, paternal rather than maternal rights and powers, gods rather than goddesses. This happened - or at least the process began - in response to warlike invasions from the east. It is hardly surprising that, in the view of feminist readers of Eisler and Gimbutas, this is where it all went wrong.

But then there is the conundrum. The symbolism of chalice and blade is the symbolism of balance, of creative union, of human wholeness. To portray these events of our immediate pre-history in terms of right and wrong, of patriarchal 'baddies' and goddess-worshipping 'goodies', is simplistic. It misses the most important point - that both protagonists in this, the first real warfare in the human story, were equally part of the human race and equally part of the same evolutionary process - and it leaves more questions unanswered than answered.

One thing is certainly true: this shift came about, at least on a scale that noticeably affected the world as a whole, no more than about 6,000 years ago. The human story (depending on how you define 'human') has already lasted 35,000, 100,000 to 200,000, maybe two million years. The human race has evolved through an enormous span of time as, we could say, 'the children of the Great Mother'. It is only during a relatively small proportion of humanity's existence that the prevailing world-view has been anything other than this. Patriarchy is a modern aberration rather than the natural order of things.

I use the word 'patriarchy' in its literal sense, meaning 'rule by men', but also as a kind of shorthand for a particular cultural bias that arrived in Europe and the Mediterranean world at the formative stage of classical civilisation. It is characterised by an imbalance of human values and modes of behaviour that, with the growth and development of technology, has gradually become a greater and indeed all-pervasive threat to life. It has spread more and more rapidly, until it now covers nearly the entire world - a world that faces enormous problems and dangers as a result.

As Anne Baring and Jules Cashford point out in *The Myth of the Goddess*, this is a situation "unique to the history of the planet", arising from nature (associated with the female) being regarded as "the chaotic force to be mastered". The God, in the name of Spirit, "took the role of conquering or ordering nature", and everything in due course has become polarised.[106] This issue lies behind all the other key issues of our time.

The question most needing an answer is the one that Riane Eisler barely looks at: where, and why, did such a world-view come about?

Where did this change begin?

Male and female roles in palaeolithic society

The relationship between the sexes inevitably has much to do with the evolution of human consciousness; and looking at this, what emerges is curious. I have found no writer who gives the same date to both the emergence of human consciousness and the onset of patriarchy. Nevertheless there are three answers which consistently came up in response to each: 4000 BCE (or thereabouts), 35,000 years ago (or so), and around two million years ago.

It is still the generally held view of the archaeological establishment that human consciousness arrived late, most likely at the time that Cro-Magnon (anatomically modern) man became fully established in Europe, around 35,000 years ago. In Victorian times it was thought that people only became truly human much more recently than that - at the 'dawn of civilisation', prior to the development of cultural hegemony and imperial power by the classical Greeks and Romans. And thirdly, there is a growing body of thought which says that human consciousness has resided on this planet for perhaps two million years, associated with the growing cranial capacity of the later hominids or, according to the more esoteric versions, in 'modern' human bodies (possibly of extra-terrestrial origin).

When it comes to the question of when patriarchy began, the answers are turned on their heads: it is the newer strands of thinking, notably (but by no means only) feminism, that consider it to be a relatively modern aberration, a pattern that has only been in place since about 4000 BCE. The traditional (i.e. eighteenth and nineteenth century) view is that male dominance, through greater physical strength together with self-centred motivation, have been 'normal' since our earliest sub-human beginnings.

This latter version, the 'Thomas Hobbes' version which was happily espoused during the period of European imperialism, surely says more about the times that produced and promoted it than the times it claims to portray. Nevertheless the modern scientific establishment, silently neutral on the subject, leaves public awareness at the mercy of suppositions based on this crude racial stereotype.

The reality of palaeolithic life, though it must certainly have been harsh in many ways, equally must have been different from this stereotype. The words 'savage' and 'barbarian' have come to mean brutish and unpleasant, but they were used by nineteeenth-century sociologists and palaeontologists to define specific stages in the development of society, approximately equivalent to 'palaeolithic' and 'neolithic'. They originally carried no emotional load. The idea that ancient peoples were 'primitives' and 'savages' and somehow less human than ourselves is received by us, it must be said, as the result of imperialist propaganda. Germaine Greer, writing of Australia in *The Guardian*, summed up the story that has been true in different versions right around the world:

> Ever since white men set foot in Australia more than 200 years ago, they have persecuted, harassed, tormented and tyrannised the people they found there. The more cold-blooded decided that the most humane way of dealing with a galaxy of peoples who would never be able to adapt to the 'whitefella' regime was to eliminate them as quickly as possible, so they shot and poisoned them. Others believed that they owed it to their God to rescue the benighted savage, strip him of his pagan culture, clothe his nakedness, and teach him the value of work. Leaving the original inhabitants alone was never an option; learning from them was beyond any notion of what was right and proper. As far as the pink people were concerned, black Australians were primitive peoples, survivors from the stone age in a land that time forgot.[107]

We would do best to let any such ways of thinking go completely; the 'whitefella' would perhaps do well to note that "in terms of hierarchy, agricultural and industrial societies resemble those of chimpanzees more than those of human foragers." [108] The notion that men have 'naturally' dominated and brutalised women is a part of this corrupted modern outlook. The reality, for those who have been termed 'primal peoples', was and is altogether more interesting.

Early human societies, however simple they may have looked in material terms, have always (in any absolute sense) been remarkably sophisticated. The balance and interplay between male and female has always been central to this. Amongst hunter-gatherers, certainly since the advent of modern human beings and quite probably since *homo erectus* first traced the outlines of recognisably human existence nearly two million years ago, there has been a more-or-less universal division of labour. Men are responsible for hunting, women are responsible for gathering. The reasons for this are perfectly rational:

> Big-game hunting might often have resulted in death or injury to the hunter rather than the hunted. In small societies, such as these early human groups and present-day forager societies, every unexpected death is a serious blow to the viability of the community, particularly the death of women of child-bearing age. Mobility would also have been more important in hunting large game: the hunter would have to move rapidly and quietly, with hands free to throw a spear or shoot an arrow. It would not be possible to do this while carrying a bag or basket of gathered food, nor a young child, who might cause additional hazard by making a noise at a crucial moment. Thus gathering and hunting became incompatible as simultaneous occupations; pregnant women and those carrying very small infants would have found hunting difficult, though gathering is quite easily combined with looking after young children.[109]

Furthermore, in ancient, palaeolithic societies, the impossibility of identifying male parentage with certainty meant that ancestry was traced through the female line; matrilineal reckoning was once universal. Humans also spend far longer in the care of their mothers than other species, so that from the earliest times the natural focus for social groupings would have been the mother.[110] Female control of domestic affairs was the norm, and generally, women were undoubtedly held in high respect. As Friedrich Engels put it:

> One of the most absurd notions taken over from eighteenth century enlightenment is that in the beginning of society woman was the slave of man. Among all savages and all barbarians ... the position of women is not only free, but honourable.[111]

The same is still true amongst those people who have retained the ancient way of life. In the words of a contemporary (male) writer:

> I have lived and worked in hunter-gatherer societies as a man; this places a limitation on what I have experienced. I learned far less about gathering than about hunting. I saw far less in the domestic sphere than I did on the land. In reality, the economic, social and political lives of the peoples I knew were as dependent on women as on men.[112]

There is little reason to doubt that in society as lived through the countless formative millennia of humanity's pre-history, the roles of men and women - and their relative social status - were equally important. The male role of hunting (and he was the most dangerous predator on the prairie) gave humans their position in the ecosystem and defined the species from an external point of view. The female role of social organisation meant survival in times of adversity, and defined human beings from a subjective, behavioural point of view.

The combination of the two was what made our species so successful. When they got out of balance it led to the first full-scale wars.

Originally (and I shall return to the early development of social groupings in some detail) human society was matrilineal. Women were thus the instruments of regeneration. The Great Mother was the source of all life and all nourishment. 'Fatherhood' and 'property' were not concepts which people understood in the way that we do today. The natural environment was common and people had a relationship with it, based on the wisdom of countless generations. Ancient, time-honoured and (in their context) irrefutable laws would have been woven around this reality. The fact is, nearly everyone knows who their mother is, nearly every mother knows who her children are. This is universally and inevitably true; but in early societies with very different social and family

groupings, it was not necessarily true that everyone, or even anyone, knew who their father was. Tracing maternal lineage was the only practical way, was in all probability embedded in religion, and until relatively recently it is hard to imagine this even being questioned.

In hunter-gatherer societies generally, and in ancient societies in particular, inheritance would have been quite a different matter from the complex legal framework we have today. 'Owning' natural resources would not have been possible. At the same time, it is human to have personal objects, personal clothes and personal tools. These would have been passed on from mother to daughter, along with the skills associated with their use; and indeed from father-figure to young man, though it was often the son of his sister or other close female relation rather than his own son. Nevertheless certain things - particularly things related to hunting - were passed down from male to male.

Malidoma Patrice Somé, in *Ritual - power, healing and community*, describes growing up in a small village in West Africa. With no pretensions to historical accuracy, he describes the traditional way of life amongst the Dagara people as having existed and held good for "tens of thousands of years." [113] He is probably right. They do a bit of farming, and also some hunting. What they have in the way of post- Stone Age technology they could mostly manage without. The roles of men and women are separate and defined, but the question of which is most important does not even arise. Each is important and the community could not exist without both. Each shares in child care, and each can aspire to become elders and shamans. Shamanic ritual is central to every aspect of their lives. Besides any purely spiritual benefits, this gives them social cohesion and psychological health. This must be the natural spirituality of all peoples who live - as hunter-gatherers do particularly - entirely within their environment. Equality and interdependence between the sexes is an important and basic part of such a lifestyle.

Climate change and cultural change

By the mid-twentieth century, only a small minority of people still lived this way; but originally it had been universal. Replacing these 'natural' values with what we must term 'modern' or 'patriarchal' ones, unravelling social forms that had evolved with human beings themselves, and which had served people well since time immemorial, has of course been neither quick nor simple. However, around 4000 BCE something occurred that gave this unravelling a profound new significance and, possibly, irreversible consequences. As Steve Taylor puts it in *The Fall*:

> For the last 6,000 years, human beings have been suffering from a kind of collective psychosis. For almost all of recorded history human beings have been - at least to some degree - insane. This seems incredible because we have come to accept the con-sequences of our insanity as normal. If madness is everywhere, nobody knows what sane, healthy and rational behaviour is any more. The most absurd and obscene practices become traditions, and are seen as natural.[114]

These 'obscene practices' include all manner of oppression, mutilation and killing, as well as abuse of the natural world. Social systems grew up based on endemic feelings of guilt and fear, resulting in an endless catalogue of cruelty, injustice and struggles for power. And even for those who do manage to succeed in the sense of gaining wealth and status, "they never find contentment and fulfilment anyway, but remain constantly dissatisfied." And all this, which has come to be seen as the result of 'human nature', is actually quite the opposite.

For such deep-seated change and loss of rationality to come about, clearly there must have been a sustained - indeed relentless - series of events and circumstances which can be seen as their cause. This was in fact the case. The process appears to have originated in Asia, at first as a localised variation of human culture which for a long time had little significance for the rest of the world. Its growth, however, came as part of neolithic developments in technology and economic life, and then became crucially magnified with a subsequent radical shift in climate.

The key factor was the increasing desiccation of vast areas of central Asia as well as north Africa and the Middle East - a subject that is dealt with in detail by James DeMeo in *Saharasia*, and to which I shall return at some length. Climate is a dynamic process, not a fixed reality, and its shifting nature inevitably has huge effects on life and evolution - including of course human life and evolution. The environmental and climatic shifts that have followed on from the last ice age are particularly relevant in this respect, and DeMeo has extensively studied the desertification of the region he calls 'Saharasia', which began around 6,000 years ago.

He identifies this as having a profound, indeed traumatic, effect on the human population, and as being the most significant historical cause of psychological 'armoring'. This is a Reichian term meaning the rigid, defensive or aggressive mind-set resulting from prolonged or acute experience of emotional distress. The region that is the subject of DeMeo's study is enormous - the central (and at that time most heavily populated) band of the world's largest land mass. Widespread desiccation and the resulting human trauma led in turn to a change from what he terms 'matrist' to 'patrist' social forms and governance, essentially the same in meaning as the shift from 'natural' values to 'patriarchal', referred to above. This was no less than a behavioural cataclysm:

> Human armoring, with its violent antisocial and institutionalized patristic cultural conditions, appeared and persisted on planet Earth for the first time about 4000-3500 BCE, in Saharasia, after it dried up. Armored patrism gradually intensified thereafter among peoples living in Saharasia, who later migrated or invaded away from the Saharasian core to affect other borderland regions, and a few regions at very great distances. These findings, derived from history, archaeology, and relatively contemporary anthropological and climatic sources, strongly support or even prove ... that the innate, or primary, core components of human behaviour are unarmored and matrist in character.[115]

Amongst the reams of evidence presented in support of these propositions - itself sometimes distressing in its relentless and detailed accounts of invasions, cruelty and human mistreatment of other human beings - is a summary of a study of rock art discovered in the Sahara. This appears particularly instructive, documenting changes in human modes of thinking in this region from about 8000 through to about 2000 BCE.

The earliest artwork depicted mainly animal life, and "reveals the smooth and steady hand of a skilled and artistically sensitive indi-vidual". This is believed to reflect the hunter-gatherer phase, when the Sahara was sufficiently well watered to be described as "a lush grassland savannah."

Later phases (c 5000 BCE) reflect changes towards nomadic herding, with the artwork emphasising cattle, and also people with dress and hair styles which suggest influence from central and southern Asia. Rock art from the final phase (c 2000 BCE), which occurred after the Sahara had begun drying up, "reflects a definite change of style and subject matter". Whereas the earlier hunter-gatherer and pastoralist stages display "a certain gentle and bold quality", the arid phase rock art "is not really art at all, but merely graffito, or haphazard scrawlings ... The principal subject matter ... [was] organized warfare, armed males, battles, death, chariots, horses and camels."[116]

These changes - reflecting the shift from 'matrist' to 'patrist' society - had already been established across the Middle East by 3000 BCE, and may have appeared in the Far East earlier than that. Their sporadic spread across Africa appear to have come a bit later. They also reached Europe in due course, though here something different had happened by then.

During mesolithic and early neolithic times, the European environment had shifted in a different way from that of 'Saharasia'. Following the end of the ice age, the climate did not dry out but gradually became both warmer and wetter. Hunting grounds shifted north, and revitalised forests covered the plains of central Europe. The process is well described by Paul Mellars in his essay on *The Upper Palaeolithic Revolution,*[117] in which he points out that a forest environment can support only 20-30% of the huntable game available on the open plains. Most of the biomass is solid wood. If the ancient ecological balance was to be maintained, the human population would need to be reduced to a third or less of what it had been. In any previous age, the human population in this region would have dwindled; indeed at first it did. Forest was one of the last habitats to which human beings adapted, even in the tropics. So the periodic reforestation of the open plains in Europe had, in inter-glacial times, meant a periodic reduction in the numbers of humans.

By the end of the last ice age, Europe had a long-established population of fully modern human beings. The preceding neanderthal population had gone and the moderns, as much as 30,000 years ago, were already establishing homesteads. Both their social organisation and their technological inventiveness represented a new level of complexity, a qualitative difference compared to any other hominid. This was of course why they had succeeded in gradually displacing their neanderthal predecessors - even though the neanderthals were better *physically* adapted to the European climate.

Around 10,000 years ago, after the ice had receded and as the forests reasserted themselves, this new breed of people adopted a novel and apparently stunningly successful response to the challenge: clearing part of the forest, collecting useful plants and animals, keeping them in the clearing and breeding them there. People were no longer a part of the natural self-regulating eco-system. From that time on they began to set themselves apart from it.

Neolithic developments: farming and herding

Neolithic farming had spread through Europe from the Middle East. It created some notable ecological disasters, partly because before the creation of the iron plough heavy soils could not be cultivated - which often meant that farmers used upland areas where clearing the trees led to rapid soil erosion. But it meant that humans prospered and multiplied where before they would have diminished.

Colin Tudge's short but invaluable essay on the 'real' origins of farming, *Neanderthals, Bandits and Farmers* (which I have shamelessly adapted for the title of the next chapter) makes a good case for farming being a reluctant choice rather than a great leap forward. It was based on existing techniques and technologies for seed collection and propogation, food storage and so on - originally developed to enhance the lives of hunter-gatherers - put together into what is now perceived as the single activity of farming. Tudge highlights post-glacial rises in sea levels, leading to denser human population with diminished access to natural food resources, as the driving force behind this change. There were other environmental challenges, including (as already noted) desiccation in Asia and forestation of the open plains in Europe.

European society was now based on increasingly sophisticated homesteads, villages and small towns - but the old ways of religion nevertheless continued and developed. This was the Goddess culture of Old Europe, epitomised by Catal Huyuk in Turkey but taking hold across a very wide area of Asia Minor, southern Europe and the Balkans. The impressive style and nature of Old European culture is gradually becoming generally appreciated; for instance a Reuters report of 2007 describes a "Neolithic settlement in a valley nestled between rivers, mountains and forests in what is now southern Serbia" as "a metropolis with a great degree of sophistication and a taste for art and fashion."

The site, which was part of the Vinca culture, "Europe's biggest prehistoric civilization", revealed "an advanced division of labor and organization. Houses had stoves, there were special holes for trash, and the dead were buried in a tidy necropolis. People slept on wooden mats and fur, made clothes of wool, flax and leather, and kept animals." According to the evidence of figurines, "young women were beautifully dressed, like today's girls in short tops and mini skirts, and wore bracelets around their arms." The findings also suggested that the community was especially fond of children, with artifacts including "toys such as animals and rattles of clay, and small, clumsily crafted pots apparently made by children at playtime." [118]

According to Riane Eisler, quoting Marija Gimbutas:

> The inhabitants of south eastern Europe seven thousand years ago were hardly primitive villagers. During two millennia of agricultural stability their material welfare had been persistently improved by the increasingly efficient exploitation of the fertile river valleys. Wheat, barley, vetch, peas, and other legumes were cultivated, and all the domesticated animals present in the Balkans today, except for the horse, were bred. Pottery technology and bone- and stone-working techniques had advanced, and copper metallurgy was introduced into east central Europe by 5,500 BC ... These early Europeans developed a complex social organisation involving craft specialisation. They created complex religious and governmental institutions. They used metals such as copper and gold for ornaments and tools. They even evolved what appears to be a rudimentary script.[119]

The 'rudimentary script', which pre-dates the strictly 'historical' period, is seen by some scholars as bona fide writing, and has interesting similarities to several acknowledged written languages; though unlike Sumerian, for instance, it appears to have been based on the need to describe and record ritual - and related spiritual concepts - rather than accountancy and bureacratic control.[120] The complex social institutions, as we shall see below when we look at the extremely ancient and basic form of organisation into clans, have their roots immeasurably further back in time than 5500 BCE. And they were not peculiar to Europe: essentially the same social forms were also used in America, where they probably arrived originally from Asia. In effect, they were universal.

Technological and economic development, however, had begun to diverge. In much of Asia, where the plains were not covered with trees after the ice age, people developed quite differently but to a similar level of technology. They continued to live off the herds as they always had done, but through domestication of the horse they became herders rather than hunters. Ultimately the herds themselves were domesticated and moved with the people, rather than people following the herds.

During the neolithic there were many different Asian steppe dwellers, variously identified as 'Indo-Europeans', 'Scythians', 'Mongols' and so on. Those which Gimbutas and Eisler focus on are known as the 'Kurgan' people, so named after the 'kurgans', or large stone burial mounds, which were built so as to mark key points in the landscape. Their culture was as sophisticated as the early farmers and settlers, but their values were quite different. To quote from an essay written by Andrew Sharratt for *The Oxford Illustrated Prehistory of Europe*:

> These peoples began to develop a distinctive culture, ornamenting their simple pottery with cord impressions ... and creating distinctive forms of objects such as zoomorphic sceptres and small pottery braziers, which could have been used for burning cannabis ... Where they came into contact with the substantial houses and settlements of cultivators, at the western end of the Pontic steppes, these hunting and herding groups began to build circular burial monuments - giving focal points to an existence otherwise spent in mobile tents. This way of life expanded westward into some of the areas formerly controlled by horticulturalists, and some groups even seem to have penetrated in small numbers along the Danube into Romania, where their typical burials and artifacts occur. This incursion had its impact on neighbouring farmers, for later Copper Age settlements were now commonly located on promontories and hilltops, and on the eastern

> frontier of farming near Kiev ... there were massive agglomerated villages of up to 200 houses, grouped together for defence.[121]

No doubt the steppe dwellers too felt threatened, with their lands encroached upon not only by settlers from the west but also by desert from the east. As noted above, during the period from about 4000 BCE onwards climate change was seriously depleting regions inhabited by enormous numbers of people in central Asia. This approximately coincides with the 'Kurgan invasons', which Riane Eisler characterised as 'The Blade'. The Kurgans' 'distinctive culture' had become patriarchal, its values male-defined. The gods that these people brought with them were quite different from the Goddess who still persisted in Europe. The marked divergence between these two cultures created a dynamic that has had a critical effect on the subsequent development of humankind.

The difference between these neolithic developments in farming and herding was crucial: the hunter-gatherer way of life - *the* way of human life up until this time - had split two ways. Farming was a development based the gathering side of ancient hunter-gatherer society. Indeed, so long as it remained at the level of horticulture rather than plough-based agriculture, it was in effect a more efficient means of gathering foodstuffs and was still largely carried out by women. By contrast, neolithic culture on the central Asian steppes developed from hunting. The new currency, cattle, accrued to the former hunters, and the balance of power and social status tipped towards the men.

Family and clan

To explain the immense implications of these changes more fully, and to give some substance to the social context in which they took place, I shall make a brief detour to look at the work of the nineteenth-century American sociologist Lewis H. Morgan.[122] He undertook what still stands as one of the most fruitful investigations into prehistoric social organisation, studying tribal societies whose customs included relics of extremely ancient systems of what he termed 'consanguinity'.

Morgan's work forms the basis of Friedrich Engels' *The Origins of the Family, Private Property and The State.*[123] He had noticed, first among the Iroquois, that the formal use of terms such as 'father', 'grandmother', 'brother' and so on, whilst they were very precise, did not match the people's actual understanding of these relationships. This phenom-enon was seen by the European outsider simply as polite or respectful forms of address, but Morgan lived with the Iroquois for a number of years and realised that such usage, describing the most intimate of relationships, was very exact and by no means arbitrary. Then, having established that this was common, in its detail, right across North America, he persuaded the United States government to assist him in his researches.

This took the form of tables and lists of questions, sent out to all parts of the world, and from the replies he discovered that exactly the same formal terms of address were in use amongst numerous peoples in Asia and, in modified forms, in Africa and Australia. Furthermore, in Hawaii and some Australasian islands he discovered a form of 'group marriage', still existing but just dying out, which corresponded exactly to the formal system of consanguinity still in use in America and elsewhere - a system in which to all intents and purposes an individual did have many 'fathers', and a whole generation of 'brothers'.[124] Morgan concluded that the formal systems outlive the actual changes in social development, and thereby survive as relics of more primitive forms of family organisation. Amongst the Hawaiians he also noted a system of consanguinity which implied a still more primitive, now extinct, form of group marriage.[125]

To summarise his overall findings: at first, people lived in groups, had children in common, and had no concepts such as 'cousins' or 'nephews and nieces'. The evolution of social organisation, and ultimately the family, has been a very gradual process which has progressively reduced the likelihood of in-breeding. The earliest form of the family was one in which all members of the group from the same generation formed a group marriage.

Later this developed into the 'Punaluan' family ('Punalua' were 'intimate friends', a group of unrelated men who were jointly married to a group of sisters and female cousins) - still a group marriage, but one in which sexual intercourse was forbidden between blood relations; and then, as a further development from this, the clan - originally a group of sisters, brothers, cousins and their children, all descended from one common ancestral mother. Parents would come together as a loose 'Pairing Family' of indefinite duration, the father always coming from outside the clan of the mother.[126]

A tribe, therefore, necessarily included at least two clans. It was, and still is, a common misunderstanding amongst modern Europeans to confuse the two terms, which are not synonymous. The tribe, and within it the increasingly complex clan system, remained a stronger, more basic institution than the family until at least neolithic times. It was still an important concept of social organisation well into the period of Greek and Roman civilisation.

A tribe was generally located in a particular geographical area; it was the political unit that related to the outside world. Tribal leaders would have included men, and may have been predominantly men. The clan was a kinship network and the basis of female power within the tribe. It was not a separate or geographical subdivision of the tribe. Nevertheless the clan's good functioning assumed geographical proximity and continuity of place. The same clan could sometimes exist across several related tribes, and each tribe included several clans. The clan had evolved to avoid children being born to close blood relations, so marriage within the clan was not permitted.

Customs of inheritance kept any property within the clan, which was matrilineal; ancestry was traced through the female line, and the clans traced their common ancestry back to one of the tribe's deities or totems. Social and religious forms of huge diversity grew up around the world, almost universally within the context of the clan. Clan leaders could be both men and women, though responsibility for internal and domestic matters fell to the women.[127]

The clan system had evolved and become established over a huge period of time. Morgan and Engels referred to it by its Graeco-Roman equivalent, the 'gens' (which in turn is related etymologically to the English word 'kin', as well as the Spanish 'la gente', the people). It had certain features of social organisation which they found to be common, more or less right across the world:[128]

- The clan assembly of all male and female adults in council elected its leaders, and had the power to depose them.
- The tribal council consisted of the clan leaders, and was the final arbiter in all matters.
- No person was permitted to marry within the clan. Originally the

clans were matri-local, so that a man would leave his clan and marry into another.
- The property of deceased persons always remained within the clan.
- Members of a clan owed each other help and protection, and especially assistance in avenging any injury by outsiders.
- Membership of the clan meant the use of particular names or classes of names, which of themselves conferred clan rights.
- The clan could adopt strangers and thereby adopt them into the tribe.
- The clan was responsible for and carried out religious rites, and had a common burial place.

This, apparently only with differences in matters of detail rather than substance, is how people had ordered their affairs for maybe a hundred thousand years or more - to all intents and purposes an endless aeon. It was people living by such a constitution who had very gradually come to inhabit every accessible corner of the world. Note that hunter-gatherers do not generally move from one area to another. As a rule, though their lifestyle is mobile, they remain within their ancestral hunting ranges, where they come to know every rock and every landmark by name and by tradition.

The process of moving into new and previously uninhabited regions I will explore, since over time it clearly happened on a very wide scale; but the intimate relationship between people and the land which they inhabited was absolutely basic to human life. It was in fact a key factor in the development of human consciousness itself. The clan system, with its totems and symbology, would have woven together more than just the people: it would have been intimately bound up in their relationship with the land in which they lived and which had sustained them for thousands and thousands of years.

Relevant information that has come to light since Engels was writing has tended to add detail to his description of clan organisation, rather than suggesting any contradictory picture. For instance, the 'Circle of Law' is presented by the native American writer Hyenemosts Storm as a "powerful system of organization for the Self Government of a Community of People." [129] Based on the concept of the Medicine Wheel and widely used in different variations across north America, it leaves our modern systems of democratic government looking crude by comparison.

The tribal council consisted of sixteen representative chiefs, eight men and eight women, each with their allotted place in the Wheel and each with a very specific function representing a particular constituency within the tribe (hunters and workers, pregnant women and nursing mothers, elders, and so on). These representatives each considered the matter to be discussed in a specific order, in a semi-ritualised manner. This ensured not only that everyone was heard, but also that this occurred according to a pre-exisitng pattern and in a way designed to maximise the chances of a satisfactory conclusion.

Such a system, with its built-in checks and balances, would have taken many generations to evolve. Each community developed its own version, each retaining its own "freedom and inherent ability for renewal" that "reflected the ever-changing circumstances and needs of many different peoples." The basic structural elements of the Circle as a Medicine Wheel would nevertheless remain the same. Storm reports a detailed example from the Blue Sky Crees, who in the mid-nineteenth century formed a community of some two thousand people spread amongst eleven camps.

Their Council met each year, as the focal point of a wider Gathering in which many people took part in dancing, trading, exchanging news and so on. The Council meeting took place in a wide circle formed by eight brightly coloured tipis, where there was room for five hundred people to follow the proceedings if they wished. It was people such as these, and not the slave-owning elite of Athens, who first created democracy.

Property and wealth

Eventually such systems of social organisation, which had provided the basic structure and stability of human society for millennia, came to be questioned and finally broken down. This did not happen easily or quickly, since the change was so fundamental. Engels traced the process through the history of classical Greece and Rome; indeed, classical history largely consists of the stormy transition from the ancient way of life based on tribe and clan, to something akin to the modern state - with the associated shift in the balance of power from women to men.[130]

Morgan had witnessed and recorded the same shift taking place amongst North American tribes, who were perhaps under similar pressures to those experienced by neolithic peoples in south east Europe.

The Kurgan people of the steppes had clearly made such a change, inviting Gods to overthrow the Goddess, re-creating their society as male-defined rather than female-defined. They in turn may have taken the ideas from somewhere further east and from further back in time. One thing does seem clear: bound up with all this was the new importance of property.

It was, according to Engels, "the formation of herds of considerable size that led to the differentiation of the Aryans and Semites from the mass of barbarians," [131] and this was a development from the traditionally male role of hunting. In a primitive society where 'property' is limited to personal effects, it was in Engels' terms "the man's part to obtain food, and the instruments of labour for the purpose." He owned the 'instruments of labour', his personal tools and hunting equipment. If husband and wife separated, he took them with him - just as she retained her household gear. So, with the creation of herds, "according to the social custom of the time, the man was also the owner of the new source of subsistence, the cattle, and later of the new instruments of labour, the slaves." [132]

It was Engels' assumption that it was the man's part to obtain "food". However, modern studies have shown without any doubt that hunter-gatherers find a lot of their staple foods from plants (sometimes as much as 80 per cent of a community's diet), which were almost always collected by women.[133]

Hunting large animals may have created excitement, status and huge feasts; and may have meant the difference between survival and otherwise in a harsh winter; but day-to-day food gathering was mostly done by the women. So, if husband and wife separated, along with her household gear she would have taken her gathering baskets and digging sticks. Engels did not have the benefit of such archaeological research, and he did not himself assert that European agriculture naturally incorporated and continued the rule of 'mother-right' - nevertheless he did note that in the beginnings of agriculture "among almost all peoples the cultivated land was tilled collectively by the gens [clan]."[134] What follows is broadly in line with his thinking.

When people started growing their crops, marking out land, and producing more food than they needed for their own immediate requirements, in this way property began to accumulate and before long wealth began to develop. In Europe, because this process was female-defined and the accoutrements of tilling the soil generally fell within what was traditionally regarded as the female province, and because descent and inheritance had always been reckoned through the female line anyway, changes in neolithic society did not at first disrupt the old social order, time-honoured structures of tribe and clan, or the old religion.

By contrast, on the steppes the new wealth accrued to the men. Cattle became the first currency.[135] But the old ways prevented men from passing it on to their sons. It was here that the reckoning of descent through the female line and the matrilineal law of inheritance were first challenged - and overthrown.

To summarise: such property as there was, if it had to do with hunting, remained with the men, and if it had to with gathering it remained with the women. When gathering developed into farming, then the property involved could become substantial, and would have been passed down the female line. This was the economic basis of the Goddess-based, matrifocal society of ancient Europe. When hunting developed into herding, again the property involved could be substantial - though the 'male line' was not so clear. It was in this context that the rule of the ancient Goddess was challenged, and with it the matrilineal ordering of society.

> The 'savage' warrior and hunter had been content to take second place in the house, after the woman; the 'gentler' shepherd, in the arrogance of his wealth, pushed himself forward into the first place and the woman down into the second. And she could not complain. The division of labour within the family ... had remained the same; and yet now it turned the previous domestic relation upside down.[136]

This change was both deeply radical and potentially dangerous. In both models - the European and the Asian, the agrarian and the pastoral - it changed in ways, two different ways, each crucially out of balance, and each inherently disrupting the ancient stability of human life by upsetting the social and economic equality between men and women. This is not necessarily a bad thing: life did not have to become unstable, but rather dynamic - the result, quite literally, was history. A new synthesis and balance could have been achieved, perhaps still will. But the Asian, pastoral model challenged the old ways in a particularly fundamental manner.

As I shall explore in more detail, this was given additional impetus from the fifth millenium BCE by climate change and desertification. Patriarchy was created, and behaviour that could be objectively described as irrational, even pathological, came to be regarded as normal. The process then spread much like a disease, from one culture to another and through one century after another, until today it has covered the globe. The imbalance is now nearly total and its effects are becoming closer and closer to terminal. The challenge we meet in the twenty-first century is immense.

Matrism and patrism

If we are to meet this challenge successfully, it is important for us to know that the task is achievable; that we are not doomed by some inevitable flaw in 'human nature' to end in self-destruction. We are not - and it is by no means only feminists, Marxists, native American activists and the like who have said so. As the eminent palaeontologist Richard Leakey clearly stated:

> Aggression is something we are taught, not an indelible part of human nature ... We are fundamentally sociable and co-operative creatures - this is how we have survived up to now and it is the key to our future.[137]

Humans evolved co-operating with one another and living in harmony with the environment. During the twentieth century the opposite viewpoint has been put, forcefully and at length, notably by the South African Professor Raymond Dart. Dart made some extremely important fossil discoveries in southern Africa, but interpreted the effects of geological processes (which had broken or stained black the early hominid skeletons) as the effects of violence or cannibalistic cooking fires, and declared both the history and prehistory of the human race to be hopelessly drenched in blood.

He has since been proven wrong,[138] but the enthusiasm with which his ideas were taken up and passed into common currency is alarming - and the assumptions that go with it are still in evidence: a recent article in my local newspaper bewailed the competitiveness and aggression of men, who have "evolved not a jot since their days in the cave."[139]

In fact, co-operation, particularly amongst men, was a hallmark of

early humanity; and co-operation has increased in importance and complexity as the species has become more sophisticated and complex. Thus the establishment, for example, of trading networks, and the social interactions and social obligations that went with them, grew incrementally in scale and contributed to people's increasing ability to cope with adverse conditions. Co-operation, rather than competition, was what marked out humans as the fittest to survive.[140]

This basic reality held true right through to the beginnings of civilisation, and there is no inherent reason why it should have changed at all. Nevertheless, change it did; and the fact that successive modern writers have felt it necessary to remind us of our essentially co-operative nature is a measure of how lost and hidden it has become. The patriachal revolution that started amongst pastoralist herders in central Asia has become established through most of the world, with economic and moral pressures completing the changes originally enforced by military conquest. Trade of course has continued, as has sufficient co-operation to maintain (mostly) the framework of society, but its nature has profoundly changed: competition and coercion have come to be regarded as the norm.

If we assume an event, or series of events, before which people retained their fundamental co-operative nature, and since which the rule has been competition and coercion, then the difference is so marked, and so widespread, that human culture can be divided into two basic types. As Riane Eisler describes it:

> Underlying the great surface diversity of human culture are two basic models of society. The first, which I call the *dominator* model, is ... the *ranking* of one half of humanity over another. The second, in which social relations are primarily based on the principle of *linking* rather than ranking, may best be described as the *partnership* model ... The original direction in the mainstream of our cultural evolution was toward partnership but ... following a period of chaos and almost total cultural disruption, there occurred a fundamental social shift.[141]

The dominator model - following Gimbutas - she calls 'androcracy', and the partnership model 'gylany'. These terms she equates to 'patrism' and 'matrism', which were originally coined in 1954 by Gordon Rattray Taylor in his book *Sex in History.*[142] Matrism ('mother-identification') refers to a form of governance based on the maternal pattern of nurturing all for the benefit of both the whole and each individual within it. Patrism ('father-identification') refers to a form of governance based on the concentration of power and resources in the hands of, and for the benefit of, a single ruler or a small elite group. Matrism means "the responsibility of motherhood rather than the exaction of obedience to a male-dominant elite through force or the fear of force."[143]

Eisler's is the feminist perspective. Engels' Marxist analysis sees the same changes that she examines as the beginning of class society, with the creation of slavery. He is also clear that "within the home, the woman takes the part of the proletariat."

James DeMeo disagrees with neither, but offers a more straightforwardly scientific presentation. Using G.R.Taylor's terminology, he lists dozens of cultural traits and classifies them as 'matrist' or 'patrist'. Many of these traits have a direct bearing on the social relationships and power balance between men and women. There is a remarkable - though intuitively predictable - level of correlation between them:

> Regions with a high degree of patrism are defined by the presence of: Female Premarital Sex Taboo, Segregation of Adolescent Boys, Male Genital Mutilations, High Bride Price, Polygamous Family Organization, Patrilocal Family Residence, Patrilineal Descent (without Cognatic Kin Groups), Patrilineal Land Inheritance, Patrilineal Movable Property Inheritance, High God, Class Stratification, Caste Stratification, and Slavery. Regions possessing few of these traits were defined as predominantly matrist in character.[144]

He then plots his findings onto a map of the world, demonstrating that highly 'patrist' cultures predominate in and near the region of 'Saharasia', whilst surviving 'matrist' cultures (or those that had survived up until the period 1840-1960) are all some distance away. The results are convincing and, together with the matrist/patrist terminology, have been followed by more recent writers. Steve Taylor, for example, presents yet another perspective on the same subject and pattern of events, which might be described as 'New Age spirituality', in his book *The Fall.* He points out that "perhaps inevitably, anthropologists have attempted to explain these correlations in terms of each other", but finds such explanations unconvincing:

> Explaining male domination in terms of war only begs the question of why these societies have a high level of warfare - and explaining the existence of high gods in terms of social stratification only begs the question of why the social stratification exists ... Ultimately, the reason why these characteristics can't be explained in terms of one another is the same reason why they all exist in the first place: because they are all effects of the same event.[145]

Whilst having a different perspective on the precise nature of this event, Taylor follows DeMeo in describing its effects - the replacement of matrist cultures with patrist. However, we still have a confusion of terminology here. 'Matrist' and 'Patrist' are not, for instance, synonymous with 'Matriarchy' and 'Patriarchy' (though they are sometimes taken to be so). A benign patriarchy, for instance, could possibly qualify as matrist; and an oppressive matriarchy as patrist. Neither do they equate with 'right brain' and 'left brain' dominance in the prevailing social paradigm, though these all of course are related. Other terms include 'matrifocal' and 'patrifocal', and (as above) 'gylany' and 'androcracy'. They have all been invented by different authors to represent slightly different shades of meaning. To clarify:

'Matrist' and 'Patrist' seem to be gaining currency, and it would be helpful to encourage them to become common usage - we need terms in general use if the concept is to become widely understood. 'Matrist' is particularly helpful, since the word 'matriarchy' is often used erroneously or misleadingly (due to a patriarchal assumption that it is the opposite and the inevitable alternative to patriarchy), and is best avoided. 'Patriarchy', however, is an accurate description of nearly all societies that historically have followed what Eisler describes as the 'dominator' model. It is also a widely used term, and understood in precisely that way. This does not make the word 'patrist' redundant, though it has a narrower meaning, as defined by DeMeo's tables of cultural traits.

I shall therefore continue to use 'patriarchy' when referring to male-dominated society as has been the general pattern during the past few thousand years; and 'patrist' when referring more specifically to the oppressive features of that society. I shall avoid the word 'matriarchy' altogether, and instead use 'matrist' - meaning a social order free from patriarchal oppression, and in which women play a full and acknowledged part in the life of their communities and wider societies.

The writers quoted above would all broadly agree that matrism and the associated 'partnership' model were the original direction in the mainstream of our species' cultural evolution. From this starting point, I shall now return to my original question of 'where did patriarchy begin' - looking first at Europe, where the essentially matrist Goddess culture survived longest and came to its fullest expression in the neolithic (chapters 2 and 3); and then at Asia, where the radical shift to patrist values and patriarchal social forms first came about (chapters 5 and 6).

Chapter 4 explores the development of human consciousness and, in particular, the psychological background to this huge shift in human thinking and behaviour. (Some readers may prefer to skip this and refer back to it as required). Chapter 7 provides a summary of all this, presented as one chronological narrative.

2 Europe (1): Neanderthals, Hunter-Gatherers and Farmers

These days, following several centuries of European empires and with maps of the Earth showing the Greenwich Meridian passing through London, it is easy to think of Europe as the centre of the world. In palaeolithic times it was the furthest periphery. Africa is the leading candidate for the title of 'cradle of humanity': current scientific thinking describes the prehistory of human population movements as first *homo erectus* and then *homo sapiens* (about a million years later) emerging from Africa, gradually migrating into southern Asia and then across the rest of the planet. Australia was inhabited by modern human beings before Europe.

By 'Europe', in a palaeolithic context, essentially I mean the western part of the Euro-Asian land mass, which was home in ancient times to 'neanderthal man', *homo sapiens neanderthalis*. Around 40,000 years ago, into the neanderthals' world came a new kind of people. These were the anatomically modern human beings, *homo sapiens sapiens*, known as 'Cro-Magnon man' after the place where their fossilised remains were first discovered.

Aurignacians and Gravettians

Where the new people came from, in an immediate sense, has not been fully established; palaeo-anthropologist Clive Gamble suggests the middle east or south east Asia. An essay by linguist and pre-historian Alexei Panshin favours the middle east, though this was not a 'migration' in the sense that we understand it today - by the time the moderns arrived in central Europe their ancestors had left the Persian Gulf no less than 10,000 years earlier:

> One of the most important centres of expansion lay in western Iran, betweeen the Persian Gulf and the Caspian Sea, where the people of

> the Zagros Mountains had developed a set of radically new stoneworking techniques ... Both archeology and genetics suggest that about 50,000 years ago, people from that area began moving out in all directions ... [including] up the Tigris and Euphrates rivers into what is now Kurdistan ... [From there] some went west to Anatolia (modern Turkey), and it was their Aurignacian culture that reached Europe soon after 40,000 BP. Others went north into the Caucasus mountains, where they replaced the local Neanderthals after 35,000 BP. [201]

The Aurignacian culture, "the first true European Upper Palaeolithic industry", was originally discovered in a cave near the French town of Aurignac. It is distinguished by several innovations in flint knapping techniques, with tools made of long slender blades rather than flakes. The culture is also noted for its artistic output including body ornamentation; "ivory artifacts, jewellery, ornaments, and art in the form of figurines and engravings are also now found within well-organized campsites." [202]

This, however, is by no means the whole story of modern human beings and their arrival in Europe. Two different cultural traditions came from the east - the Aurignacian, which arrived shortly after 40,000 years ago, and the Gravettian, which began displacing the Aurignacian about 29,000 years ago:

> The DNA evidence ... seems to reflect both an earlier migration, which accounts for about 10% of contemporary European mtDNA, and a later one which accounts for another 65%. It is widely accepted that these two components can be plausibly associated with the Aurignacian and the Gravettian.[203]

There is also tentative linguistic evidence to support the same proposal. Most writers on the subject have tended to lump these together into one, to talk about the 'Cro-Magnons' as if they were one homogeneous group, and the ensuing cultural "great leap forward" as if it was the work of a mere moment. In fact it took 5,000 to 10,000 years - equivalent to the span from neolithic times to the present - during which period there were major shifts in both population and climate. Whilst the first wave of newcomers were developing artistic skills such as had not been seen before, further east the other 'modern' people were achieving technological expertise of a new order.

The Gravettian culture was developed by the big game hunters in the river Don region around 33,000 years ago. Besides highly sophisticated stoneworking techniques and the use of spear throwers, they invented animal traps and fish traps, and they may have used darts to kill birds and small mammals. They are also known for their large skin tents, which were constructed over frameworks of mammoth bones. This was a culture geared to survival in the cold northern climate, and the key to its success was its many advances in domestic technology:

> Their greatest achievement was in their use of more humble materials. They were trapping hares and foxes for their skins, which they sewed into warm clothing by means of ivory needles with precisely drilled eyes. By 27,000 BP, or perhaps earlier, they were making nets and baskets and even weaving cloth on some form of loom. This more intensive use of resources led to a rapid increase in the average lifespan and a dramatic growth in population. It also created the potential for large numbers of people to live together on an extended basis, and by shortly after 30,000 BP some ... were dwelling in semi-permanent villages.[204]

At this time Europe was still dominated by the Aurignacian culture, which had arrived from the middle east some five thousand years earlier. Given the Aurignacians' artistic achievements, "it is tempting to speculate that there may have been mutually beneficial interaction between the two peoples." However:

> After 30,000 BP the climate began falling back into extreme Ice Age conditions which the Aurignacians were not prepared to withstand. The last of the Neanderthals died off at this time, and it has recently been suggested that the Aurignacians would have perished as well if the Gravettians had not come to their rescue.[205]

So it was these people, the second wave of 'moderns' to arrive in Europe, who were best adapted socially and technically to life in glacial conditions

- and who were ultimately to inherit the continent from their neanderthal predecessors. The Gravettians are named after a cave at La Gravette in the Dordogne, notable for its associations with carved 'Venus' figurines (a tradition that spanned several cultures). Amongst their technical achievements, as noted above, are as many which relate to clothing and the home as to hunting and fishing. Weaving and sewing, in particular, were notable advances as compared to the Aurignacians.

Moving into new areas, where the climate was exceptionally harsh, would have required substantial planning. Traditional mobile and temporary living structures, for instance, would have been worth reviewing, particularly by those who were going to be giving birth to children. Adequate clothing - and the space both to make it and to store spare supplies - may have been the difference between life and death in some situations.

Food supplies would have been sufficient only in the warmer portion of the year, and storage would have been of greatly enhanced importance. Collecting plant foods in sufficient quantities may even have been impossible without encouraging their propogation and growth in places easier to access than their natural wild habitat. All these considerations point towards the establishment of homesteads - which is in fact what began to happen. They are also considerations that would have fallen primarily to the women.

This is a major area of speculation, but one that I believe fits well with the known and established facts: the manner of the Gravettians' entry into Europe was crucially influenced by the thinking and the priorities of the women. This, I would suggest, is the earliest beginning of the European Goddess culture.

The mammoth hunting trails

The neanderthals and their territory had long been known about, and their hunting grounds were very well stocked. In a world where the primary economic activity is hunting, where subsistence is the norm and 'wealth' not much more than a measure of one's relative comfort in winter, the nearest equivalent to a modern gold mine or oil well was a good hunting ground. And the richest, most prestigious hunting - at least in the northern hemisphere - was for mammoth. The neanderthals were rich.

Yet whether or not these riches were the goal of the moderns in coming to Europe, it is not true (as many have imagined, including famously H.G.Wells) that the neanderthal population suffered as the native Americans did much more recently when their territory was invaded by Europeans. The process of modern humans replacing neanderthals in Europe was in fact long and protracted - creating conditions affecting human development that were significantly different from those in Asia or other parts of the world.

The Gravettians in particular were hunters of mammoth, the largest animal in the world. One dead mammoth could provide food, clothing, shelter, fuel and many other useful things - including much-valued ivory - for a great many people.[206] Mammoths lived in the northern periglacial regions, and had no other predators; but were hunted by people in larger and larger numbers. By the time the glaciers withdrew and their natural habitat diminished, they were already dying out, perhaps becoming the stuff of legend. Much later, American mammoths, along with many other species of 'mega-fauna', appear to have been hunted to extinction as part of what has become known as the 'Pleistocene Overkill':

> Very soon after human beings entered these [newly colonised] land masses for the first time, the local fauna began to go extinct, with the biggest animals suffering most. Thus Australia lost thirteen genera of large animals after 40,000 years ago ... In the centuries after the first human beings arrived in North America around 13,000 years ago, no fewer than thirty-three out of thirty-five genera of large mammals disappeared. These included camels, giant beavers, peccaries (American pigs), several types of elephant including mammoths and mastodonts, giant ground sloths and the glyptodont - which was an armadillo the size of a bread van ... South America's large animals suffered even more a couple of millennia later as the human beings spread down from the north.[207]

This 'blitzkrieg' model of colonisation has certainly been called into question; it was not the equivalent of the massacre of American buffaloes in the nineteenth century. The results of tracing extinctions in Australia "show conclusively that the megafauna was not wiped out across Australia at the same time but persisted in some regions for at least 20,000 years after humans first arrived." [208] Neverthless, these animals were particularly vulnerable to humans because they had evolved without predators, and successfully hunting large animals produced the palaeolithic equivalent of prosperity.

In Europe, this same breed of people had probably first arrived along the mammoth-hunting trails. They were socially and technologically developed such that they could adapt to inhabiting northern latitudes, which the neanderthals only moved into as hunting grounds during fine weather.[209] So the 'moderns' were able to colonise these regions by default, since no-one else was living there. The change from neanderthals to moderns took place during the build-up towards the most recent ice age, and the last remnant neanderthal population existed in southern France and Spain.

There has been long and exhaustive discussion as to whether neanderthals were a different race or a different species from modern humans, whether or not they were ancestral to modern humans, and how they compared to their successors in terms of culture and technology. There is a growing consensus that they were 'human' in a very real sense, but that they were replaced by the moderns rather than being ancestral to them. The key factor in the moderns' relative success is that they had far larger and more effective social networks - so much so that this in itself is an important reason to believe that moderns replaced neanderthals rather than evolving from them. The crucial survival value of wider social networks is described by Clive Gamble:

> Alliances between individuals and groups provide the struts in a social framework along which individuals can move in search of alternative resources should theirs fail. Among modern fisher-hunter-gatherers such partnerships based on exchange, marriage and family extend over huge areas. They involve time being set aside for visiting, and competitions such as song contests and poetry recitals ...
>
> Story tellings not only confer prestige on an individual but also serve as a repository of knowledge about how to cope with periodic subsistence crises. Where long term survival information is coded in

> such oral traditions it is common to find it sanctified and linked to ritual performances. Unlike ordinary storytelling this leads to accurate repetition so that the vital information is not lost or embellished by the present generation. Periodic crises in the Arctic may not always happen in an individual's lifetime, but on a longer timescale they certainly will ... Obtaining, updating, and preserving such knowledge thus involves complex and time consuming social practices understood to be indispensable for long term survival.[210]

Both the moderns and the neanderthals, so far as we can tell, lived in small groups, but the moderns' kin-relationships and trading connections were far better developed over a far larger geographical area. Clive Gamble and Christopher Stringer, in their book *In Search of the Neanderthals*, suggest this meant that individual neanderthals related to a 'breeding population' of no more than 175-500, with little or no contact beyond their localised range. The moderns, by contrast, had established connections over distances which were relatively huge,[211] and this would have been a crucial factor for survival during times of severe weather or natural disaster.

These two types of humans had evolved separately, and in very different environments, for hundreds of thousands of years. They had already co-existed - and had undoubtedly known about each other - for an enormous length of time; for far longer, in fact, than the time which has since elapsed from when the neanderthals became extinct. For much of this time their tool technology - and, by inference, their lifestyles - were the same or very similar.

The two populations occupied the same ecological niche, and there is nothing to suggest that they were antagonistic to each other - rather that each had maintained a respectful distance. Eventually Europe was colonised by moderns, but even then the neanderthals continued to live alongside them, or adjacent to them, for thousands of years.

Nevertheless gradually, and perhaps inevitably, the moderns replaced their predecessors right across the continent. Stringer and Gamble do not see this as any kind of violent replacement; rather they cite a computer-simulated model produced by Ezra Zubrow, an anthropologist from the State University of New York. He shows that a modest difference in subsistence skills - amounting to about a two per cent margin in mortality per generation - could have resulted in neanderthal extinction within a thousand years.[212]

In fact it took far longer, and this extended period of co-habitation would surely have been important. It meant that the development of modern human beings, at least in this respect, was different from their development in any other part of the world. Interchange between the two types of human - on a level of knowledge, skills and culture, as well as quite probably genetic - was a unique occurrence, with profound consequences which are only now being fully examined and considered.

The legacy of the neanderthals

Neanderthals were a cold-adapted species, having evolved in peri-glacial Europe some 200,000 years ago. They had come into existence as part of their landscape, which they had then inhabited for far longer than any modern human population has ever inhabited any environment at all. Their relationship with this environment must have been more intimate, their knowledge of it more comprehensive, than anything we can now imagine. And we can only guess at how their brains, larger than ours but differently configured, functioned - for instance - in terms of memory and dreaming.

As 'modern' a writer as Chris Stringer can say that the neanderthals had no real art or culture, and therefore no real humanity. But now we have reports in the press of a neanderthal flute,[213] carved out of a bear bone 45,000 years ago. And whoever made that flute surely already knew how to make one out of softer material like wood or reed, and was certainly part of a tradition that already knew how to make music. How old is music? Archaeology can most likely never tell us.

No one has ever examined a neanderthal brain, but what can be inferred from the size and shape of their brain cases, and from what we know about modern human brain function, leads to some tentative but interesting conclusions. A simplistic way of describing the difference could be to say that the moderns had a highly developed brain for dealing with the practical side of life, and the neanderthals with dreams and intuition. Both would have had each of course, but with the balance reversed.

This would have given the neanderthals as much potential for the artistic and magical side of their existence as modern people have for developing their technical expertise. We could imagine the neanderthals being highly advanced compared, for instance, to Australian aboriginals and their understanding of the dream time, or the Tibetans and their explorations into other realms of consciousness; and that these areas of expertise were important and valuable to them.

On a purely practical level, neanderthals developed in an environment where they had to cope with long, dark winters when there was little opportunity for going outside their cave and its immediate environs. An active dream life and the creative use of the imagination and inner visualisation would have been entirely functional, perhaps even necessary for their psychological survival. How they expressed themselves we do not know; we do not know if they could sing, though they could play music, and almost certainly danced. They may have told stories and immersed themselves in mythology, but they definitely never wrote books. The new people, by contrast, had the ability to make carvings, paint pictures, do intricate bead work and inscribe meaningful shapes on pieces of bone - but before their arrival in Europe, though their history was already very long, they had scarcely done so.

The taller, more 'gracile' Cro-Magnons had evolved in the tropics, and had adapted to deal with an environment where the dangers came from competitors and predators far more than from meteorological causes. They were quick-witted and resourceful, and ultimately more successful; but the neanderthals, when it came to knowing how to survive and live well in this particular region of the world, must have had something to offer. Their relationship with the landscape and climate of Europe was immemorially ancient: they were shaped by it. Whether by conscious design or unconscious example, over the generations they must have passed on some of this knowledge.

Archaeology can, of course, tell us little as to how the populations of neanderthals and moderns related to each other during the protracted period in which they shared the European land-mass. It does suggest that the later neanderthals learned some techniques for making stone tools and building shelters from their Cro-Magnon contemporaries, particularly through the apparently hybrid 'Chatelperronian' technology, which for many years was regarded as a mystery:

> Discovered in western France, it is a curious mixture of the typical Neanderthal flake technology and the modern human blade technology, including bone and ivory objects, and was therefore considered an intermediate technology by people in evolutionary transition between Neanderthals and modern humans ... [The] discovery of the two Neanderthal individuals with the Chatelperronian assemblage at the St Cesaire rock shelter in western France effectively finished that idea. Neanderthals, it seems, had adopted some of the tool-making techniques of the newcomers to their land.[214]

However, archaeology cannot answer the critical question: did the two populations regard *each other* as people? Certainly most modern scholars avoid any assertion that modern humans are biologically superior to neanderthals,[215] and the possibilities are huge:

> In an area as large as Europe, with its varied environments and over a timespan of perhaps 10 millennia, many different kinds of interaction could have occurred (and probably did occur), ranging from avoidance to tolerance to interbreeding, and from conflict and economic competition to friendship and an exchange of ideas. As Paul Graves has suggested, if the Cro-Magnons passed on some of their technological innovations to the Neanderthals, perhaps the Neanderthals reciprocated by sharing their long experience of dealing with the Ice Age environments of Europe.[216]

There is growing archaeological and genetic evidence, though still inconclusive, that there was at least some interbreeding. There is also the surprising fact that Cro-Magnons were taller and more 'gracile' than modern-day Europeans, suggesting some racial inter-mixture since. A recent New Scientist article goes so far as to say that "a broad consensus seems to be emerging about our ancestry, and it includes interbreeding as an important element".

Imagine a modern eskimo, and a tropical African. The eskimo is comparatively short and stocky, a racial development which makes him better able to retain body heat, which has come about in response to life in the cold northern climate. The African is taller and more slender, more suited to a hot tropical climate.[217] The process of differentiation has been going on for 100,000 years and the racial differences are marked, but the two are most certainly still members of the same species. Now imagine a similar parallel process taking place, separately in glacial Europe and tropical Africa, but over a period of a million years or so. The resulting differences, between neanderthal and Cro-Magnon, are very great: but are they enough to result in two separate species, or are the differences still merely racial?

Geneticists at the Max Planck Institute in Leipzig have now succeeded in unravelling the neanderthals' genetic code, and have discovered that they were "more similar to modern humans than previously thought." In particular, "Neanderthals shared with modern humans a variant in a gene known as FOX P2, known to play a key role in the development of speech." [218]

Recent DNA research in the United States has further suggested that the two were in fact part of the same species - and that modern humans did in fact inherit a gene, as the result of cross-breeding with neanderthals, which has been important in the development of 'cognisance'. American geneticist Bruce Lahn has shown that:

> One variant of [the neurological gene] *microcephalin* appeared about 40,000 years ago and has since swept through the population, propelled by the power of natural selection. The new variant is found in 70 per cent of living people ... The obvious interpretation is that the new version arose 40,000 years ago via a chance mutation ... [but] on the basis of sequence differences between the old and new versions of the gene, [Lahn] concluded that the two are so different that they must have diverged at least 1 million years ago ... "These dates roughly correspond to human [sic] -Neanderthal divergence 1 million years ago, and the time when they coexisted in Europe 40,000 years ago" ... If Lahn is right, a gene potentially underpinning the power of the modern human brain originally arose in Neanderthals.[219]

The 'great leap forward'

Their interaction certainly had an effect - perhaps a profound effect - on the future development of humans and their culture, primarily in Europe. It was here that material culture took enormous steps forward, in particular with the 'venus' figurines and the cave art of southern France. The latter were such vast and mystical masterpieces that some commentators regarded everything that went before as being less than truly human.

Right across Europe and into Asia, what took place has been described as "the first great flowering of human arts and culture", when sculpture, symbolic religion and abstract thought began to make their mark in the archaeological record:

> The first people that really seem to impress the palaeo-anthroplogists are those of the late Palaeolithic, of around 40,000 years ago. These people apparently started to innovate. They began producing a greater range of tools and refining the designs, and they began serious cave painting, which quickly reached a very high standard. This seems to represent a shift in consciousness - deliberate innovation, and not just a tendency to do whatever was done by the generation before. And ... the first bona fide farmers - or at least proto-farmers, appeared at this time too.[220]

It is also from here on, and in this region, that the first human habitations appear that are "structural campsites with storage pits and base camps (which are properly called villages)", along with an increase in the extent of trade. "The distance over which raw materials - now including shells and lumps of fossil resin - were transported was much greater." [221] The increase in scale was dramatic:

> Middle Palaeolithic raw materials generally came from within a radius of 50 km (31 miles) ... In early Upper Palaeolithic Europe, distinctive chocolate-coloured, high quality flint was transported from quarry sites in the Holy Cross Mountains of Poland over distances of up to 400 km (250 miles).[222]

The raw materials used to make ornaments travelled greater distances still; whilst relative uniformity of style - in tool making and in artistic expression - covered enormous areas and suggests a system of social networking that represents a qualitative step forward compared to any earlier peoples. It is surely significant that it was also at this time, due to the increase in life expectancy associated with advances in domestic skills and technology, that it first became normal for children to grow up with living grandparents as well as parents.

Stringer and Gamble conclude that "the huge changes in behaviour that took place in the early Upper Palaeolithic resemble the flick of a switch and *not* the slow upwards movement of a symbolic dimmer." [223] In other words there was an abrupt shift from 'ancient' to 'modern' human beings.

Others stress that this was the culmination of a long period of preparation, so that "as far as human evolution is concerned, the Upper Palaeolithic is less significant than the appearance of Middle Stone Age tools in Africa around 250,000 years ago," [224] whilst modern humans' blade technology "appears first in Africa, a little less than 100,000 years ago," [225] and some see the Upper Palaeolithic as "merely a regional phenomenon". All the same - whether it represents the culmination of a long period of development, or a sudden change - its importance as a new chapter in the human story is not disputed.

"Human anatomy has not changed over the past 100,000 years in any way that suggests a sudden leap in mental capacity"; nevertheless "a spectacular flowering occurs in human behaviour in the period between 50,000 and 30,000 years ago." [226] This has even been described as the "magic moment in evolution" [227] when we suddenly became human after millions of years of evolutionary struggle. As palaeo-anthropologist Jared Diamond has characterised it:

> As recently as 35,000 years ago, Europe was still occupied by neanderthals, primitive beings for whom art and progress scarcely existed. Then there was an abrupt change. Anatomically modern people appeared in Europe, and suddenly so did sculpture, musical instruments, lamps, trade and innovations. Within a few thousand years neanderthals were gone. Insofar as there is any single moment when we could be said to have become human, it was at the time of this great leap forward 35,000 years ago.[228]

No one seems to give any credit for this phenomenon to the neanderthal people who had been displaced and (to some unknown extent) absorbed by modern humans. In fact what went before was the separate evolution and development of two different types of human beings.

It is here worth noting once again that there are two essential components to art: imagination and execution. Modern humans had long possessed the technical proficiency to create artistic output, but had seemingly rarely bothered to do so. Neanderthals had the ability to make music and, we can well imagine, to fill the long dark winters with song, stories and imaginative visualisation - but had apparently never carved a carving or painted a picture. After their meeting, there was art, and something resembling modern culture. Is it inconceivable that this came about *as a result of* their meeting, and perhaps their inter-breeding?

It does in fact seem likely that whilst the Cro-Magnons represented the 'cutting edge' of human evolution, the strand of consciousness that had evolved amongst the neanderthals was catalytic. What can be proposed is that something happened, a connection between the two peoples was made, and it had far-reaching consequences.

We do not know the nature of the connection, or how close it was. We do not know for sure whether a trace of neanderthal blood still flows in modern veins. If it does, we carry the genetic potential for neanderthal consciousness; and this could be important, in a world where technical expertise has become overbearingly dominant, and where imagination and intuition have been banished to the margins.

Although we are here considering enormous spans of time on the basis of relatively few firmly established facts, there are more than enough indications that there is an important connection between the interaction of neanderthals and moderns, the subsequent 'great leap forward', and the ensuing developments right down to the emergence of the Goddess culture of early neolithic Europe. It is also worth examining the possibility that parallel cultural developments in central Asia, though significantly different, also had their origins back in palaeolithic times when 'modern' human culture was first taking shape in a recognisable form.

Before looking further at these connections and differences, it would be useful to get a clearer picture of the nature of ancient human society generally, and the overall context within which all this took place.

Hunter-gatherer society and the primary relationship with the land

The human story that culminated in modern people arriving in Europe and developing culture such as is still recognisable today, is enormously long, comprising the periods known as the 'Lower' and 'Middle Palaeolithic'. Following on from their arrival, we have the 'Upper Palaeolithic' and the displacement of 'ancient' people with 'modern'.

The dynamics of population movements in these distant times were undoubtedly quite different from those recorded by history, and particularly from those carried out by farming cultures. These dynamics help to explain why it was that in Europe, by neolithic times, there was a distinctive Goddess culture - and why this contrasted with the neolithic culture in Asia.

It has been generally assumed that ancient cultures and societies can be described as 'hunter-gatherers'. There has been considerable debate as to how far back this was so: Richard Leakey is convincing in his argument, based on the archaeological reconstruction of an East African campsite at least 1.5 million years old, that this was true for *homo erectus.*[229] He presents hunting and gathering as being the hallmark of human life, the crucial difference as compared to pre-human hominids.

Some would say that humanity arrived earlier, with *homo habilis*, the first of the *homo* lineage and the makers of 'Oldowan' tools in East Africa up to 2.5 million years ago.[230] Bruce Chatwin described meeting Professor Yves Coppens, "one of the most lucid minds in the fossil man business," who lined up a series of 'endocasts' - imprints from the inside of fossilised skulls - so that various hominid brains could be compared:

> The moment he passed from *australopithecus* to man [*homo habilis*], I had a sense of something startling and new. Not only does the brain increase in size (by almost half), but also in shape. The parietal and temporal regions - the seats of sensory intelligence and learning - are transformed and become far more complex. Broca's Area, a region known to be inseparable from speech co-ordination, makes its first appearance. The membranes thicken. The synapses multiply: as do the veins and arteries which irrigate the brain with blood. Inside the mouth, too, there are major architectural changes, especially in the aveolar region where the tongue hits the palate. And since man is by

> definition the Language Animal, it is hard to see what these changes are about unless they are for language. The subsequent stages of human evolution - through *homo erectus* to *homo sapiens sapiens* - do not, in Coppen's view, warrant the status of a separate species.[231]

Fossilised limb bones of all the early members of the *homo* genus suggest fatigue stress possibly associated with frequent endurance running necessary to capture prey.[232] Certainly with *homo erectus*, a recognisably human body shape has arrived: tall and athletic and suited to a hunting lifestyle - which was distinguished by the on-going co-operation of a group of males as a hunting band (as well as a group of females in gathering food for the whole extended family).

The strong suggestion is that this hunter-gatherer lifestyle - together with the ability to garner a living in a variety of environments - formed the distinctively human way of life from around two million years ago until relatively recently.[233] Contemporary hunter-gatherers, of course, have enormous differences in lifestyle from one place to another; nevertheless those still existing can give us important clues as to what ancient society was like.

Generally speaking, hunter-gatherers exploit the natural resources available to them very efficiently. Prehistoric humans' place in the natural world was as the most effective predators, and as the most 'generalised' species in terms of adaptation to different habitats. The combination enabled them to occupy all the world's land masses successfully.

Nevertheless, the fact that they could does not on its own explain why they actually did. If there were particularly favourable conditions to move into, or particular dangers to escape from, then no doubt they would have done so. But continual expansion fuelled by population growth and a desire to control natural resources is a modern way of thinking, born of a farming-based culture, and not relevant to the ancient world. Furthermore, as Hugh Brody points out in *The Other Side Of Eden*:

> This difference is established in stereotypes of 'nomadic' hunters and 'settled' farmers. However, the stereotype has it the wrong way round. It is agricultural societies that tend to be on the move; hunting peoples are far more firmly settled.[234]

His insight into the fundamental difference between hunter-gatherers and farmers is highly illuminating and deserves emphasis. The nature of hunter-gatherers' culture makes them resistant to moving into new and unknown territory: from a long-term perspective, hunter-gatherers are indeed mobile, but within a traditional range which does not normally change. Farmers, on the other hand, live in a homestead and work a fixed land holding, but their population is far more likely to grow, or at least to grow more quickly; over the course of generations they, or their offspring, will be looking to move on. As a result they have colonised huge areas of the world in a relatively short space of time.

Such colonisation is in fact an inevitable function of farming, but not of hunting and gathering. It has been a feature of farming culture since it first emerged in the Middle East and south east Europe, and particularly in the past three hundred years or so, whilst hunter-gatherers have been pushed to the geographical margins:

> The settlement of Europeans in the Canadian West during the late 1800s, for example, was amongst the largest and most rapid movements of human beings in history. Since the beginnings of agriculture, all over the world, on new-found lands, in the *terra nullus* of colonial frontiers, migrants have made their family farms. There they have many children, who also have many children, pushing the frontier outwards until it reaches its limits ...
> Being willing to go to unknown and harsh places, in defiance of aboriginal resentment; taking part in colonial wars of conquest and 'pacification'; accepting the relentless need to remake, with Herculean efforts, a land of forest or marsh or rocks or sand into a patchwork of pasture and fields; knowing little comfort and little respite from hard work; setting pleasure at the far end, the distant terminus, of a journey of hardship; making the endurance of this hardship a religious achievement ... These are the qualities that define what Europeans (and other expansionist agricultural cultures) see as the signs of success and civilisation.[235]

For all that it is the subject of countless heroic Hollywood films, Brody sees in this the signs of a sickness akin to schizophrenia, the results of

God's curse in banishing mankind from the Garden of Eden - "on the one hand, a passion to settle, on the other, a fierce restlessness." [236] This cursed restlessness replaced not merely individual hunter-gatherer cultures that had each been viable for millennia, but a primary relationship with the land and landscape - without any such need to 'remake' it - which had been the very context for human evolution.

Pre-neolithic, pre-farming colonisations had, of course, also moved into huge areas of the world, but much more slowly. The process had clearly been absolutely different. Hunter-gatherer peoples' connect-ion with the land they live in, intimately bound up with their spirituality, will have taken many generations to establish and refine. Bruce Chatwin's *The Songlines* describes this particularly well in an Australian context, with the beings from the dreamtime first walking through the landscape and naming its physical features as well as all the animals, so bringing them into existence.

These names are incorporated into songs, and these songs form the basis of the people's oral tradition. Chatwin even suggested that the real reason that humans developed large brains was "for singing our way through the wilderness." [237] In Australia, each individual hunter has a particular line he can walk, for which he has received the song. The songlines stretch right across the continent, and the limits of tribal territory are defined by the points on these lines where one person's song ends and another's begins.

In North America, Hyemeyohsts Storm similarly describes a select group of people called the 'Singers', who were trained to sing tens of thousands of words of poetry - including the mythology and history of their people, as well as 'Journey Songs'. These were symbolic and extremely detailed, such that only a trained Singer could successfully pass them on; and "after travellers learned the entire song from a Singer, they would have memorized a map of the physical terrain of where they wanted to travel." [238] The 'Journey Songs' provided precise details of the route, landmarks, and resources necessary to the traveller, over immense distances - and, if sung backwards, back home again.

As suggested in chapter one, the clan system, which existed right across the world and stretched back into the Dream Time with its totems and symbology, would have been intimately bound up in the people's relationship with the land; and it was precisely this relationship that was expressed and recorded in the mythology of tribe and clan. In Canada, Hugh Brody reports that songs and stories have been recited in Canadian courts during native land rights cases - since they are the nearest equivalent that the native peoples have to 'title deeds'.[239] In Australia, mainstream academics recognise that 'chains of connection', criss-crossing the continent, were integral to aboriginal culture:

> These linked individuals and local groups through networks of kin and alliance and crossed language and cultural boundaries. In many areas of central Australia they still do. Movement of raw materials from the coast into the interior and vice versa, as well as shared song cycles, myths, and initiation rites are tangible evidence of a pancontinental system.[240]

Bruce Chatwin saw the system of songlines as the basis for trade, friendship and co-operation; yet more than this, he saw the songlines as a universal phenomenon, spreading out from beyond Australia. "They were the means by which man marked out his territory, and so organised his social life. All other successive systems were variants - or perversions - of this original model":

> The main Songlines in Australia appear to enter the country from the north or the north-west - from across the Timor Sea or the Torres Strait - and from there weave their way southwards across the continent. One has the impression that they represent the routes of the first Australians - and that they have come from somewhere else ...
>
> I have a vision of the Songlines stretching across the continents and ages; that wherever men have trodden they have left a trail of song (of which we may, now and then, catch an echo); and that these trails must reach back, in time and space, to an isolated pocket in the African savannah, where the First Man, opening his mouth in defience of the terrors that surrounded him, shouted the opening stanza of the World Song, 'I AM'.[241]

The resulting worldwide network is reminiscent of the 'ley lines' that have been traced in the United Kingdom. Guboo Ted Thomas, a native Australian elder who visited Glastonbury (England) in the 1980s, certainly understood them to be the same thing. It seems reasonable to assume that this is - or at least was - a universal feature of hunter-gatherer life; the basic human means of mapping the landscape and of defining people's relationship with it.

We could even conjecture that it is an essential part of being human, that it goes right back to the time when humans first stepped out across the planet, that its development was vital to (and went hand-in-hand with) the development of human intelligence and consciousness, language and culture. "All were embedded in the physical context of the environment. The sense of self, of 'I', of the body, was intimately bound up with the life of the immediate kin, the tribe, and the ecological context of life." [242]

This intimate and detailed relationship with the land was and is a primary tool for survival. It recorded and mapped out routes for movement across the landscape, landmarks and vital resources; it is what would have given some semblance of order and stability in a very uncertain world. When people moved into new territories, it would never have been easy to let go of their relationship with the land they left.

Prehistoric colonisation

People did not evolve living 'close to nature'; they were part of nature. They were the most successful species at adapting to a variety of climatic and environmental conditions, but that did not give humans mastery over the rest of the environment - rather it defined their place within it. Their function in the eco-system, now virtually forgotten, was at least as important as that of microbes for instance, or fruit trees. There was a purpose to life, which was carried out simply by humans being human, living their lives as best they could in the circumstances which they found.

So in what circumstances would hunter-gatherer people have moved, of their own volition, from their established territory into somewhere new? The answer to this can be no more than informed guesswork, but the question emphasises that prehistoric 'colonisation' would have been done in a very different way and with a very different mind-set than that carried out by farming cultures since neolithic times, or by more modern 'civilisations'.

Clive Gamble's *Timewalkers* - a study of prehistoric global colonisation, which he himself says is a subject "not often investigated" - begins with the observation that humans are "the only animal with a near-global distribution". This was taken for granted by European explorers in recent centuries, who scarcely questioned where all these people and their myriad cultures had come from, and their "lack of curiosity about a signal fact concerning our own species now strikes me as one of the central issues in the development of archeology." [243]

Gamble points out that the rhythm of world colonisation has been staccato, with only intermittent periods of great movement and exploration; and that these have been the result of new developments in social organisation rather than in physical or mental abilities. The two great movements of population spread in the ancient world - the first by *homo erectus* beginning around a million years ago,[244] the second by *homo sapiens* from about 100,000 years ago - did not begin with the first appearance of these "new faces in the fossil record". According to Gamble they occurred as the result of "an expanded web of relations", through which sufficient information became available within the "tribal encyclopedia", at first to enhance chances of survival during times of local food shortage.

This in turn led to "selection pressure for calculated migration", which "benefited the fitness of individuals who belonged to a more complex social unit.[245] In other words, the more sophisticated and extensive the social organisation, the greater the chances of survival for those individuals within it; which in turn meant enhanced evolutionary selection for people who were naturally adapted to the pleasures and the challenges of living in complex social units.

In the case of *homo erectus*, their social units were highly complex compared to any pre-human species, but far less so than *homo sapiens*. It is of course arguable whether *homo erectus* should correctly be called 'human' - though Richard Leakey, whose team discovered the 1.6 million-year-old 'Turkana boy' in northern Kenya, certainly believed that they were: "The origin of *homo erectus* represents a major turning point in human history ... leaving an essentially apelike past and embarking on a distinctly humanlike future." [246] Clive Gamble states that "the changes in behaviour required to complete this process [global colonisation] are what made us human" [247] - and this clearly first became effective with *homo erectus*.

The question of when 'human beings' first appeared on the planet will be considered more fully later. It does appear, as Richard Leakey and others have pointed out, that it was far earlier than many have maintained. Marek Kohn highlights the discovery of stone tools on the island of Flores (east of Bali) which has never been attached to the Asian mainland. They are dated to at least half a million, perhaps 900,000 years ago, implying that "south-east Asian hominids had far more sophisticated technological and planning abilities than their simple stone tools suggest." [248]

"This would mean that *homo erectus* was not only in possession of much greater technological capacities than we thought; it would also be proof that language existed at this time, for no sea-going voyage is plausible without such a capacity." [249] Such sophistication and complexity do not, in themselves, fully explain the phenomenon of human expansion to colonise the whole of the 'old world', though clearly they are what would have made it possible. It would be a mistake, however, to imagine (as some, from a modern perspective, seem to) that ancient people were less than fully formed modern people, who somehow looked forward to the time when they could expand and colonise the world. Returning to Clive Gamble's study of 'timewalkers' (prehistoric pioneers):

> Prehistoric colonization is not a remote equivalent of recent maritime empires ... The long wait to get out of sub-Saharan Africa or across to Sahul is usually explained in terms of waiting for the new gifts to evolve to make it happen ... [which] removes purpose by making all timewalkers wait passively for change from outside. Only then did they realize their purpose to expand ... [but] these checks to expansion do not provide sufficient reason for the delay. *The limits are set internally and so are integral to social life.*[250]

Gamble sets out a particular chronology for different parts of the world being populated. People moved first to regions where their lifestyle could remain most similar to that assumed for their original habitat in the African savannah - not into regions that happened to be closest (such as equatorial forest), where the climate may have been more favourable but it would have been less easy to adapt hunting and gathering to the environment:

> The two easiest habitats - tropical savannahs and temperate grasslands - are colonized first ... Once away from these habitats with their plant and animal resources life becomes harder. There may be huge growth and productivity, as in a tropical rain forest. But diversity and abundance are not everything ... Only those tundras which appeared in mid-latitude Europe and Asia during the Pleistocene ice ages came anywhere near the productivity of the temperate grasslands.[251]

Siberia, for instance, provided "a cold version of the African savannah with a fauna to match ... northern forms of lions, hyenas, rhinos, and elephants (woolly mammoths), with bison in place of buffalo, horses in place of zebras, dholes in place of wild dogs, foxes in place of jackals, wolves as the coursers in place of cheetahs, and many kinds of deer in place of many kinds of antelope, with the giant deer *Megaceros* browsing the treetops in place of the giraffe." [252]

So to say that ancient humans colonised 'the world' is overstating the case, but this first expansion of people out of their formative habitat is most remarkable for the fact that it happened at all. Gradual and limited as it was, it nevertheless represents the first concrete expression of humanness across a significantly large area of the world.

Modern humanity - filling up the corners of the world

The second great wave of population spread began around 100,000 years ago and involved modern human beings. This was different from the earlier migrations in that there was already a hominid population in existence over large areas of Eurasia - *homo erectus* and the various 'archaic modern' humans who had evolved from them in different regions and in different conditions.

As suggested, it was the neanderthal people in Europe who were the most 'advanced' of these, in that their lifestyles - technologically and socially - most closely matched those of the moderns. After *homo sapiens* had emerged from Africa, it was a very long time before they entered Europe: migration was first into south and south east Asia - where we do not know how sparse, or how primitive, the population of *homo erectus* and their descendents appeared to our modern forebears.

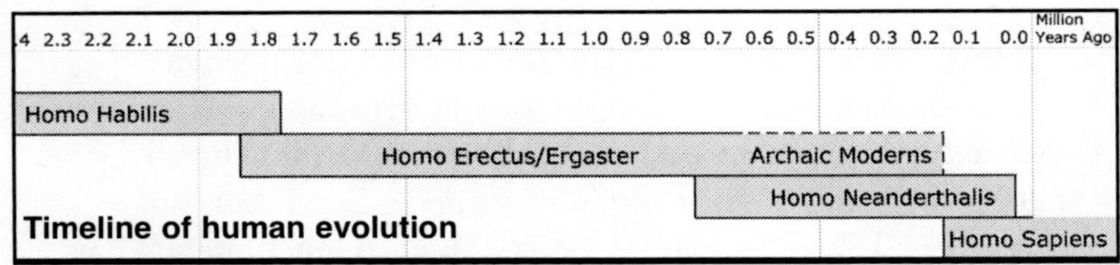

Palaeolithic (Old Stone Age)
3 million years ago: Distinctively human-like footprints left in volcanic ash deposits, East Africa
2 to 1.5 million: Hunter-gatherer lifestyle established in Africa
1 million (or more): Asia and Europe first populated by 'homo erectus' originating from Africa
Population remaining in Africa sometimes known as 'homo ergaster'
200,000: 'Anatomically modern man' first lived in Africa
100,000: Both modern and neanderthal remains found in the Middle East
100-70,000: Colonisation of south and south east Asia
Neanderthal population in Europe and western Asia
60-50,000: First human colonisation of Australia

Upper Palaeolithic
40-35,000: Modern humans arrive in Europe (Aurignacian culture)
30-25,000: Gravettian culture reaches Europe
Colonisation of Asian steppes
'Goddess figurine' culture in Eurasia
Beginning of most recent Ice Age
Last of the Neanderthals
20,000: Last glacial maximum
20-15,000: Classic period of cave art in western Europe

Mesolithic (Middle Stone Age)
15-10,000: Ending of last Ice Age
Colonisation of America from north eastern Asia

Neolithic (New Stone Age)
10,000-6,000: Development of horticulture in Middle East and then Europe
Goddess culture in Asia Minor and Europe
Herding culture on Asian steppes
6,000-4,000: Desiccation of 'Saharasia'
Kurgan invasions of Balkans and south east Europe
Beginnings of plough-based agriculture
First historical civilisations of Middle East and eastern Mediterranean

> These early humans were primarily denizens of the sea coasts, who moved quickly along the shores of the Indian Ocean and also spread inland along the great rivers. By 70,000 years ago they had got as far as New Guinea and the coast and rivers of China. At that point they halted, or even retreated somewhat, as the onset of the most recent ice age had rendered much of the world unsuitable for habitation by modern humans. Especially between 65,000 and 55,000 BP, all but the most favourable areas were locked in bitter cold and drought. In time, however, the climate began to moderate, setting off a second great wave of migration.[253]

People reached Australia 50,000-60,000 years ago, a move that involved a sea crossing of at least 60 miles and all the technical expertise, planning and provisioning that would have been required - suggesting that 'modern' behaviour was already established then. Before that, people "were not everywhere. They had a restricted range within the Old World. They avoided many environments where the living was not easy". But after 50,000 BP "they are now part of modern humanity, separated by a rapid transformation, seen by some as the Human Revolution, from the earlier Ancients." [254]

Modern people reached Europe around 40,000 years ago. Siberia and peri-glacial Asia next became part of the populated world, and the Americas are assumed to have been colonised from Asia at the end of the last ice age, when there existed a land bridge across the Bering Straits. The islands of the Pacific were the last region to be populated: humans did not finally arrive in New Zealand until about 1000 CE.

So the process of populating the world took perhaps 100,000 years; it happened very slowly, and it was carried out step by step, deliberately. Maori mythology, for instance, tells us that Aeoratoa was known about before people ever came there, and that a special fleet of 'great canoes' was built to accomplish the move. Something similar, less grandiose perhaps but surely at least as significant for the time, must have taken place in order to reach Australia - the first occasion that people had sailed beyond the horizon to reach a new land.

Most migrations, of course, did not involve sea crossings - but it is likely that they involved a similar type of deliberation. The people who moved "quickly" along the shores of the Indian Ocean actually took 30,000 years to progress from Africa to China.

The most recent continental colonisation, that of the Americas, appears to have been completed in only 1,000 to 2,000 years. Mathematical models have created the impression that a human 'blitzkreig', fueled by excessive energy and protein intake provided by 'Pleistocene Overkill', slashed and burned its way through the plains of the north and the plateaux of the south at a steady and inexorable rate of 16 kilometers per year. In fact, even if the human advance had been this rapid (and there is growing evidence that it began much earlier than so far supposed), this is actually most likely to have meant a move of about 200 miles after a whole generation.[255]

The nature of hunter-gatherers' culture makes them resistant to moving into new and unknown territory; but equally it is true that all people are inherently curious, enterprising and innovative. This appears to be contradictory, but it is not: it means that the expansion of humans into the whole world was a historical process, rather than an inevitability pre-ordained by its arrival at present-day reality. In Clive Gamble's words, "Humans went everywhere in pre-history because humans have purpose ... I can say this for the simple reason that we can now see they usually chose *not* to expand." [256]

The common pattern of human life was "a limited number of inhabitants, who lived in small isolated groups in the areas most favourable for settlement ... Each area was occupied by a large number of small primitive clan communities separated by extensive unoccupied areas." [257] Where unexplored places lay beyond the traditional homelands of ancient peoples, they would certainly have known about them - even where they lay across the sea. Exactly how is largely glossed over by palaeontologists, who leave us to assume that it was all down to individual explorations and chance crossings of the waters during storms, but let us not underestimate the power of active dreaming and creative visualisation in pre-literate societies. Either way, the key factor is human curiosity, enterprise and innovation.

Let us also not be bound by modern modes of thought that assign basic motivations of economics and population growth to any process of 'colonisation'. In a period of expansion that stretched over 100,000 years there was no such driving force, and any such factors would have been secondary. People can do quite extraordinary things, essentially because they choose to do so, perhaps for reasons that would make very little sense to us today - but because, in their own terms, they have purpose.

The reality, I would suggest, is that a population group lived in a certain place, and that beyond that place was another place, known about but unknown, distant but related, where it was understood (in a religious sense perhaps) that people would one day travel and live. It could have been generations before 'the right time' arrived, or before the god/esses prompted the move, or before particular weather conditions or other natural circumstances made it necessary or possible.

It could have been generations again before the beings from the dreamtime had made the new place fully known, had taught the people their new songs, had given meaning and significance to the physical features of the new land - before the human relationship with that new landscape had been thoroughly created. This could only have happened at a pace that moved, like the turning of the seasons, without urgency. And still 100,000 years would have been plenty of time to populate the world.

3 Europe (2): Godesses, Gods and the Holy Grail

After modern people had arrived in central-northern Europe, they not only established themselves, but continued to live there successfully even as the climate became progressively colder. With the approach of the glacial maximum, as the neanderthals died out and some areas became completely uninhabitable, the moderns continued to thrive in the more southerly regions. Life expectancy was actually on the increase. Whatever their survival strategies, they worked well. It is likely, in Europe, that these strategies were essentially shaped by the women. If so, then this was the basis for the Goddess culture that lasted through to neolithic times.

These were the beginnings, in a very real sense, of what we now call civilisation. A sparse population grew significantly with the steady spread of agriculture. By the time this way of life reached its high-point in the first half of the fifth millenium BCE, it stretched from north and south of the Black Sea all the way to western Europe.

Archaeologists have divided this area into a number of cultural regions, each perhaps based on the ancient homeland of a tribe or group of related tribes, though the cultural differences were less significant than the similarities. The physical evidence speaks of the gradual increase in villages and small towns, technological sophis-tication, social equality, female religious imagery, and the absence of weaponry or fortifications.

The Goddess Religion

Starhawk, the contemporary American feminist and witch, states unequivocally that her tradition ("according to our legends") stretches back to 35,000 years ago. Marija Gimbutas presents a similar picture based on archaeology, arguing that the Goddess worship of Old Europe and Anatolia is traceable well before 20,000 BCE - that is, well before the peak of the last ice age - and "can be detected or inferred over a vast expanse of the Eurasian land mass":

> She does this by building up a network of 'Goddess' artifacts and imagery. The key items, recognized for some time, are female figurines. Hundreds have been unearthed, in several styles. Some are apparently pregnant, some have exaggerated sexual features, others are more austere. Archaeologists, accepting them as images of female divinity (although not all do), have applied the restrictive label *Venuses*, which Gimbutas rejects ... She [also] exhibits linear motifs and gives them Goddess interpretations.[301]

Of course 'Goddess artifacts and imagery', even if they signify a relationship with spirit that understands creation in terms of being birthed from a Great Mother, does not necessarily mean a religion in the sense that we understand it today. That, after all, would simply be a mirror image of patriarchal religious form. It is worth bearing in mind that "just because prehistoric societies - and primal peoples - didn't worship domineering male gods, it doesn't mean that they worshipped benevolent female goddesses." [302] Indeed, it may well have been that 'goddesses' as personifications of spiritual principles were unknown much before 'gods' appeared as well. Nevertheless:

> Early human beings clearly revered the female form, and felt a great sense of awe at women's reproductive powers. Judging by the massive numbers that have been found, particularly through-out Europe and the Middle East, female figurines seem to have been their major art form. They also made a massive number of carvings and drawings of the vulva, [and] had a custom of staining vulva-shaped cavities with red ochre (to represent menstrual blood).[303]

These figurines, together with "a medley of carvings and ceramic designs covering many millennia", appear to represent a form of spirituality that continued unbroken for more than 20,000 years. They also suggest a people who held actual living women in similarly high esteem, and whose culture was based equally - or largely - on female thinking and values. Their religion was most likely not a self-conscious religion at all, certainly not a religion with alternatives to which one could be 'converted', but simply a natural part of the flow of life. 'Belief' in the Goddess would be an extension of belief in motherhood. As Steve Taylor says, questioning whether there was ever a Goddess religion in Old Europe:

> Their sense of the sacredness of nature ... was closely connected to both the hunter-gatherers' and simple horticultural peoples' life. An important difference between them and later peoples is that to them there was apparently no separation between religion and the rest of their lives, and no sense of the divine being separate and apart from the world. To them God or Spirit was everywhere and in everything. This was obviously part of the reason why these peoples had such a deep respect for nature: because they saw it as an expression of Spirit. In fact, it's doubtful that the concept of gods - as higher beings who watch over the world and control its events - had any meaning to them whatsoever.[304]

In fact, the feminist and Goddess protagonist Riane Eisler does not disagree with this at all: "To say that people who worshipped the Goddess were deeply religous would be to understate, and largely miss, the point. For here there was no separation between the secular and the sacred ... religion was life, and life was religion." [305]

> When our ancestors began to ask the eternal questions (Where do we come from before we are born? Where do we go after we die?), they must have noted that life emerges from the body of a woman. It would have been natural for them to image the universe as an all-giving Mother from whose womb all life emerges and to which, like the cycles of vegetation, it returns after death to be again re-born.[306]

She gives tentative suggestions as to how this began to develop, over time, into what we would now recognise as religious form. Early burial sites feature red ochre, assumed to be a surrogate for menstrual blood, and cowrie shells - "shaped in the form of what [religious historian E.O.] James discreetly calls 'the portal through which a child enters the world'." These suggest the importance of a female deity and appear to have been part of rites intended to bring the dead back through re-birth. Even more specifically, as James notes, they 'point to mortuary rituals ... closely connected with the female figurines.'

In addition, there is evidence in cave paintings - and even the preserved impressions of human feet - which strongly suggest the use of ritual dance:

> These cave sanctuaries, figurines, burials, and rites all seem to have been related to a belief that the same source from which human life springs is also the source of all vegetable and animal life ... They also suggest that our early ancestors recognized that we and our natural environment are integrally linked parts of the great mystery of life and death and that all nature must therefore be treated with respect. This consciousness - later emphasized in Goddess figurines either surrounded by natural symbols such as animals, water and trees, or themselves partly animal - evidently was central to our lost psychic heritage ...
>
> The paleolithic remains of female figurines, red ocher in burials, and vagina-shaped cowrie shells appear to be early manifestations of what was later to develop into a complex religion centering on the worship of a Mother Goddess as the source and regeneratrix of all forms of life ... [which] survived well into historic times.[307]

She also quotes James Mellaart as saying that the symbolism of upper palaeolithic art shows "strong similarities to the religious imagery of Catal Huyuk," [308] the celebrated centre of neolithic Goddess culture in Asia Minor. It would be an over-simplification to imagine that human life in Europe followed an uninterrupted flow from 35,000 BP right through to the neolithic - but this, if anything, emphasises the all-pervasiveness and durability of the prevailing spiritual beliefs. Marija Gimbutas made a particular study of the "numerous express-ions of the divine female which persisted for many thousands of years ... from the Upper Palaeolithic through the whole of the Neolithic, Copper and Bronze Ages, up to historical times." [309]Anne Baring and Jules Cashford, in reasearching *The Myth of the Goddess*, discovered "such similarities and parallels in the goddess myths of apparently unrelated cultures that we concluded that there had been a continuous transmission of images throughout history." [310]

Besides the images noted above, they pay particular attention to the moon cycle. As well as its obvious relationship to the female menstrual cycle, it is "an image in the sky which was always changing yet was always the same", with its different phases (including the invisible dark phase) all being part of the whole. This provided an image and an understanding of the universe as an inter-related whole, as well as a symbol in which "the visible 'came from' and 'returned to' the invisible - like being born and dying, and being born again." [311] Artifacts which appear to be representations or recordings of this 28-day cycle have been found dating far back into the palaeolithic.

The biggest challenge to palaeolithic cultural unity in Europe was the advancing ice age. During the last glacial maximum (c 20,000 years ago), conditions were such that ice sheets and the Alps completely divided south west Europe from southern central Europe:

> From 21,000 to 17,000 BP, glacial conditions grew so extreme that much of Europe was uninhabitable. Ice fields spread south from Scandinavia and north from the Alps, and the narrow corridor between them became a bleak polar desert. This created an impassable barrier between eastern and western Europe which destroyed the cultural unity that had endured for thousands of years. At the absolute peak of the cold, human habitation was reduced to a few relatively temperate refuges, and even in those the harshest of steppe conditions seem to have prevailed. There was one such refuge in southern France and north western Spain, and a second in Italy. A third was in the northern Balkans, and a fourth in the Ukraine.[312]

By the time temperatures began to rise, linguistic and cultural differences were well established: the mosaic of European ethnicities began to take form from that time onward. All the same, the excavation of neolithic Catal Huyuk revealed "obvious Upper Palaeolithic influences", which can be traced via the mesolithic site of Lepenski Vir on the Danube,[313] with artwork harking back to "the theme of complex and female symbolism" found in palaeolithic cave art, and "numerous cult practices of which red ochre burials, red-stained flooors, collections of stalactites, fossils, shells, are but a few examples":

The Neolithic culture of Catal Huyuk and Hacilar have provided

> extensive information about a long-missing piece of the puzzle of our past - the missing link between the Paleolithic Age and the later, more technologically advanced Chalcolithic, Copper and Bronze Ages ... A continuity in religion can be demonstrated from Catal Huyuk to Hacilar and so on till the great 'Mother-Goddesses' of archaic and classical times.[314]

This continuity was not limited to Catal Huyuk and Hacilar, nor even to Asia Minor and the Middle East. The figurines, for instance, have been found from western Europe, through to Mohenjo-Daro in India, to the east; and from Malta in the south to Scandinavia and Siberia in the north. Also found at Catal Huyuk and other Anatolian sites were bulls' horns, depictions of bull leaping, and paintings of the labrys - the double-headed axe. All of these were later important in Cretan culture.[315]

Baring and Cashford point out that "The Mother Goddess, wherever she is found, is an image that inspires and focuses a perception of the universe as an organic, alive and sacred whole, in which humanity, the Earth and all life on Earth participate as 'her children'." [316] There seems no reason to doubt that the Goddess religion was based on a spiritual understanding and relationship with nature that was once universal, and that it reached its most developed form in neolithic Asia Minor and Europe.

The origins of farming

After the end of the Ice Age, both the human population and the level of human artistry declined for some time before neolithic farming gradually gave people a more effective way of exploiting the natural resources available to them.[317] Farming, as already discussed, appeared in Europe primarily as an adaptation to forestation; but this was not simply and suddenly a triumph of human ingenuity over the vicissitudes of nature. According to Colin Tudge:

> From at least 40,000 years ago - the late Paleolithic - people were managing their environment to such an extent that they can properly be called 'proto-farmers' ... They were not simply hunting and gathering, but also coercing their prey to behave more amenably, and

> perhaps encouraging favoured plants. Dramatic as they appear, then, the changes of the Neolithic Revolution were not really revolutionary, but merely a consolidation of established trends.[318]

These trends had grown up piecemeal over thousands of years. Farming involves a number of separate activities - such as plant propagation, land preparation, harvesting, and storage - which these days we see as one integrated system, but which had originated one by one as means to enhance the effectiveness of hunting or gathering. This process of innovative 'proto-farming' had developed over the same period as the developments in artistic and cultural life described in the previous chapter. But Tudge emphasises that eventually bringing these activities together into a completely new way of life was at best a reluctant choice. "People did not invent agriculture and shout for joy; they drifted or were forced into it, protesting all the way":

> Farming in Neolithic times was obviously harsh: the first farming peoples were less robust than the hunter-gatherers who had preceded them, and suffered nutritional, traumatic and infectious disorders that their forebears had been spared ... Hunter gatherers clearly had a varied diet that included scores of different plants while farmers were commonly confiined to just a few staple crops that sometimes failed and must often have been mouldy.[319]

Richard Rudgley expands on this theme, quoting from the results produced by a special conference on palaeopathology:

> The study of the sample of skeletal remains from South Asia showed that there was a decline in body stature, body size and life expectancy with the adoption of farming. A broadly similar result was obtained by the analysis conducted on skeletons from pre-historic populations in Georgia, USA - i.e. the health of the hunters was markedly better. In the case study of the Levant region there was a slight increase in the level of health with the initial adoption of farming, but this was followed by a marked decline once intensive agriculture and husbandry were fully established. Of the 13 regional studies, 10

showed that the average life expectancy declined with the adoption of farming.[320]

The archaeological record also shows the appearance of 'industrial diseases' such as arthritic knees and lower spines, and osteoarthritis in the neck vertebrae.[321]

With the post-glacial rises in sea levels, and the consequent loss of coastal regions which had provided a particularly good living to hunter-gatherers, population densities on higher ground rose sharply. The commonly held assumption that population growth in itself led to the breakdown of traditional ways of life is a product of modern thinking and experience, and would by no means have been inevitable. However, the maintenance of growing populations in the face of major environmental challenges would have had a huge effect. For instance:

> What is now the Persian Gulf must have been a very favoured spot ... The land was flat and the climate balmy. There was no shortage of water. There would have been fish and shellfish galore, and great flocks of water birds, with gazelles and fallow deer and fruiting trees ... But as the Ice Age ended the sea flooded in ... People, hordes of them, were obliged to move inland to what then was uplands. The population of what had been the coastal plain was already high ... but now they all had to crowd into a much smaller space and were obliged to farm to support the augmented population.[322]

In the middle east, where wild grasses and grains particularly lent themselves to domestication, farming began as a way of maintaining this increased population density. Horticulture as a way of life first appears in the archaeological record in the 'fertile crescent' of the middle east by 10,000 BCE (and perhaps as early as 12,000 BCE); this spread steadily as generation by generation the population grew still larger and more land was needed for cultivation.[323] Farming spread into Europe from the south east.

It meant much harder work, and far more time taken up with attending to the necessities of survival. It meant that larger human populations could not only be maintained, but steadily increased; and it meant that the accumulation of what we now call 'wealth' gradually became possible. Life may also have become (or seemed) more secure, but in all probability it became less pleasant, it lost something essential. The Biblical story of the Fall comes inevitably to mind: "to condemn all of humankind to a life of full-time farming, and in particular of arable farming, was a curse indeed." [324]

It is important to note that 'farming' covers a multitude of different technological and cultural practices. In particular there is a large and important difference between what is generally termed 'horticulture' and what is regarded as 'agriculture'. The shift from horticulture to agriculture was in many ways a greater change than the shift from hunting and gathering to horticulture.[325]

It had always been the case that more than half the food, perhaps two thirds, was derived from gathering plants (plus eggs and small creatures); and, as has been noted by several authors, early horticulture was almost certainly introduced by women as a development from food gathering. This is particularly well described by Margaret Ehrenberg in *Women in Prehistory*.

Regarding food production:

> As women are responsible for plant food gathering in virtually all foraging societies about which we have information, and are responsible for growing plants in horticultural societies today ... it is very likely that they would also have been responsible for these tasks in the past. It also follows that women would have been in a position to hit upon the various stages towards the cultivation of plants, as well as all the vital concomitant inventions associated with it.[326]

Horticulture is, essentially, food gathering made more efficient by the application of relatively simple techniques to encourage food plants to grow in larger quantities and in convenient places. These techniques, using simple tools such as hoes and digging sticks, would almost certainly have been based on women's expertise and observations as food gatherers. In this sense farming was the invention of women.

The adoption of horticulture meant that a 'base camp' became a permanent home, since crops would need attention in different ways through all the seasons of the year. It included little domestication of livestock, and certainly no large herds or flocks. This form of farming was essentially the preserve of women, whilst meat was still hunted by men.

Agriculture, by contrast, is characterised by the use of the plough, and increasingly with other heavy equipment, carts, and draught animals. It dates from the late neolithic or early bronze age. (In Europe and the Middle East it dates from the fourth millennium BCE - in other words it coincides with the Kurgan invasions and their aftermath). It is marked by a change to men carrying out most agricultural work, thereby taking control of the primary means of food production. It often took the form of mixed agriculture, with herds and flocks alongside arable farming, the use of manure to maintain soil fertility rather than moving from one plot to another every few years, and also the manufacture of secondary products such as cheese and wool. The introduction of this type of farming coincided with the decline in the social status of women.

Agriculture also meant that farm production could expand into areas where land had previously been marginal. It meant greater accumulation of wealth, both in land, herds, and equipment. It led to more efficient production of food and ever more rapid population growth. It meant the beginning of craft specialisation, and paved the way for social stratification. The shift from horticulture to agriculture marked the shift from matrist to patriarchal social values.

It was the expansion of this type of farming which was the subject of Hugh Brody's observation that farming culture regards the endurance of hardship, particularly in the opening up of new frontiers, as a religious achievement. At the same time, he points out that for people in this culture "a love of place is secondary to the importance of prosperity" and even that "given the right price, everything is for sale." [327] And this, in turn, is part of the spiritual malaise which he describes as going back to the eviction from Eden:

> They move, they settle, they create a home, and they find - or their children or their children's children find - that they must move on. Exile is the deep condition. The longing to be settled, the defensive holding of our ground, the continuing endemic nomadism - I suspect that we share them all ... Agriculturalists, humans who live by remodelling the land, are the peoples whose story is some version of Genesis. We live outside any one garden that can meet our needs and

> growing population, so we must roam the earth looking to create or re-create some place that will provide a more or less adequate source of food and security.[328]

All the same, in evolutionary terms, this new way of life can be viewed as a success. Where previous hominid races had succumbed to adverse environmental changes, *homo sapiens* found a way to survive and - at least in a material sense - to thrive. And once people came to rely on re-modelling the environment for the sake of their food production, there was no turning back:

> Once begun, farming obliges people to farm even more, as their populations rise and the wild creatures suffer, eventually to collapse to a new and greatly impoverished level. The farmers do not increase their efforts because they enjoy it, or because it is necessarily easier than hunting and gathering. They are simply the victims of their own success.[329]

The resulting culture was female-defined and still sufficiently close to the natural time-honoured order of things to be compatible with the continuity of religion. Nevetherless it was already a major change from the traditional palaeolithic lifestyle, particularly in that it meant a rising population and the establishment of substantial homesteads. It spread through Asia Minor, into south east Europe and along the Mediterranean coast by 6000 BCE, and to central Europe by 5000 BCE. In its wake, "Old European society grew from small agricultural village communities in the earliest Neolithic, to expanded composites of social units in the 5th millennium BC" with small towns containing several thousand inhabitants.[330]

It spread first along the major river valleys, with their rich soils and easy availability of water. The arrival of farming did not mean the automatic and immediate end of hunting, nor the sudden demolition of European forests. The Mesolithic hunter-gatherers still inhabiting these areas lived alongside the newcomers with their new ideas, adapted to them, traded with them, and gradually become one culture.[331] Indeed, it is an assumption that there were 'newcomers' at all; it may well have been simply new ideas - or a new way of putting together already existing ideas - taken up by the existing population.

Longhouses and grandmothers

'Linear Pottery Culture', so named because of the distinctive decorations on its pottery,[332] was the direct descendent of hunter-gatherer society. And its particular developments - its modes of food production and social organisation - suggest a clear and growing emphasis on what had traditionally been the female roles amongst hunter-gatherers, such that "elder women, the great clan mothers, received the highest social respect." [333]

The feminist archaeologist Margaret Ehrenberg is extremely cautious in her interpretations of archaeological data. Even with regard to Minoan Crete, for example, she avoids making any firm statement claiming significant social or political power for women. However, when it comes to the Linear Pottery Culture of early neolithic Europe she concludes that "the evidence ... is consistent with a high degree of economic, and hence political, involvement by women ... together with higher than average status for women ..." [334]

This was based on women having become the main producers of food, which in turn was based upon the new technological developments (horticulture) being taken up in the context of ancient systems of consanguinity and clan property rights. These had always served to maintain the balance between the sexes amongst hunter-gatherers; the social organisation that developed, as can be deduced from the archaeological evidence of living spaces, was matrifocal and matrilineal:

> One of the most distinctive aspects of the Linear Pottery Culture is the large, rectangular longhouses, about a dozen of which are usually grouped together to form villages occupied by several hundred people.
>
> The shape and size of houses of any society will be, at least in part, a reflection of its social organisation, and particularly of family structure ...
>
> According to [Melvin] Ember, in matrilocal societies, where women stay in the same settlements after marriage, larger houses used by extended family units are more common than in patrilocal societies, where smaller houses are occupied by nuclear units. Sisters and their

> unrelated husbands are more likely to share household tasks and live under one roof, than are brothers sharing houses with unrelated wives.[335]

Ehrenberg compares it to the Iroquois, who lived in what is now New York State and who were extensively studied by anthropologists in the eighteenth and nineteenth centuries. Their land was owned communally and cultivated by the women "as a team", presumably based on clan associations. They also lived in a forest environment similar to that of post-glacial Europe. What she notes as one of the most striking similarities, however, is their houses:

> In each Iroquois house an older woman, or matron, who was usually the grandmother of the children in the house, lived with her daughters and their husbands and children. Each smaller unit had an area and hearth of its own, but food supplies were communal and distributed by the matron, who had the power to exclude undesirable men from the house or to withold food from them. This gave women the very powerful right of veto over virtually all male activities, including making war. Although discussion in inter-village or inter-tribal matters was in the hands of the men, it was impossible to implement a decision unpopular with the women.[336]

This was the reality in matrilocal societies. James DeMeo cites matrilocality as an important factor underpinning matrist cultures in general, since it provides the woman with emotional and economic security that are not dependent on her husband:

> The entire matrilineal and matrilocal family unit is therefore very much in tune with deeper biological factors, such as childbirth, breast feeding, and the absence of economic motivations or coercion regarding marriage and divorce. All of the above factors reverse themselves ... under the patrilocal and patrilineal kinship system.[337]

All of this echoes the description of a society in which male power in the tribe and female power in the clan were held in balance, as presented by

Morgan and Engels in their description of life in "the old long-houses":

> The stores were in common; but woe to the luckless husband or lover who was too shiftless to do his share of the providing. No matter how many children, or whatever goods he might have in the house, he might at any time be ordered to pick up his blanket and budge ... The women were the great power among the clans, as everywhere else. They did not hesitate, when occasion required, 'to knock off the horns,' as it was technically called, from the head of a chief, and send him back to the ranks of the warriors.[338]

It would be reasonable to assume that such things were similar in early neolithic Europe, where a new kind of life was coming about. It was based on fixed places to live and work, with the seasons marking the planting and growing cycles rather than the movement of animals and people across the landscape. Nevertheless there was a substantial degree of continuity with palaeolithic culture. Life in Europe was becoming settled as well as plentiful - and peaceful:

> The image of the Old European most of us carry within us today is of those frightfully barbaric tribesmen who kept pushing southward and finally outdid even the Romans in butchery by sacking Rome. For this reason one of the most remarkable and thought-provoking features of Old European society revealed by the archaeological spade is its essentially *peaceful* character. 'Old Europeans never tried to live in inconvenient places such as high, steep hills, as did later Indo-Europeans who built hill forts in inaccessible places and frequently surrounded their hill sites with cyclopean stone walls,' reports Gimbutas. 'Old European locations were chosen for their beautiful setting, good water and soil, and availability of animal pastures.' [339]

However, it is important to point out that the 'essentially peaceful' character of this society needs some qualification. The Iroquois, for instance, regarded themselves as being "in a state of war with every other tribe with which [they] had not expressly concluded a treaty of peace." [340] They were "the terror of the whole country from the Great Lakes to the Ohio and the

Potomac." [341] With regard to ancient Europe, Ronald Hutton has claimed that "Old Stone Age artists had portrayed human bodies stuck full of weapons, indicating that either war or executions were already a feature of society." [342]

Nicholas Mann's interpretation, however, is that "No evidence of warfare has ever been found, unless the paintings of men pierced by lances in the cave at Cougnac c. 15,000 BCE depict inter-communal strife. The motifs at this cave, however, suggest it was a place of male initiation. The two transfixed men out of more than three hundred representations probably had a significance other than that of war." [343]

In any case, it must also be made clear that 'war' in this context would have been restricted to raiding, and not conceived of on a scale that would require or provoke the construction of 'hill forts in inaccessible places' or military engineering of any sort at all. Military expeditions, even amongst the fearsome Iroquois, were freelance affairs carried out by volunteers, for which the consent of the tribal council was not even required.

The basis for social organisation in Old Europe would undoubtedly have been the tribal system based on the clan, as detailed in Chapter 1.[344] This included responsibilities amongst clan members for "help, protection, and especially assistance in avenging injury by strangers." [345] Security for the individual, who could rely upon receiving protection from other members of the clan, contributed to society's overall 'peaceful character'. Violent death, however, carried an obligation of blood revenge:

> First mediation was tried; the gens [clan] of the slayer sat in council, and made proposals of settlement to the council of the gens of the slain, usually offering expressions of regret and presents of considerable value. If these were accepted, the matter was disposed of. In the contrary case, the wronged gens appointed one or more avengers, whose duty it was to pursue and kill the slayer. If this was accomplished, the gens of the slayer had no ground of complaint; accounts were even and closed.[346]

This description, based on nineteenth century research in America, is not necessarily relevant to prehistoric Europe. At the same time it has the feel of something which goes back to time immemorial, and it certainly has echoes in the other continents of the world.[347] It would be naive to assume a complete lack of violence in the ancient world of the Goddess; at the same time, the containment of violence to a level that did not disrupt the *essentially* peaceful nature of society is enormously significant.

The Goddess culture of Old Europe, like all those following the old ways of the clan, was one in which there were "no soldiers, no gendarmes and police, no nobles, kings, regents, prefects or judges, no prisons, no lawsuits - and [yet] everything takes its orderly course. All quarrels and disputes are settled by the whole of the community affected ... only as an extreme and exceptional measure is blood revenge threatened." [348] This form of European society appears to have remained stable, innovative and productive for 2,000 to 3,000 years.

Crete: 'the key to our lost evolution'

An off-shoot that arrived in Crete around 6000 BCE traced its mythological ancestry back to the goddess Europa. Relatively isolated from the turbulance that would before long arrive on the mainland, it continued through into historical times as Minoan civilisation. Crete was probably first colonised from Anatolia, by immigrants who brought the Goddess culture with them, as well as neolithic agrarian technology. For a period of 4,000 years there was steady progress, in crafts including pottery, weaving, metallurgy, engraving and architecture, as well as increasing trade and the evolution of the characteristic Cretan art. By 3000 BCE these developments represented a fully-fledged civilisation, which around 2000 BCE entered what is known as the 'Middle Minoan' or 'Old Palace' period.

This particularly remarkable ancient culture was not excavated by archaeologists until the last hundred years or so, and when it was:

> Archaeologists were dumbfounded. They could not understand how the very existence of such a highly developed civilisation could have remained unsuspected until then ... Most strikingly, as excavations progressed and more and more frescoes, sculptures, vases, carvings, and other works of art were unearthed, there came the realisation that here were the remains of an artistic tradition unique in the annals of civilisation. [349]

Presumably the reason for this being so unexpected is that the reality of Cretan culture was subsequently suppressed by the Greeks and Romans. Certainly on Crete there existed a peaceful, matristic and extraordinarily accomplished society, enduring for 1,500 years in a world where everywhere else had succumbed to hierarchical domination, endemic warfare, slavery and cruelty. It managed to thrive in the midst of a world "heavy laden with profound and irreversible changes", in which "vast geological catastrophes occurred. Civilizations perished. Half the world's population became refugees. And wars, previously sporadic, came with hastening and ferocious frequency." [350] As such it represents the great possibility that was lost, the example of how civilisation could have developed if the shift to patrism had not come about.

Eventually Crete, too, succumbed to geological catastrophe and ferocious warfare, but the message from this era seems clear: it is possible to enjoy the benefits of civilised culture whilst still leading a 'natural' life - living an egalitarian existence within the environment, and thanking the Goddess for its gifts. Only patriarchal propaganda suggests that modern civilisation necessarily means an end to all this.

Riane Eisler therefore called Minoan Crete "the Goddess-worshipping key to our lost evolution." [351] She devotes a whole chapter of *The Chalice and the Blade* to the subject, describing in detail a culture where "the Goddess was still supreme, there are no signs of war", and where "the economy prospered and the arts continued to flourish" in spite of the chaos and brutality into which the world around it had fallen.

Crete's artistic tradition records a society in which "for the last time in recorded history, a spirit of harmony between women and men as joyful and equal participants in life appears to pervade," and she quotes Nicolas Platon in his appreciation of a tradition unique in its "delight in beauty, grace, and movement" and in its "enjoyment of life and closeness to nature ... the fear of death was almost obliterated by the ubiquitous joy of living."

She cites archaeologists and art historians as having used superlatives such as "the enchantment of a fairy world" and "the most complete acceptance of the grace of life the world has ever known," with "magnificent frescoes of multicoloured partridges, whimsical griffins, and elegant women, the exquisite golden miniatures, fine jewellery, and gracefully moulded statuettes." But the implications of the archaeological finds are not merely artistic attainment: "sharply distinguishing it from other ancient high civilisations," Cretan society appears to have had an equitable sharing of wealth and an absence of poverty, even amongst the peasants.

Crete was not richer than, for instance, Egypt or Babylon, but the economic and social gulf which separated social classes in these cultures was far less marked in Crete. The island's economy was basically agrarian, with the addition of stock breeding, industry, and particularly trade - with a large mercantile fleet that dominated the entire Mediterranean.

The basis of social organisation was at first the traditional matrilineal clan, though around 2000 BCE society became more centralised. "During later stages there is evidence of centralised governmental administration at several Cretan palaces. But here centralisation did not bring with it autocratic rule." Use of new technology was not merely for the benefit of a powerful few. Though there was an affluent ruling class, it was not maintained by massive armed might "or the kind of exploitation and brutalisation of the masses that is so striking in other civilisations of the time."

The development of writing and a sophisticated bureaucracy enabled the island's increasing wealth to be "judiciously used to improve living conditions, which were, even by western standards, extraordinarily 'modern'." This included extensive drainage systems, sanitary installations, and domestic conveniences, together with "viaducts, paved roads, look-out posts, roadside shelters, water pipes, fountains, reservoirs" and "large-scale irrigation works with canals to carry and distribute the water." All this would have been paid for out of the royal coffers.

Cretan palace architecture is described as "unique in civilisation, since rather than being "monuments to authority and power," the palaces were "a superb blend of life-enhancing and eye-pleasing features" including "vast courtyards, majestic facades, and hundreds of rooms laid out in the organised 'labyrinths' that became a catchword for Crete in later Greek legend." This typically allowed for many apartments constructed over several stories, at different heights, arranged asymmetrically round a central courtyard. "Long lines of store-rooms with connecting corridors were used for the orderly safekeeping of food reserves and treasures. And vast halls with rows of elegant columns were used for audiences, receptions, banquets, and council meetings."

A further essential feature of all Minoan architecture was its gardens, whilst the buildings themselves were designed for privacy, good natural light, and domestic convenience. And above all, "attention to detail and beauty." Details included "gypsum and tufa pilasters and tiles, perfectly bonded composed facades, walls, light-wells and courtyards. Partitions were decorated with plaster, with murals in many cases, and with marble facings" using both local and imported materials. "Not only the walls but often the ceilings and floors were decorated with paintings, even in villas and country houses and simple town dwellings ... The subjects were drawn mainly from marine and land plants, religious ceremonies, and the gay life of the court and the people. The worship of nature pervaded everything." [352]

Redressing the female/male balance

It is easy to see why the rediscovery of Crete, and Marija Gimbutas' revelations from Catal Huyuk and Old Europe, have been so exciting to so many people. Some of these archaeological sites have in recent times become the focus for what is essentially religious pilgrimage by goddess worshippers. So it is important to note that this 'goddess culture' did have a place for gods. Starhawk acknowledges this, saying (whether as a matter of historical fact or poetic license) that "Male shamans dressed in skins and horns in identification with the God and the herds; but female priestesses presided naked, embodying the fertility of the Goddess." [353]

The understanding of life, for men in particular, had been based since time immemorial on understanding the movements of animals. And since all these animals had come from the Goddess, and those that were hunted had been given to the men by the Goddess, there would never have been much question over where men stood in the natural order of things.

Marija Gimbutas suggests that the relative paucity of male figures in the archaeological record of Old Europe was "because his cult must have taken place in the wild, not in homes or temples", though male images were not "less divine ... man's sexual and physical power was esteemed as magically enhancing female life-giving powers." [354] The male aspect is examined in depth by Kenny Klein, in his pioneering exploration of Wicca from the male point of view, *The Flowering Rod*:

> Religion centred around an Earth Mother, who birthed all that is and ever would be, and a God who embodied the skills these people used for everyday survival, the skills of a hunter. He was part man and part animal, to show the interdependence of hunter and hunted. He could teach wisdom and skill to those who hunted reverently, and drive insane those who did not ... When the great hunt of the Autumn was finished, the hunters would gather around the hunted antlered animals. Then stones were gathered, one stone for each animal killed. The stones were sewn into the belly of the biggest of the animals killed in the hunt. A priest in an antlered head dress cast the animal into a round lake, a lake in the shape of the Mother's fertile belly. In this way the hunters assured that the animals that had been hunted so that the people could eat would be reborn.[355]

This description of a palaeolithic origin for Gwynn ap Nudd's *Cauldron of Annwn* may owe much to the imagination, but it does concur with ancient images on cave walls and would seem to contain an essential truth. Nevertheless with the spread of farming, though the God did not lose his antlers, he did lose some of his potency.

As Old European culture developed through the neolithic era, regular community festivals developed into new forms, expressing the new relationship between the people and the earth; but here we find a suggestion that the balance between the sexes had in fact tipped towards women. Baring and Cashford, for instance, quote James Mellaart: during the sixth millenium BC "agriculture finally triumphed over the age-old occupation of hunting and with it the power of woman increased: this much is clear from the almost total disappearance of male statues." [356]

It is undoubtedly true, as Riane Eisler says, that "there is little indication that the position of men in this social system was in any sense comparable to the subordination and suppression of women characteristic of the male-dominant system that replaced it." [357] Nevertheless there is reason to see the female-defined nature of this society as being oppressive towards men in certain ways. To avoid looking at these does a disservice to history, as well as failing to provide a full understanding for the ultimate failure of Old European culture to survive the challenges which it was to meet.

Eisler does state clearly that Crete "was not an ideal society or utopia but a real human society, complete with problems and imperfections" [358] but these imperfections tend to be glossed over in the very real need to start putting right the imbalance of information which has been available to us for so long. However, they were important. For instance, sex researcher Mary Jane Sherfey highlighted the introduction of male circumcision during early Mesolithic times "in a society in which women expected and demanded to experience frequent and regular orgasmic satisfaction":

> Men must have shown considerable resistance to such a barbaric act of symbolic castration which, as initially practiced, must have taken its toll in actual castration and in lives through infections and blood poisoning.[359]

There is nothing wrong with women experiencing frequent and regular orgasmic satisfaction; but the use of surgery on men to help ensure such an outcome suggests an element of exploitation. Overall, whilst men's power as expressed through the hunt and its associated rituals was diminishing, so women's power was growing. The ancient balance was changing. In many places, in different ways, archetypal male figures were ritually sacrificed to the Goddess at regular intervals. Stories of the 'Year King' and suchlike are widespread, and plentifully recorded in, particularly, J.G.Frazer's *The Golden Bough.*

Such practices were not so cruel or oppressive as those later inflicted by the patriarchy upon women, and it may be simplistic to see them as men being subordinated to women's sexual needs before being systematically culled. There could be some advantage in having the alpha male impregnate as many women as possible before being replaced; but the sacrifices were real, and they certainly indicate a shift away from the ancient balance of the sexes.

The Europe into which the Kurgans rode was one in which men had become to a significant degree disempowered, where they had "lost their ancient role and struggled to find their new identity and elevate their own usefulness in a woman-dominated world." [360] The warrior on horseback would have been a terrifying sight, "a host whose on-slaught was like a hurricane" in the words of one Sumerian scribe.[361] But he is not just, or always, a threat. He is a powerful archetypal figure: and one that answers to the very space left by the absence of hunting as a primary male role. He first rode into Europe more than 6,000 years ago, surely dressed up as impressively as possible. His effect would have been more than visual: he would have been a psychological bombshell. He could of course inspire fear if that is what he wanted to do; but would he not also have been attractive, in a profound way, to those who had never seen him in the flesh before?

Though the imagery is medieval, the same archetype inspires Parsifal in the Arthurian cycle: a simple youth living with his mother in the forest, he sees five armed knights ride by. He is awe-struck, and wants only to be one of them. This story describes a necessary part of the young man's psychological growth, enshrined in folk tales and eventually written down as part of the Grail Legend in twelfth century France. Robert A. Johnson explores male psychology in *He*. This passage seems particularly pertinent:

> Parsifal grows up in a primitive, peasant way, wears homespun clothes, has no schooling, asks no questions, and is completely untutored. Early in his adolescence he is out playing one day when five knights came riding by wearing all their impressive equipment: the scarlet and gold trappings, the armour, the shields, the lances, all the accoutrements of knighthood. They dazzled poor Parsifal so completely that he dashed home to tell his mother he had seen five gods. He was on fire with this marvellous sight and decided to leave immediately to join the five wonderful men.[362]

Whatever the physical effect of incursions into Europe by mounted warriors, the Goddess culture would have had little or no defence against the psychological impact of this image. Although this was an alien concept in the world described by Marija Gimbutas, it is hard to imagine any real response except, sooner or later, for the Europeans to come up with their own equivalent.

Life for the prehistoric hunter had been very hard: a constant battle for survival as evidenced archaeologically by cracked bones and short lifespans. Farming became an effective answer to this; but at what cost? For the men, it was no doubt safer to have one of their number sacrificed annually than for the whole company to risk death and injury every week hunting large wild animals. But the change, particularly in its effect on male psychology, must have been profound.

Human sacrifice, specifically the symbolic sacrifice of men at particular seasons of the year, is a phenomenon that has been well documented. But conventional historians tend to hold it up merely as evidence of the ancients' barbarity. The new breed of feminist historian rarely mention it, though Baring and Cashford in *The Myth of the Goddess* suggest that sacrifice in general "might be best understood as a symptom of a radical disorder of the psyche in which the person or tribe has claimed for itself the powers of the deity ... the earliest collective expression of what has come in this century to be called psychosis." [363]

They go on to look particularly at ritual regicide, in which "the sacrifice of the 'old' king then ensured that the forces of decay would be arrested, just as the installation of a 'young' or 'new' king would renew life for the whole community;" [364] this being one example - though far less barbaric than later ones - of psychosis as "the ultimate defence against *unconscious* terror."

It must have been an important element in cultures that were actually far more advanced than most have given them credit for. I suggest that its purpose was to help maintain the balance of energies - perceived at the time in socio-magical terms - in societies that required some means of imposing cohesion since the ending of the primary role of hunting. I shall refrain from exploring the subject further here, but leave this as a suggestion: the Old European Goddess culture - though its advantages and virtues were great and demand acknowledgement - included inherent weaknesses that contributed to its own ultimate demise.

The Kurgan invasions

Into this 'Golden Age', of the feminists as well as of the Greeks, came hordes of horse-riding, sword-wielding warriors from the East. With them came new - and warlike - gods, who are said to have replaced, or subordinated, the Goddess;[365] but this is something of an over-simplification.

The Goddess culture was, after all, based on principles and traditions that had been created to ensure a balance between male and female, with an understanding that both were integral parts of the whole. In stark contrast, the invaders "introduced the idea of an opposition between the powers of light and darkness, imposing this polarity on the older view in which the whole contained both light and darkness in an ever-changing relationship." [366]

In doing so they created a radical change in the male element, rather than introducing it for the first time:

> An alien Sky God appeared, whose prime attribute was the thunderbolt, or nickel-iron meteorite, from which were forged the weapons for which we name the Iron Age ... This Sky-God raped and ravished the Earth Mother and forcibly married her, supplanting Her true mate ... When men had the Antlered God as the archetypal role model at the center of their worship, they viewed their maleness and their sexuality as part of their worship ... But as the Iron Sky God came into Europe, the role of men's sexuality shifted. Stories of rape were interwoven with native mythologies. The Sky God possessed women, and the Earth. Men's sexuality was no longer defined as an act of beauty and worship, but as an act of possession.[367]

Here, then, is a key element of patriarchy. This new development was symbolised by an extraordinary phenomenon: the creation of fixed marks in the landscape in the form of burial mounds or 'kurgans'.[368] As noted in Chapter 1, these mounds appear to have been created as a response to incursions onto the steppes by the 'cultivators'. Conflict between the two cultures originally arose when the horticulturalists began settling the traditional Kurgan ranges in the Ukraine; their settlements here were the first to be built as fortifications.[369] In clearing the incomers off, the Kurgans may have discovered that pillage can be far more profitable than hunting or herding.

There followed a long series of incursions, over several thousand years, characterised as the 'Kurgan invasions' into south east Europe. This warlike behaviour steadily spread, and everything started to change:

> By the fifth millennium BCE ... we begin to find evidence of what [James] Mellaart calls a pattern of disruption of the old neolithic cultures in the near east. Archaeological remains indicate clear signs of stress by this time in many territories. There is evidence of invasions, natural catastrophes and sometimes both, causing large scale destruction and dislocation. In many areas the old painted pottery traditions disappear. Bit by devastating bit, a period of cultural regression and stagnation sets in. Finally, during this time of mounting chaos the development of civilization comes to a standstill.[370]

Even in the west, "profound changes occurred. Settlements are now found outside the ecological niche of valley bottoms, with some defended by palisades built of tree trunks. These changes signal the shift from a peaceful, unfortified lifestyle, to one that required protection against invasion." [371] Gradually models of power and domination based on male hierarchies and warfare became the norm everywhere. Where the indigenous population (and remnants of their culture) survived, there was a new ruling class based in hill forts and maintaining their power by force.[372] It took several thousand years, but by the time of the Greek city states and the Macedonian empire, this was the established reality.

Our attention has been drawn to this period by feminist historians, who tend to see the whole series of events as entirely negative and destructive. However, both of these societies had stepped away from the ancient ecological balance - which implies also the balance of the sexes - and each in different directions.

In Europe, neolithic farming meant, progressively, the end of hunting as a primary way of economic life, the gradual end of the key male role that had been a central factor in our species' evolution. Ultimately this activity, which had originally defined humans' place in the natural order, was to become no more than a leisure pursuit.

The incursions of Kurgan people into Europe had a profound effect; but the feminist analysis of this effect does not tell us why they were so successful, nor why the Old European Goddess culture was not sufficiently resilient to survive - though it had survived everything else, including the ice age, for 30,000 years. Simply to say that the Kurgans

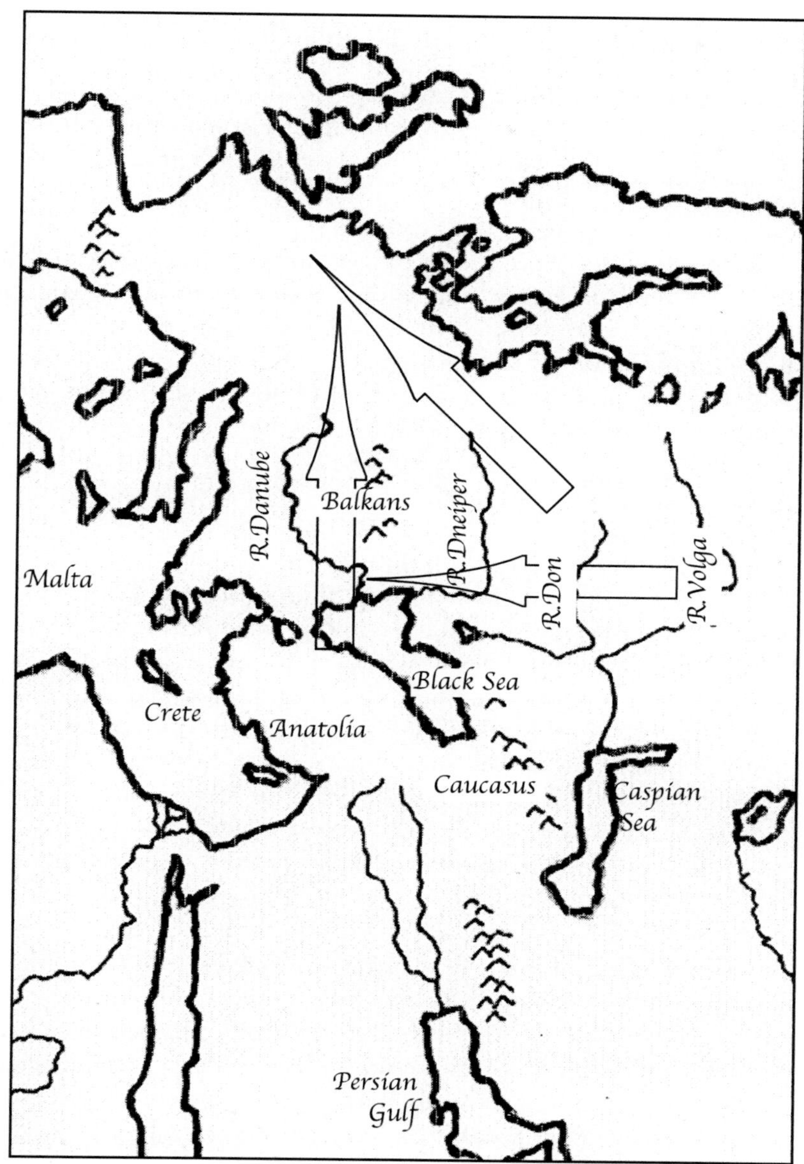

Southeast Europe and the western steppes
Showing 'Old Europe' and the Kurgan incursions:
(1) 4,400-4,300 BCE, (2) 3,500-3,000 BCE, (3) 3,000-2,900 BCE.

were more violent and better equipped for violence is not enough; what we are looking at is not an imperial conquest, but a profound cultural shift that has gradually been adopted nearly everywhere on the planet.

The end of the reign of the Goddess

The cultural shift was indeed both profound and gradual. The essentially matrilineal 'gens' (or clan) system, the kinship network that was common to pre-patriarchal societies, survived well into Greek times, though overlaid with father-right and militaristic functions.[373] And although rulership now fell to Kings rather than Queens, in many cultures the hereditary rights of Kings depended on the royal blood of their mothers or their wives, rather than their fathers. Thus Egypt was ruled by a married partnership of brother and sister; whilst elsewhere in the Mediterranean world:

> Kings ruled in Italy, but they reigned as viceroys of women. They ruled by permission of the wives or mothers who were the hereditary heirs to the throne, as in Egypt, Persia, and Mycenae ... Livy tells in shocked tones of Tullia, the wife of Lucius Tarquinius, who 'driving into the Roman Forum in her chariot, unabashed by the crowd of men present, called her husband out of the Senate house and was first to greet him King'. Tullia, an Etruscan lady, was only performing the expected function of a royal wife; for she was the daughter of the old king and queen, and therefore it was in her power to make a new king.[374]

The truth of all this is still remembered in folk tales, where the man of humble origin becomes King by virtue of his marriage to the Princess.

The old ways of the clan persisted for many centuries, and the examples from the classical world quoted above represent an intermediate situation. Ultimately, in order to take power within their communities so as to fight effectively for power in the world, men first had to take power from the women. This was gradually put into effect until the wife, rather than being her husband's equal, was reduced to being his household's chief servant. In Engels' words:

> The overthrow of mother-right was the world historical defeat of the female sex. The man took command in the home also; the woman was degraded and reduced to servitude, she became the slave of his lust and a mere instrument for the production of children. This degraded position of the woman, especially conspicuous among the Greeks of the heroic age and still more of the classical age, has gradually been palliated and glozed over, and sometimes clothed in a milder form; in no sense has it been abolished.[375]

The social history of Greece and Rome is largely the story of the Goddess culture's step-by-step dismantling. The Athenians, for instance, are remembered as the inventors of democracy; but ninety percent of Athens' population at that time were slaves - this was not democracy as we understand it.

Around the Mediterranean there was a new cosmopolitan merchant class. Some of Athens' most influential and wealthy inhabitants were foreigners, and were not part of the local tribe or clans; so according to the old law they could take no part in the political process. The introduction of 'democracy' was actually taking power away from the traditional clans and transferring it to the new class of merchants and traders.[376] At the same time, "the old sense of participation with nature had been replaced by a desire to dominate it, and the powerful new male gods reflected this." [377]

The old ways of the Goddess had become an excessive restraint, their practitioners a danger to the new male power structures - but they would not go away completely. They were deep magic, based on countless generations of life being focused on The Mother. They were never completely wiped out. Their essential elements remained, in the mystery religions around the Mediterranean for instance.

The Roman Emperor Constantine took Christianity and turned it into a state religion, a tool for eliminating 'Paganism' [378] and imposing patriarchal uniformity. After a further 1,500 years this had still not been completely accomplished, though the medieval witch burnings were sufficiently conclusive to pave the way for the industrial revolution.

Right through this period there have been widespread taboos against women in childbirth, menstruation, and all things that symbolise female power. Midwives became secondary to professional gynaecologists. Men took power actively and deliberately, and developed their own magic: forging iron, searching for the philosopher's stone, creating technological marvels. The story since the industrial revolution has been wholesale destruction of the natural environment, massive population growth, and indeed the oppression and exploitation of everyone to serve the system and its ambitions. Modern society is an extraordinary achievement, but seemingly still based on the fear that if women take back their power then it will all come to an end.

This process started a very long time ago, somewhere in ancient Asia. Today, it has reached close to its limits. Every one of us is thoroughly affected, every one of us willingly or unwillingly contributes to it, and history must surely take a new turn.

4 Palaeopsychology

The prehistoric origins of the shift to patriarchy will be explored in chapters 5 and 6, which look at the developments in ancient Asia that were such a contrast to what took place in Europe. First, however, it is necessary to have some understanding as to why human beings would have reacted to changes in climatic conditions and other environmental challenges in such a way as to alter the general quality of life - not just in the short term, but for thousands of years. James DeMeo's *Saharasia* has been cited as the major ground-breaking work in this respect; but we do now have a growing body of writing which can help us to understand the psychological reality behind our modern predicament. This chapter presents a review of such work.

To discuss the subject of human consciousness at all is to enter an intellectual minefield - since there is so little understanding, and particularly so little agreement, as to how the human mind works and how it came to do so. Nevertheless, it is far too important to avoid, so I present here what makes sense to me, in the hope that it will help to shift the direction of debate about human consciousness and the human psychological process to one that can contribute to real practical solutions.

There is, of course, endless confusion over terminology. The word 'awareness', for instance, is commonly used and with many shades of meaning. It has therefore been avoided here, though 'self-awareness' and 'human consciousness' seem to be closely linked concepts. I have also avoided discussing the 'subconscious' mind, generally understood to be that part of our minds from which instinctive behaviour, and responses 'programmed' by our life experience, emanate.

Since I am firmly of the opinion that programmed responses (and any other forms of inflexible thinking) in humans are the result of distress experiences that can be healed and freed up, I find the idea of the 'subconscious' unhelpful, at least in this discussion. I begin from the premise that people have their consciousness fully and creatively functional at all times, from childhood onwards, except to the extent that something has interfered with it.

On the human condition

Consider the suggestion that all human beings are born with a great potential for flexible intelligent thinking; with a natural attraction to other human beings and a natural propensity to behave towards them in an affectionate, co-operative manner; with an innate ability to derive enjoyment and satisfaction from life; to be enthusiastic, optimistic, curious and communicative; to meet life's challenges, dangers and disappointments with the attitudinal advantages implied by these abilities; and, if for any reason circumstances cause such optimal functioning to be temporarily lost, they have the ability to effect a full recovery once those circumstances have changed. Individual humans are born with this potential intact, and only as they grow older do they learn patterns of negative and destructive behaviour. This is also likely to be true for the human race as a whole, as it 'matures' from its relatively simple beginnings towards its uncertain future.

This description of the human condition is based on the work of Harvey Jackins, founder of the Re-evaluation Counselling movement. Since it does indeed describe 'optimal functioning', and it would be odd to expect evolution to select for anything less, it must carry credence. Taken as a working hypothesis, it casts an interesting light on the history and prehistory of our species. It clearly does not describe the 'average' or 'normal' adult human alive today (although we all may have glimpsed such a reality when life has been going particularly well); and Jackins estimated that people who are these days considered 'normal' operate on average at 10% of their emot-ional and intellectual potential.[401]

Clearly modern society is not based on any assumption that human behaviour is naturally or universally benign, although we might well imagine - even long for - a utopian existence in which it is. If we accept the hypothesis, then the question is: What has changed? What has gone wrong? And why?

Marija Gimbutas, Riane Eisler and others have shown that these questions are worth asking - that there was a time, at least in some parts of the world, when human life was different. In Minoan Crete, for example:

> The entire relationship between the sexes - not only definitions and valuations of gender roles but also attitudes toward sensuality and sex - was obviously very different from ours. For example, the bare-breasted style of dress for women and the skimpy clothes emphasizing the genitals for men demonstrate a frank appreciation of sexual differences and the pleasure made possible by these difference ... As [Jacquetta] Hawkes writes, "The Cretans seem to have reduced and diverted their aggressiveness through a free and well-balanced sexual life." Along with their enthusiasm for sports and dancing and their creativity and love of life, these liberated attitudes toward sex seem to have contributed to the generally peaceful and harmonious spirit predominant in Cretan life.[402]

This raises questions that go well beyond the artistic and economic achievements of ancient Crete. Wilhem Reich believed that "the existing social order is sick and, to the extent that it opposes biological urges and needs, creates pathos in people who otherwise would remain healthy." [403] The maintenance of this psychological health, from which their artistic and architectural achievements would have flowed, must have been the most important hallmark of Cretan culture.

The work of the sex researcher Mary Jane Sherfey, who worked with William H. Masters and Virginia Johnson, is relevant in this context. She developed a particular interest in the reasons for premenstrual tension, and in *The Nature and Evolution of Female Sexuality* (first published in 1966) she followed her own research and came to the conclusion - with extensive biological detail - that "the human female is sexually insatiable in the presence of the highest degrees of sexual satiation." [404] PMT, therefore, is the result of women's biologically determined sexual drive being suppressed in the supposed interests of social stability and the growth of civilisation. For this statement, she was widely heralded by the early feminists.

Sherfey's book deals mainly with the nature of female sexuality; its evolution - and the history of its suppression - were intended to be the subject of a second volume that never appeared. There has been speculation as to what happened to her, including conspiracy theories that suggest she was deliberately silenced. However, the evidence from within the book itself suggests that Sherfey - a scientist with no feminist pretensions of her own - was uncomfortable with the unavoidably radical conclusions of her own research:

> The suppression by cultural forces of women's *inordinately* high sexual drive and orgasmic capacity must have been an important prerequisite for the evolution of modern human societies and has continued, *of necessity,* to be a major preoccupation of practically every civilization.[405]

Whatever the reason, we are left with little more than a few footnotes as pointers to her thinking on this aspect of prehistoric human development. What she does give us, however, opens up a view of early human society that is dramatically different from most of those imagined by - for instance - modern novelists:

> The nature of [women's] sexual responsivity described is too close to that of certain higher primates to be ignored ... Primate females will perform coitus from twenty to fifty times a day during a peak week of estrus, usually with several series of copulations in rapid succession ... They will emerge from periods of heat totally exhausted, often with wounds from spent males who have repulsed them. I suggest that something akin to this behaviour could be paralleled by the human female if her civilization allowed it.[406]

Of course the human female does not 'come on heat', the cycle of menstruation being a far more sophisticated mechanism; nevertheless contemporary women assure me that - with the probable exception of periods spent nursing young children - the scenario described above could be substantially true.

It goes without saying that our civilisation absolutely does not allow it, so that such a proposition is likely to remain unproven either way. However, if we question whether anything biologically determined should be described as 'inordinate', and if we recall that Cretan society in

Minoan times was a successful civilisation whilst certainly not being preoccupied with suppressing women's sexual drive nor human sensuality in general, the questions raised are profound.

Amongst the higher primates, bonobos (those genetically closest to humans) famously and with prolonged and widespread enthusiasm 'make love not war', and this contributes enormously to their social cohesion. Amongst humans, 'something akin to this behaviour' does not have to imply 'wounds' and 'spent males', since (as with all our instincts) human sexuality is subject to conscious human choice. Hence sexuality is *able* to be suppressed, but physical and psychological health require that it should best be incorporated into appropriate social and ritual activity.

It is actually this, social and ritual forms which act as a container for the healthy expression of our natural sensual selves, that our modern (patriarchal) society does not allow; and the example of Minoan Crete which shows that it is possible.

Sherfey herself allowed that this could have been the case "within one or possibly several types of social structures which would have prevailed through most of the Pleistocene [inter-glacial] period." [407] However, she went on to say that not until the "ungovernable cyclic sexual drive of women" had been "gradually brought under control by rigidly enforced social codes" could "family life become the stabilizing and creative principle from which modern civilized man could emerge." [408]

So much, surely some will say, for modern civilised 'man'. In any case, the notion that women's sexual drive would (or before 'civilisation' did) over-ride the instinct to protect and nurture children who have already been born, is clearly a biological and evolutionary nonsense. Freud asserted that, of necessity, "civilisation has been built up on the denial of instinctive urges ... mainly those of sex" [409] - but this of course is true only of *patriarchal* civilisation.

James DeMeo's work illustrates the fact that positive attitudes to sex and sensuality go hand in hand with a positive relationship with the rest of the natural world, whilst repressed sexuality correlates with a drive for 'economic development' at the expense of both nature and the more subtle and gentle of human values.

These days we have increasingly mixed attitudes towards the formerly all-pervading notion of 'progress'. One thought that is barely entertained, though, is that we may actually be *less* human than our predecessors were, at or before a certain stage of our species' development. Yet it is a perfectly plausible suggestion: modern life is well stocked with people apparently lacking in 'common humanity', whilst no species other than that proclaimed as *homo sapiens* is actually so unintelligent as to wreck its own environment. As Stuart Wavell has pointed out in *The Sunday Times*, human beings are in a sense "the least intelligent of all living species", because we can no longer live within our environment, but seek to control it.[410] Of course, the biological fact of human intelligence is not here being called into question; the suggestion is rather that something has happened, as a result of which most of us - at least collectively - are unable to exercise that intelligence constructively and effectively.

It is part of the problem that we see ourselves as separate from our environment at all. The modern-day debate about climate change, for instance, focuses on to what extent global warming is part of a natural and inevitable cycle, and to what extent caused by human activity; but the two are really different aspects of the same phenomenon. Humans and their behaviour are, actually, part of the process of nature and integral to the environment. If we deny this and set ourselves apart from the natural world, this will inevitably lead to its degradation. There is no genuine separation. As James DeMeo says, the 'emotional desert' that inwardly afflicts people and the desert caused by desiccation of the landscape are, in the patrist world, part of the same vicious cycle:

> We treat nature very similar to the way we treat our infants and children, the way we were treated ourselves in infancy. While an unarmored or less armored individual may stand in the middle of a vast and ancient forest, or on a pristine shoreline or mountain-top and feel a powerful and expansive bioenergetic connection to nature, a feeling of being part of the larger web of life, another more armored individual feels only anxiety in such a situation, or they feel nothing at all, and may even start to calculate the amount of money which can be made from cutting down all the trees, or 'developing' the last untouched spot on the coast or mountain range.

He even goes on to suggest that:

> Saharasia created a new kind of homo sapiens, a dried-up life- and love-hating specimen who is emotionally better adjusted to existence within a toxic deforested wasteland than within the throbbing and pulsing web of life. We are caught in a suicidal symbiosis - an emotional conspiracy - with the desert itself, expanding and enlarging the deserts even into our own emotional and social structures.[411]

Reich's 'sex-economic' theory

DeMeo, based on the work of Wilhelm Reich as well as a wide-ranging review of archaeological research, shows that the earliest human societies were co-operative and egalitarian, sexually uninhibited, free from warfare, free from the domination of one sex by another, and from oppressive political regimes - and that these attitudes and modes of being are inter-related, together forming the profile of people in their 'natural' state. Humans, we could say, evolved so as to function well, without the need to waste energy on unnecessary conflict. However, emotional trauma has led to psychological 'armoring':

> The process of human *armoring* (as Reich called it) against impulse, feeling, and emotion, begins in the cradle as the child is purposefully (though often unconsciously) traumatized by contactless and emotionally deadened adult carers, who themselves had been subject to similar trauma in infancy. Additional traumas and repressions, particularly those of a sexual nature, were heaped upon the older child and adolescent, by which time the fully armored character structure crystallizes. Examples of the specific traumas I studied ... are infant cranial deformation, swaddling, genital mutilations, the bride price, and various other pleasure-censoring or very painful childrearing and adolescent rituals.[412]

Such overtly cruel practices, however, represent only the extreme cases. Human children come into the world expecting and needing the loving attention of their carers; merely a significant lack of this will induce some degree of anxiety and trauma.

Reich did not provide a convincing analysis of where this process of armoring began historically, and DeMeo's work is an exploration of precisely that question. His presentation can perhaps be criticised for failing to see the social and economic preconditions which were already in place prior to the late neolithic, and for focusing solely on Saharasian desiccation and avoiding other traumatic climatic challenges. Nevertheless he is the first serious researcher to have examined the issue of what, exactly, went wrong with human beings to have caused us to arrive in our current state of endemic conflict and insecurity.

What becomes clear is that modern society (whether we take the view of Freud and Sherfey or of Reich and Jackins) now depends on rigid and oppressive patterns of behaviour being in place - and that once in place, they become self-perpetuating. These patterns should realistically be described as pathological, and they have appeared over the past 6,000 years, profoundly altering the original nature of human society.

DeMeo describes Reich's theory as an "alternative to mechanistic genetic determinism for the passing on of [violent or destructive] behaviour traits from one generation to the next" since "a culture free from inhibition of innate, biologically mandated pleasure drives would maintain itself in a social, co-operative and loving manner." He presents it as the "spontaneously honest, loving, social and peaceful core to human nature" having been affected by "some powerful, prolonged and widespread anxiety-provoking trauma."

This has resulted in "chronic sexual frustration and undischarged emotional-energetic tension - the 'fuel' of pleasure-anxiety, armoring, and sadistic aggression" which over generations becomes embedded as social institutions and traditions:

> Once the armor is formed and generally exists culture-wide, it becomes a force for its own self-perpetuation, this time wholly from *within* the culture. After the outside force had worked its traumatic damage, social structure would change and institutionalisation of trauma would occur. Newborn infants, mothers and children would then be attacked and repressed by ritual traditions, by distorted and damaged social institutions which would rationalise a thousand different methods for the denial of pleasure and infliction of pain, implanting new barriers of fear, compulsion and anxiety into male-female relations ... People thereafter would become their own

> traumatic oppressors, and would hence only 'feel comfortable' with neighbours and leaders who would likewise support the continuation of the same harsh and repressive ways of living.[413]

'Harsh and repressive ways of living', of course, extend beyond the sexual and domestic sphere and lead to the creation of slavery, and then class-stratified societies of increasing complexity. The initial cause of such changes on a world-wide scale, he identifies as the effects of desertification across the region identified as 'Saharasia' between about 4000 and 3000 BCE:

> During extreme drought and desertification, food supplies dwindle and famine sets in; as this happens, children tend to suffer most severely ... [they] will not recover full physical or emotional vigor once food supply is restored, and will suffer lifelong physical and emotional effects ...
>
> Individuals who have suffered through severe famine during childhood will raise their own children differently from prior generations, even during times of plenty ... In regions which experience repeated widespread droughts ... new patterns emerge, focused upon basic survival, and with little or no emphasis upon pleasurable emotional bonding or social living. Social conditions become disturbed and emotionally diminished, much in keeping with the surrounding landscape, which is drying out and withering away.
>
> Once so anchored into social institutions, the new drought- and famine-derived behaviour patterns reproduce themselves in each new generation, irrespective of subsequent turns in climate towards wetter conditions. Warfare, which often appears as a secondary effect of drought and famine starvation, compounds the damage ... Combined with other traumas related to forced migration, these environmental forces are quite sufficient to initiate the process of armoring among previously unarmored peoples.[414]

DeMeo presents extensive and detailed evidence for this taking place. However, he barely touches on the existence of a natural recovery process. In fact, since it would be impossible to mobilise an army of Reichian psychotherapists sufficient to solve the world's problems as he describes them, he offers little hope for the future. However, traumatic experience has not only occurred during and since the period he focuses on. Natural disasters and climate change have always been a part of life on earth; and on a local or personal level, experiencing trauma has always been and will always be a possibility. At some point during any individual's lifetime, it is a likelihood. For humans to function well, our functioning needs to include a viable recovery process, and evolution will surely have equipped us with just that.

The natural recovery process

The need for a recovery process is emphasised by humans' long period of growth and maturation, which makes the likelihood of experiencing trauma more acute, particularly in childhood and before the individual has reached emotional maturity. It has been estimated that, if humans were born at the same stage of development as most mammals, the gestation period would need to be at least 12 to 15 months.[415] The large size of the human brain and skull has resulted in birth at an earlier stage of the growth process, and a relatively longer childhood than any other species.

The brain reaches virtually adult size whilst body growth is only forty percent complete, and this is followed by an adolescent growth spurt - unique to humans. Furthermore, "humans become human through intense learning - not just of survival in the practical world, but of customs and social mores, kinship and social laws. In other words: culture." [416]

This unique growth pattern, which allows for a large brain and an extended period of learning and cultural assimilation, also means an extended period of vulnerability, both physical and emotional. Here lies the answer to a key question posed by Wilhelm Reich:

> Why does the armoring of the human species exist at all, since it contradicts nature in man at every single step and destroys his natural, rich potentialities? This does not seem to make sense. Why did nature make a 'mistake'? Why only in the human species? Why not also in the deer or the chipmunk? Why just in man? His 'higher destiny' is, clearly, not the answer. The armor has destroyed man's

> natural decency and his faculties, and has thus precluded 'higher' developments.[417]

As a species we have adapted to deal with the emotional risk, inherent in our long period of maturation, by developing the ability to suppress painful emotional experience. Once suppressed, it can remain so indefinitely, allowing for continued mental and emotional functioning rather than catatonic collapse. The level of such functioning will, however, be adversely affected to some extent.

It would be more than extraordinary if this ability to suppress negative emotional material was not matched by a natural ability to release it and recover from its effects when circumstances become favourable.

This ability does exist, and in one way or another forms the basis of any workable system of psychotherapy. DeMeo hints at it in his discussion of Reichian therapy. Harvey Jackins is explicit, calling it the 'discharge process' and describing it as something potentially available to all human beings, as a normal part of life that has been hidden or forgotten:

> The distressed human spontaneously seeks to claim the aware attention of another human. If he or she is successful ... discharge ensues. Discharge is signalized externally by one or more of a precise set of physical processes. These are: crying or sobbing (with tears), trembling with cold perspiration, laughter, angry shouting and vigorous movement with warm perspiration (tantrum); live, interested talking; and in a slightly different way, yawning, often with scratching and stretching. Discharge requires considerable time for completion ... The residue of the distress experience is being recalled and reviewed (not necessarily with awareness). Rational evaluation of the information received during the distress experience occurs automatically following discharge. It occurs only to the degree that discharge is completed. On completion, the negative and anti-rational effects of the experience are completely eliminated.[418]

However, "as a result of long-term conditioning of the entire population", any attempt to claim such attention in a social context "is almost always rebuffed". Modern (patriarchal) cultures actively discourage precisely those physical reactions which make up the natural emotional healing process. Along with Reich's 'armoring', or perhaps as part of it, the ability to recover from the effects of a distress experience has been suppressed.

This, and the theory which supports it, are described in more detail below. But first, is there evidence for such a naturalised recovery process outside the context of modern therapeutic practice?

Malidoma Patrice Somé describes in detail a traditional funeral ritual amongst the Dagara people of West Africa. There, funerals are occasions that provide every member of the community, whether or not they are closely related to the person who has died, with the opportunity to express any and all of their grief about anything. The result is a collective cathartic experience that goes on for several days. Within a protected ritual space, everyone is expected to express their grief, anger, sorrow, fear - whatever has emotional power - through crying, shaking, dancing, shouting and wildly running about.

This occurs whenever somebody dies, so that grieving and emotional discharge are a normal part of the social life of the community. In what Somé describes as the 'indigenous world', people "understand the expression of emotion as a process of self-kindling or calming which not only helps in handling death but also resets or repairs the feelings within the person," and the whole population remains emotionally and psychologically healthy as a result.[419]

It is not possible to say how widespread such practices once were. Somé does refer to the 'indigenous world' as a whole, but this kind of activity is not likely to have been properly appreciated or understood by nineteenth-century anthropologists in the wake of western imperial conquest. Nevertheless we can allow ourselves to believe that our species, in its 'natural habitat' before the advent of agriculture and then civilisation, had resources available in a social context that would have made possible recovery from trauma and painful emotional experience. As a result, the continuing ability to make full use of intelligence and creativity would have been maintained.

Distress would have been less widespread, since patterns of distress would not have become culturally embedded. In some regions at least (and probably most), distress experiences were integrated into the life of the community and understood as a potential source of strength and character. Those who suffered serious trauma in early life - through accident, illness or bereavement, for example - were 'marked out' by its lasting effect on their lives, and it was they who became the shamans. It was recognised that those who suffered the depths of the underworld were best able to attain the spiritual heights - and they were therefore given special training and special status:

> Psychological problems might show themselves in peculiarities of behaviour. Young potential shamans could be violent and frenzied, sometimes collapsing inexplicably into states of unconsciousness. Such youths would often withdraw voluntarily or at the command of spirit voices into the wilderness, eating only tree bark and fungus, and engaging in bouts of self-injury. The parents of the afflicted child, recognising the 'shamanistic sickness', would consult the old tribal shaman and often place the youth under his care.[420]

Such people today are too often seen only as life's casualties. Once they were key to healing, for themselves and for the community as a whole.

Re-evaluation Counselling

In the 1940s, Harvey Jackins was an American trades union activist with an interest in psychotherapy and related subjects. During the 1950s he developed a technique for dealing with the psychological 'distress patterns' that are laid down as the result of painful emotional experience and that remain undischarged. He gradually built up a body of theory that both supports 'Re-evaluation Counselling' as a therapeutic process and that describes the cumulative effects of distress patterns on the development of society.

He saw the class system as having been created and held in place by the interaction of these patterns. According to this theory, all of us have to some extent become affected by such patterns, though in different circumstances some people will take 'oppressor' roles and some 'victim' roles, neither being the experience of our true humanity. The result is a society whose nature is oppressive. It has become increasingly sophisticated, but its earliest form (beginning some 6,000 years ago) was the slave society.

The full 're-emergence' of everyone from these patterns would result in the ending of all class differences, together with related oppressions such as racism and sexism, oppression of other minority groups, lack of adequate care for the environment, freedom from addictions, and so on. This in turn would allow for the establishment of a truly 'rational' society. To the extent that such re-emergence has not been achieved, exploitation and mistreatment of all kinds will continue.

The basic counselling technique ('Re-evaluation Counselling') can be used by professional counsellors, but Jackins saw the professional counsellor/client relationship as mirroring society's other oppressive patterns. He encouraged the use, amongst lay counsellors, of the techniques he had pioneered ('co-counselling'), where there is a peer relationship between two or more counsellors who take turns in counselling each other. By the 1970s, the 'RC' or 'co-counselling' movement had grown worldwide. Jackins died in 1999, but it still continues to flourish.

Re-evaluation Counselling theory starts from the assumption, supported by empirical evidence from thousands of people's experience arising from their counselling practice, that all people in their essential nature are benign. We are born with the potential for almost unlimited enjoyment of life, and if we were to grow up or live entirely free from interference we would all be entirely co-operative, intelligent, flexible in our thinking, mutually supportive, personally powerful (though not in an oppressive sense), inquisitive, creative - and generally glad to be alive. It is only distress that prevents this.

A 'distress experience' is any experience that arouses negative feelings: fear, anger, loneliness, despair, embarrassment, tension ... and when this happens we temporarily cease to have control of ourselves through our full human intelligence, instead reverting to animal instinct in order to escape the danger or otherwise threatening circumstances. This in itself is not a 'bad' thing, in fact it can be a very effective survival mechanism.

If we need to escape from an avalanche or the attack of a wild animal, for instance, it is best not to think about it - however intelligently - but to rely on instinct to get us out of trouble as quickly as possible.[421] Having done so, however, we will continue to feel disturbed and upset. Though the acute fear may subside, that part of our intelligent thinking which was suspended will remain suspended until we can fully discharge the fear from our bodies. This will commonly be done by shaking. Other negative experiences may be discharged by crying, sweating, laughing or yawning.

Imagine a small child who has suddenly been scared or upset. Imagine her running towards her mother, who is waiting, arms outstretched. The child runs towards her with an anguished expression on her face. Once there, still upset but now in a safe place, she will burst into tears - and if she is held in those loving arms for as long as she needs it, she will recover. This simple description of the discharge process often happens naturally for children, but actually holds true for all people of all ages.

It works best if someone is available to witness and support the person discharging. If the discharge is allowed to proceed without being interrupted, halted or postponed, the person will recover completely. The incident will be stored in the memory as useful experience, and fully functioning intelligence will be restored straight away. However, if discharge is not possible, or is actively discouraged, then recovery is not effected and the experience is stored as a 'distress pattern'. A portion of the individual's normally flexible intelligence is replaced by a rigid and emotionally charged image of the incident, and any future situation that is sufficiently similar will 'restimulate' the original feelings - even though they may be entirely inappropriate in the new circumstances.

A common example would be someone in an adult relationship who becomes restimulated by an aspect of their partner's behaviour. Such a person will commonly become angry or upset, most likely blaming their partner for the feelings which arise. They are probably reacting to an emotional issue which is actually from the past and, for instance, to do with their parent of the same sex as the present-day partner. This situation will persist until circumstances are sufficiently favour-able for discharge to take place (usually when a deliberate effort is made to remedy the situation).

There is no absolute time limit on this and, as suggested, there may be some survival advantage in the ability to suppress negative emotions in some circumstances. However, the longer life continues without discharge taking place, the more likely that restimulation and further negative experiences will occur. The original distress pattern thus becomes reinforced and overlaid by further layers of distress - making the original feelings ever more difficult to access.

If this is never adequately addressed, the individual's thinking becomes progressively more rigid and reactive, and in extreme cases pathological. Even when people carry a relatively 'tolerable' level of distress, there is likely to be sufficient built up over the years to require many hours of counselling - particularly as adults often take a while to loosen up and feel safe enough to allow discharge to come.

It should be noted that, once the prevalence of rigid distress patterns becomes endemic in a culture, one of the primary causes of distress amongst children is the behaviour of their own parents. This is partly due to the unconscious acting out of patterns that the parents themselves were subjected to as children, and partly due to confusion of the recovery process (crying etc) with the distress itself - so that well-meaning adults will discourage children from discharging ("there there, don't cry, it's alright now").

None of this is to say that these are 'bad' parents, who do not love their children. (Indeed, RC theory asserts that everyone is always doing their best, given the particular circumstances of their own lives). Nevertheless patterns tend to be passed on from one generation to the next, and over time this results in social institutions based on rigid, patterned thinking, and which become self-perpetuating in the same way. Ultimately the whole of society becomes oppressive in its nature, its people operating well below their potential, having effectively traded their flexible intelligence and creativity for the illusion of safety from danger, discomfort and difficult feelings.

The question of how all this began is asked within Re-evaluation Counselling, but Jackins never addressed it in detail. He was not a prehistorian; but he did say, in noting the destruction of 'natural communities':

> Before human beings got organised into class societies, there was much hardship and difficulty in living, but there apparently was little deliberate exploitation of humans by humans. We can presume from present patterned behaviour by humans that there could be occasional oppression when someone had acquired a pattern of greed or impatience or anger from some accidental catastrophe, or by contagion from someone who had been accidentally hurt badly and then acted out the hurt pattern at the other person in a way that 'seemed' advantageous

to the dramatiser. But the natural affection between intelligent people who lived together as associates and families and bands would probably have made sharing and mutual support the dominant themes in the simple groupings that grew from families into clans and tribes.[422]

Indeed, it is precisely this natural affection, and the co-operation that springs from it, that gave human beings the evolutionary edge over other species. However, with the establishment of agriculture this gradually gave way to coercive patterns of behaviour and social development. Once greed, violence and the concentration of power had taken hold, the result was warfare - and the enslavement of war captives. The first class societies consisted of slave-owners and slaves:

> These persisted for about 6,000 years, and in persisting allowed the invention of many new forms of oppression as a way of keeping the oppressed divided against each other for the benefit of the oppressors. The internal contradictions of the slave societies led to their collapse and downfall as the slave 'empires' became unwieldy. Their breakdown allowed the subsequent feudal class societies to arise, consisting primarily of serfs and nobles but fostering the emergence of a much larger contingent of middle-class people within the religious bureaucracies and as supervisors, knights and scribes.[423]

This does not explain where the patterns of greed and war-making came from in the first place, though it does summarise the historical process very well.

There are, no doubt, a number of effective ways to address our emotional and psychological problems on a personal level. Particular emphasis is given here to Re-evaluation Counselling because it also provides an analysis of the social and political context, explicitly describing society's ills as the collective result of individuals' ills.[424]

The patristic/patriarchal warrior horsemen who rode out of Asia to invade the Goddess's Europe in the fourth and fifth millennia BC had not always been there; nor did they appear out of nowhere for no real reason. The pain that they inflicted was the result of their own pain, however it was suffered, and however it had gained sufficient momentum to become expressed on such a scale as war.

So what is (or isn't) human consciousness ... ?

The work of both Wilhelm Reich and Harvey Jackins gives us a picture of how patriarchy came about; a picture that is gaining clarity as more attention is paid to the subject. A growing number of writers are presenting the view that this development has become a serious problem, one that needs addressing with some urgency. And as noted in the opening chapter, the subject is inextricably bound up with the evolution of human consciousness, which inevitably had much to do with furthering reproductive success, and therefore with the relationship between the sexes.

I use the term 'human consciousness' as if its meaning were obvious, as if everyone knows what it means, but this is an enormous assump-tion to make. In fact it is clearly not true. Informal discussions on the subject soon reveal, for instance, that many people consider an important part of human consciousness to be what psychologists define as 'the unconscious', i.e specifically *not* consciousness in the sense of being self-aware or consciously focused.

In order to discuss the appearance of human consciousness on the planet, some clarification is required.

For the purposes of this discussion, human consciousness is taken to be that which sets us apart from other creatures. This does not include what Jung and his students define as the 'unconscious', which is often described in terms of a force of nature, as a 'deep sea' or whatever, different from the part of our minds that is distinctively human. The unconscious equates to what others, principally those interested in esoteric spirituality, generally describe as 'universal consciousness', with which the whole of creation is imbued; or perhaps it would be better to describe it as the part of our minds that can perceive and relate to 'universal consciousness'.

It is doubtless true that this (un)consciousness has evolved to become more sophisticated and complex as life forms have become more sophisticated and complex physically, and that this has reached a particular level in humans; nevertheless it is not unique to humans, this is merely a matter of degree.

From a biological point of view, in comparing humans to other species, what is said to mark us out tends to be very basic in terms of consciousness and behaviour - bipedalism, the use of tools, understanding of language and so on. But on closer examination we find that such things already exist, at least to some extent, in the animal kingdom. The higher apes and aquatic mammals such as dolphins often seem to be 'as human' as us (or even more so) in one respect or another. American psychologist Julian Jaynes has extended this reality into territory that most people assume, even take for granted, is occupied specifically by human consciousness:

> Consciousness is not what we generally think it is. It is not to be confused with reactivity. It is not involved in hosts of perceptual phenomena. It is not involved in the performance of skills and often hinders their execution. It need not be involved in speaking, writing, listening, or reading. It does not copy down experience, as most people think. Consciousness is not at all involved in signal learning, and need not be involved in the learning of skills or solutions, which can go on without any consciousness whatever. It is not necessary for making judgements or in simple thinking. It is not the seat of reason, and indeed some of the most difficult instances of creative reasoning go on without any attending consciousness. And it has no location except an imaginary one! [425]

In other words, we can react to external stimuli without consciously focusing on them (even whilst we are asleep); the continuity of consciousness is an illusion caused by the fact that we cannot be conscious of when we are not conscious; we play the piano or drive a car without thinking consciously about what we are doing - and our performance is likely to be inhibited if we do (though we may have used our consciousness in learning those skills in the first place); similarly, if we focus consciously on the mechanics of verbal communication, we will probably fail to communicate; our memory, though subject to recall when needed (such as when we notice that something is unexpectedly changed or missing), is not so good at consciously recalling details simply at will; and concepts are not held consciously (rather we consciously call up concrete images which act as symbols for the concepts).

Jaynes cites experiments to show that learning is, at a simple level, a Pavlovian process of repeating actions which provide rewards, and that even complex learning situations, though they can benefit from conscious activity in understanding the problem or the goal, are basically carried out by the same means; that making judgements, for instance about the relative weight of two objects, is carried out unconsciously (though consciousness is required to set up the 'structions' that define such judgements in more complex situations); that simple reasoning is automatic and based on past experience; and that, though creative reasoning to find new solutions to complex problems may be based on extensive conscious attention, the answer famously comes in the 'eureka moment' whilst sitting in the bath. And finally, that consciousness is not located in the brain; in fact that it has "no location whatever except as we imagine it has."

Jaynes convincingly shows that all these things, so often assumed to be the province of the conscious mind, are in fact based in the unconscious - which, except perhaps for a certain degree of sophistication, we share with the natural world as a whole. In other words, this has plenty to do with 'consciousness', but it tells us what *human* consciousness is not, rather than what it is.

So, what then does a distinctively *human* consciousness consist of? What actually sets human beings apart from the rest of creation? Before examining Jaynes' answers to this, I shall consider the more fundamental questions of what are human beings? And how long have they been around?

First, in the words of Harvey Jackins, "rational human behavior is qualitatively different from the behavior of other life forms" and is not merely the most complicated version of animal behaviour:

> The essence of rational human behavior consists of responding to each instant of living with a new response, created afresh at that moment to precisely fit and handle the situation of that moment as the situation is defined by the information received through the senses of the person. (Other living creatures typically respond with pre-set, inherited response patterns - 'instincts' - or with conditioned, equally rigid modifications or replacements of the inherited response patterns, acquired through experiences of stress). This ability to create new, exact responses may be defined as human intelligence. It operates by comparing and contrasting new information with that

> already 'on file' from past experiences, and constructing a response based on similarities to past situations but modified to allow for the difference.[426]

So human intelligence emerged as a new development in the evolutionary story. But how did such an ability evolve? How does it relate to 'human consciousness'? And where does the 'comparing and contrasting' of new information take place? The nature of mind, as Richard Leakey has pointed out, "has troubled, tantalized and eluded philosophers and psychologists alike":

> Operational definitions, such as 'the ability to monitor your own mental states, and the corresponding capacity to use your experience to infer the experience of others' may be objectively accurate, but they don't capture the essence of what each of us *feels* 'mind' to be.[427]

What this essence consists of, and how it came to be, is perhaps the defining question concerning human nature, such that the world's great thinkers have struggled to answer it completely. Nevertheless, knowing that my own answers are less than complete seems no reason to avoid outlining them here, beginning with what we can find of its history.

... And when did human consciousness appear?

'Becoming human' has been a very long process. As humans, we have inherited the phenomenon known as consciousness, the 'inner I' that Thomas Hobbes recognised more than 300 years ago: "Given the similitude of the thoughts and passions of one man to the thoughts and passions of another ... he shall thereby read and know what are the thoughts and passions of all other men upon the like occasions." [428]

This ability, which is pre-human, clearly contributed to reproductive success amongst our primate and hominid ancestors; and "once established, there is no going back, for individuals less well endowed would be at a disadvantage." [429] It is the key to proficiency in the 'social chess' that is such a feature of all primate social life, and the best explanation for the evolution of a primate - and human - intelligence so much greater than is needed for a simple life of gathering fruit and plants, hunting a few animals, and finding a comfortable tree or a dry cave to sleep in. As Nicholas Humphrey has noted, human hunting skills are not much greater than those of other social carnivores, and their gathering strategies are similar to those of chimpanzees or baboons. "Complex social lives. That's what makes [us] so intelligent." [430] Richard Leakey agrees:

> In higher primates, the greatest reproductive success (in both males and females) is shaped much more by social skills than by physical displays, either of strength or appearance. The complex interactions of the primate social nexus serve as an exquisite sorting system, in which the individuals with an edge in making alliances and monitoring the alliances of others may score significantly higher in reproductive success.[431]

With intelligence itself being the key to reproductive success, then inevitably the species will gradually become more intelligent. With the reason for this success being the 'inner I', the ability to use intelligence to understand and predict the behaviour of others through an awareness of our own, then conscious thought has begun. At what point in evolution did this capacity become distinctively human?

Human consciousness is often thought of as a fixed, definitive thing; but if we view it as a dynamic process, beginning when it first became self-conscious, then even millions of years ago is not an impossibly distant time for the first outlines to have been traced out in the landscape, and correspondingly in the human mind. It is not necessary to imagine that human consciousness (or, correspondingly, language) at that time was highly complex; only that it was *human*, an adequate vehicle for the expression and pursuit of truly human thoughts, feelings and actions.

Effectively this means that, along with language, consciousness "emerged gradually in the human career" as "part of an evolutionary package built around the hunting-and-gathering way of life." [432] As already suggested, this development began with *homo habilis* and reached a defining and significant stage with the appearance of *homo erectus*, close to two million years ago:

> In addition to important changes in overall body form and life patterns, *homo erectus* was at the forefront of a surge in brain size, a boost in mental capacity. It was, I believe, at the real beginning of the burgeoning of compassion, morality, and conscious awareness that today we cherish as marks of humanity.[433]

Homo erectus has so far been the most successful hominid species. They existed for at least one and a half million years - *ten times* the span so far negotiated through this precarious life by modern human beings. During that time they populated most of the world; they adapted to live in widely varied environments right across Africa, Asia and Europe. Their adaptation to physical environments was generalised rather than specific - they were not entirely limited and controlled by changes in climate. By using means that, by and large, we would have to describe as technological, they successfully transcended the need to exist within the localised habitat in which their species had evolved.

This was a great and truly human achievement; indeed, perhaps *the* defining human achievement. We can assume that a significant level of human culture and social cohesion had been arrived at by at least a million years ago, when they first began colonisation beyond Africa. I would agree with those palaeo-anthropologists who believe that *homo erectus* had some form of language, and that they had an understanding and expression of aesthetics, as well as (by primate standards) social organisation which was not just more complex but exhibited an extra dimension.

They surely told stories, shared knowledge and understanding across the generations. They must have had, in a way that was a qualitative difference between them and their australopithecine predecessors, human intelligence. The first conscious human act, actually or metaphorically, was to set out on a journey ... the making of a decision, to behave differently from our animal forebears. Rogan Taylor gives us an interesting perspective on this in *The Death and Resurrection Show:*

> We are beasts of this earth who have undergone a peculiar event, a change into something rich and strange. It must have first happened somewhere, sometime, to someone. We are a transformed animal, a

> creature with culture. We may think we are normal, but we are not. We are changelings. The foundation of the human personality must lie in this experience of change. For without such a revolutionary event, we would never even have noticed ourselves.[434]

The gradual ongoing process of change that followed, including the growth in brain capacity and the progressive development of language, would have come about in tandem with the evolution of consciousness. The concept of the Journey, of tracing out the 'song lines' and forming a relationship with the flora and fauna, is central to the evolution of human consciousness. Richard Leakey, quoted above concerning the development of human intelligence through the complexities of social interaction, arrived at this conclusion about our interaction with our habitat:

> The way people arrived at answers about their world followed much the same path individuals take in coming to understand one another. In all of the mythologies that we know, and by extrapolation in mythologies long extinct, many of the important elements, such as animals and physical forces, are endowed with humanlike emotions and motives. The mind that evolved subjective consciousness as a tool with which to understand the complexities of social chess used the same formula to understand the complexities of the rest of the world.[435]

This is crucial. People's understanding of the world around them came through the same mental pathways as their understanding of (and empathy for) each other, which in turn had been the stimulus for the evolution of their intelligence. Nicholas Mann presents a similar theme:

> It would not be correct to think that without saying the prayers the sun would not rise, or that the world was stuffed full of anthropomorphically animated 'ghosts' or spirits. No. The world mirrored the people and the people mirrored the world, and the two participated in an existence where there was no sharp separation between them ... 'Reality' was the total of all the inner and outer world. There was no division of sacred and profane. All of life was sacred.[436]

It was this step, into the realms of the spiritual and the sacred, which uniquely marks out human consciousness. People became people as a result of the nature of their relationship with their environment. They travelled through it, they named places, they told stories or sang songs about the spirits that inhabited those places, they passed these songs and stories on so that others could experience the same archetypal journeys.

From the first microcosmic steps across the savannah to global-scale migrations, such journeys have always taken place. They are all at once a response to environmental pressures, a search for the promised land, and an answer to a spiritual calling: *The Hero's Journey*. Human conscious-ness, as well as implying the ability (based on human intelligence) to conceive and plan such an enterprise, is also a phenomenon both cultural and spiritual:

> Experience of a sacred dimension is found in all cultures whether their organization is simple or very complex. This suggests that the sacred is not a *stage* in the history of consciousness but an element in the *structure* of consciousness.[437]

This is not to say that humans became truly conscious through developing an understanding of the sacred, but that sacredness is an essential element of consciousness, which has contributed to the way humans have evolved in a practical and physical sense.

Human consciousness, of course, can most easily be recognised and identified by its outward manifestations. The first of these, the essential item to take with us on this journey into consciousness, was probably something as simple as the shoulder bag. There have been many much greater inventions since, but it was the simple carrying bag - the natural adjunct to making a conscious decision and setting out on 'the journey' - that made the difference in being human.

It is widely believed that we had to develop the full use of language, a high degree of philosophical thought, artistic expression and indeed navigational skills, before we really attained 'humanity' in a meaningful way. Not so. All we needed was a shoulder bag, and these must have been in use at a very early stage.

Of course bags, being made of perishable materials, do not show up in the archaeology of Stone Age sites. Nevertheless their use can certainly be inferred, for instance from the undeniable fact that non-perishable items such as flint nodules and tools were transported over great distances, by people who undoubtedly had the intelligence to make "a basket, a rawhide sling, a fibre belt or an animal-skin shoulder-bag" in order to carry them. "The existence of simple man-made (or woman-made) containers seems to be not just an innovation that would have made life easier for Lower Palaeolithic people, but one that was essential to their very existence." Similarly the baby-sling, which has been described as "the first characteristically human artifact." [438]

If you were to see some beings coming over the hill, walking on two legs and with limbs and features equivalent to our own, then however hairy they were, however apelike their features, however long their arms and bowed their legs, if they were walking along and *carrying bags on their shoulders*, you would recognise these creatures as human beings. And if they were to walk off back up the hill and into the sunset, silhouetted on the skyline with those bags still on their shoulders, then we could all relate to what they were doing: being human.

This is a light-hearted way of looking at the origins of humanity of course, but I am in good company - for instance, Ursula LeGuin: "The earliest cultural inventions must have been a container to hold gathered products and some kind of sling or net carrier," [439] and:

> I am an adherent of what [Elizabeth] Fisher calls the Carrier Bag Theory of human evolution ... If it is a human thing to do to put something you want, because it's useful, edible, or beautiful, into a bag, or a basket, or a bit of rolled bark or leaf, or a net woven of your own hair, or what have you, and then take it home with you ... if to do that is human, if that's what it takes, then I am a human being after all.[440]

Humans, with the help a skin bag, a basket, a wooden bowl or a pottery jar, can do that distinctively human thing, the storing and sharing of food:

> The introduction of food gathering ... would both have necessitated and been made possible by the invention of the container. More food might be gathered than was needed immediately by one individual,

> either for giving to someone else or for later consumption. With the exception of parents feeding very young offspring, this behaviour is unusual among other animals.[441]

Such outward manifestations of human consciousness are in our cultural developments and inventions. These can be observed and objectively discussed, along with the distinctively human behaviour that may go with them. The details of consciousness itself are not so easy to tease out - for after all, as Julian Jaynes put it, "We shall never be able to understand consciousness in the same way that we can understand things that we are conscious of.[442]

Metaphors, analogs and song lines

The 'ego' has had a very bad press in recent years, but this is the one thing which animals do not have though we do.[443]

For Jungian psychiatrist and writer Robert A. Johnson, it is quite straightforward - the ego *is* human consciousness: "Jung compared the ego - the conscious mind - to a cork bobbing in the enormous ocean of the unconscious." [444] And this human consciousness evolved out of the unconscious, "the real source of all our human consciousness":

> The Original Mind of humankind, the primal matrix out of which our species has evolved a conscious mind and then developed it over the millennia to the extent and the refinement that it has today. Every capacity, every feature of our functioning consciousness, was first contained in the unconscious and then found its way from there up to the conscious level ... [Jung] saw a creative force at work ... the huge unconscious psyche of nature has slowly made a part of itself conscious ... nourished by a continuing stream of contents from the unconscious that rises gradually to the level of consciousness.[445]

This 'stream of contents' arrives in the form of symbols, and these have facilitated the evolution of conscious thought and of language. The medium for these two inter-related developments has been metaphor. Returning to Julian Jaynes, he begins by stressing the importance of metaphor in the development of language:

> It is by metaphor that language grows. The common reply to the question 'what is it?' is, when the reply is difficult or the experience unique, 'well, it is like ...' [and the resulting metaphors] with repetition become contracted into labels. This is the major way in which the vocabulary of language is formed. The grand and vigorous function of metaphor is the generation of new language as it is needed, as human culture becomes more and more complex.[446]

He gives lists of examples - the *face* of a clock, the *leg* of a table and so on - and points out that many of our words are based on metaphors from other languages, Latin and Greek for instance, which we no longer recognise as being metaphorical. The word 'galaxy', for example, derives from the Greek word for 'milk' (i.e. 'the Milky Way'). These days we also use the word 'star' as a metaphor for a celebrity performer, and hence appears the phrase 'a galaxy of stars' meaning a whole collection of celebrities. If the popular press succeeds in familiarising this use of the word 'galaxy' so that it becomes (in Jaynes' sense) a label, then we may end up referring to a galaxy of flowers, cutlery or motor vehicles, as the word comes to mean simply 'a large number of similar items collected together'.

Jaynes describes understanding *as* metaphor - in other words we consciously understand something when we arrive at a satisfactory metaphor for its meaning, in terms of something better known or more commonplace. This may be metaphor in the literary sense, or, in a scientific context, "the feeling of similarity between complicated data and a familiar model". In grasping this metaphorical description, or feeling this similarity, we understand.

He then introduces the term 'analog':

> An analog is a model, but a model of a special kind ... A map is a good example. It is not a model in the scientific sense, not a hypothetical model like a Bohr atom to explain something unknown. Instead it is constructed from something well known ... And the relation between an analog map and its land is a metaphor. If I point to a location on a map and say, 'There is Mont Blanc and from Chamonix we can reach the east face this way,' that is really a shorthand way of saying, 'The

> relations between the point labeled 'Mont Blanc' and other points is similar to the actual Mont Blanc and its neighbouring regions.' [447]

And from there he defines human consciousness as an analog of "what is called the real world":

> It is built up with a vocabulary or lexical field whose terms are all metaphors or analogs of behaviour in the physical world. Its reality is of the same order as mathematics. It allows us to shortcut behavioural processes and arrive at more adequate decisons.[448]

So, we 'grapple' with intellectual problems and 'see' their solutions, and we do this in the metaphorical space where our consciousness resides. In order to do so, we have an 'analog I' - that same 'inner I' recognised by Thomas Hobbes as the means by which we can understand each other - in other words, an ego. This, the tiny cork that has bobbed up to the surface of the vast ocean of unconscious mind and the natural world's evolutionary process, is what marks out human beings as different.

Jaynes apologises for the density of his arguments in presenting this understanding, and I must do the same for summarising him in what must seem an extended digression. My purpose here is to achieve some clear understanding of what humans, and human consciousness, really are, before returning with this clarity to what has gone before.

Whilst Julian Jaynes' description of consciousness is excellent, his belief that it appeared only recently, well into the historical period of classical civilisation, is much less credible. Recent archaeological evidence, discovered since the 1970s when he was writing, has shifted our understanding of human development; whilst his inference that peoples who have not developed civilisation for themselves could not be fully conscious or fully human, is with good reason no longer acceptable. We are better served by the Jungian perspective, in which consciousness and language have evolved in tandem over the millennia.

Jaynes' work has been given scant recognition by the scientific establishment. A researcher with somewhat parallel ideas, who has similarly been regarded as something of a maverick, has latterly enjoyed a revival of interest: the Russian psychologist Lev Vygotsky in the 1930s developed a thesis based on the insight that complex mental processes depend on an 'inner voice' of silent speech. This helps to confirm that human conscious thought developed along with language. Whilst an animal's mind "is mobilised to make sense of events as they are occurring," for humans:

> Saying or hearing a word, or reading a word in print, will unlock a wealth of images, associations and experiences in our heads. Hearing words such as 'alligator' or 'hovercraft' will sting our brains into action, creating a surrogate experience that is almost as good as an actual alligator or hovercraft before our eyes.[449]

Humans must always have had this ability, though its potential has only gradually been realised as human consciousness, along with language, has gradually been developed and refined. Words and metaphor have been key elements in this process, and human consciousness is the ability to make use of them. What Jaynes described as "the first and most primitive aspect of consciousness" is spatialisation. This is what we use to construct the mental space that all the other word-associations and metaphors inhabit, and the spatial quality that all things must have if we are to be conscious of them at all.

This is what people had when they first emerged from the dream time. This is what made people people: the creation of a mental mapping system, tracing out the song lines and the ley lines in the landscape - and correspondingly in our minds; an 'analog' of external reality, a system for naming its inhabitants, the first perception of ourselves as being partially separate from the gods and the ancestors, the beginning of language growth through metaphor, the ability to sing songs and tell stories, the decision to set out on a journey - both physical and metaphorical. The decision to consciously become.

All this may have happened a very long time ago. As Richard Leakey contends, it marks the difference not between *homo sapiens* and the earlier hominids, but between the genus *homo* and its predecessors. Everything since then has been part of the human story, everyone since then has carried things in bags upon their shoulders. As more and more archaeologists and palaeontologists are gradually coming to agree, language - however rudimentary - almost certainly began with the genus *homo*; and with it came human consciousness, at least in its 'most primitive aspect', and the enormous process of human development that has followed.

So, two million years ago or so, somewhere in Africa, human consciousness began. Though it had little visible effect on the rest of the planet for a very long time, eventually it was to cover the whole world. By the time of the neolithic, the 'new stone age', it was significantly shaping the environment, re-creating the world according to the images and ideas emerging from the conscious inner landscape of human beings.

5 Asia (1): The Indo-European Question

On the steppes of central Asia, people developed a similar level of technology and culture to that in Europe, but in a very different style. Neolithic developments in technology and lifestyles were all, to some extent at least, responses to shifts in climate and related environmental factors. Thus the development of agriculture in Europe was a response to the forestation of the central European plain. In Asia, post-glacial forestation took place in northern latitudes but the open plains, the steppes, remained open and supported a large population of herd animals - and a herding culture among humans.

The multiplicity of human cultures and lifestyles is proverbial, and across the huge expanse of territory from Iberia to Mongolia there would have been endless variations in the way people lived and garnered a living. Russian archaeologist Natalia Shishlina makes a particular point that "the Eurasian steppe must be seen as a mosaic of environments, each of which offers different opportunities and resources."[501] Nevertheless, as a way of looking at an overall trend that makes sense, we can say that whilst European farmers domesticated the cow, the sheep and the goat, the distinctive feature of human culture on the Asian steppes was that they domesticated the horse; whilst the Europeans grew crops on their land, the people of the east followed the herds of game animals, with horses to make them more mobile and able to carry the paraphernalia of a complex lifestyle.

Farming can imply deforestation, and herding can imply over-grazing; both can contribute to environmental degradation and, historically, may sometimes have been the decisive factor in turning marginal land into desert. The natural process of climate change, however, has always driven change and evolution amongst the planet's species, including humans; and at a critical time around 4000 BCE it began to affect Asia far more severely than Europe: north Africa and much of Asia began to be subject to severe environmental trauma through lack of rainfall and resulting desiccation. This is the backdrop to what follows.

The 'original Indo-Europeans'

The herders of the neolithic steppes were the first, according to Engels, to overthrow 'mother-right' and to establish a patriarchal society. According to Gimbutas and Eisler, this was the original 'Aryan' or Indo-European culture, with its warrior kings and sun gods, which placed a "higher value on the power that takes, rather than gives, life,"[502] and which perpetrated the long series of incursions and invasions into Old Europe that ultimately brought to an end the Goddess culture. This viewpoint is not without its critics, however. Alexei Panshin, in his essay on *The Paleolithic Indo-Europeans,* writes:

> It used to be taken for granted that the prehistoric and early historic periods were an era of vast migrations and awe-inspiring conquests ... [and] the presence of Indo-European languages everywhere from England to India was assumed to have resulted from the emergence of horse chariot technology, which is well documented as having occurred shortly after 2000 BC. The original Indo-Europeans were imagined as a horde of aristocratic Bronze Age warriors who came hurtling out of the steppes, overwhelming the simple peasant cultures of Europe ... Despite its troubling racist overtones, that point of view was still dominant in the 1960s, but it had started to lose ground by the 1970s ... Even the Mycenaeans - who had been considered a prime example of invading Indo-European chariot-warriors - were reassessed as being a purely local development.[503]

This approach to the Indo-Europeans he writes off as being "born of the era of European imperialism in the late 19th century, which exalted war-making abilities as a prime example of Darwinian survival of the fittest,"[504] which is a very good point. However, as the work of Gimbutas and others since the 1970s has confirmed, and as DeMeo has documented at length, there is exhaustive archaeological and latterly documentary evidence for an extended 'era of of vast migrations and awe-inspiring conquests'.

It certainly began well before 2000 BCE and the invention of the war chariot; herders on the steppes had not only domesticated the horse, but had also developed stabbing weapons made from bone or flint - effectively short swords - well before the Bronze Age and the use of hardened metals.[505] However, the feminist perspective is by no means 'exalting the war-making abilities' of the Asian invaders - quite the opposite - and neither does it describe the Old Europeans as 'simple peasants'.

There are, nevertheless, plenty of reasons to doubt that these 'war-making invaders' were the 'original Indo-Europeans', or Aryans, with some kind of racial predilection for murder and mayhem. In fact, as one writer sympathetic to Gimbutas' general thesis puts it: "While Gimbutas's gylanic society may have existed ... it must have been Indo-European itself, or predominantly so; and the nature of the change that subverted it is more problematic." [506]

For Indo-Europeans go back a very long way - far further than 2000 BCE. They spread very far and wide, and developed a number of different types of culture.[507] This does not challenge Gimbutas' basic thesis, but it does call into question the 'troubling racist overtones' implied by naming the invaders 'the original Aryans', as if they were the inevitable forerunners of the Third Reich.

It also needs to be emphasised that the nature of the change brought about by these invasions was not - as Riane Eisler suggests - a development of 'peripheral isolates', as might be inferred from Systems Theory.[508] These were absolutely not "seemingly insignificant nomadic bands roaming the less desirable fringe areas of our globe" whilst "the first great agricultural civilizations spread out along the lakes and rivers in the fertile heartlands." [509] The Asian steppes are very much at the centre of the Eurasian land mass, and of palaeolithic developments in culture; it was Europe that could better be described as peripheral. This is easy to forget, from our modern Euro-centric point of view, particularly as the amount of research undertaken and information available from the former Soviet Union lags considerably behind Europe.

This situation is gradually becoming rectified, though there is much still to come to light.[510] A review of the available evidence from someone such as Alexei Panshin, an American of Indo-European descent who has family connections with Voronezh on the river Don, is therefore especially valuable. His insight is particularly helpful in making the case for the early spread of Indo-European culture and language; beginning far earlier than the Bronze Age, or even the Neolithic.

'Indo-European' actually refers to a language, which is assumed to be the forerunner of a multitude of others (including both Latin and Sanskrit) ranging from the Celtic west to the Indian sub-continent. Although its existence is well accepted, there are no documents written in this language, it can only be inferred from remnants surviving in later languages; and there has never been any Indo-European race or culture clearly identified.

There have been many attempts, including the 'Kurgan Hypothesis' as originally proposed by Marija Gimbutas, and others identifying the 'urheimat' or ancestral Indo-European homeland as Anatolia, Lithuania, or possibly even India. Most of these date 'PIE' (the original 'Proto Indo-European' language) at between 4500 and 2500 BCE. However, as Alexei Panshin points out:

> By the 1980s it was becoming apparent that the conventional dates for Indo-European origins had to be off not merely by a few centuries, but by thousands of years. The earliest known Indo-European languages - Mycenaean Greek, Hittite, and Sanskrit - were already far more divergent in the second millennium BC than, say, French and Italian are today. This suggested that their common ancestor must have been spoken not around 3,000 BC, as formerly assumed, but well back in the Neolithic ... [so that] it was not force of arms but rather the ability of farming to support a greater population that had enabled them to outbreed and eventually absorb the small Mesolithic hunting bands ... However ... it [now] seems that the Neolithic farmers who entered Europe from the Near East and North Africa were the source of no more than 20% of European DNA, with the other 80% going back to the Paleolithic. Apparently the farming folk ... were themselves the ones who were assimilated.[511]

This led to yet another theory: 'Palaeolithic Continuity'.

Panshin sees Indo-European as an off-shoot of an even older 'Eurasiatic' language, which was spoken by the people who brought

Gravettian culture into Europe before the height of the last ice age.[512] This is at least plausible; and it would mean that both protagonists in the warfare that later came about through the Kurgan invasions were Indo-European - or at least Eurasiatic. But the truth is that there have been endless theories as to the origins of the Indo-Europeans, and the number of places suggested as their 'homeland' rivals those claimed for King Arthur's Camelot. I do not intend to go into the pros and cons of these various theories and hypotheses, except to agree with Panshin's basic proposition that since "there was both genetic continuity and cultural continuity" during the major transition in Europe from the Mesolithic to the Neolithic, "there must have been linguistic continuity as well," [513] so that the origins of Indo-European would have been earlier.

This does not, of course, mean that there was no development of a patriarchal, horse-riding culture on the steppes before or during the neolithic - and indeed Panshin describes the phenomenon of the 'patrilocal band', which he suggests was a social structure developed by hunters on the ice age steppes, and which he contrasts with the "matrilineal cultures of the south." [514] Neither does it mean that these people were not Indo-Europeans - in fact he cites ancient Indo-European kinship terms as a proof of this proposition.[515] What it does mean is that the roots of the split between patri-focal herders and matri-focal horticulturalists go back considerably further than the neolithic.

In most regions of the world, hunter-gatherers provide at least half their food from gathering plants; but on the glacial steppes there was an abundance of animals to hunt and relatively few edible plants. So, more than 20,000 years ago, there came about a geographical imbalance between the relative importance of hunting on the one hand and of plant-food gathering on the other.

This implies greater economic importance for men rather than women on the Asian steppes, where "the Upper Palaeolithic was spread primarily by small bands of hunters who travelled fast and light" [516] - just at the time when their European counterparts were beginning to establish homesteads, together with substantial advances in domestic crafts, implying increased economic and social importance for women. The next chapter will return to all this in more detail.

The beginnings of warfare: arable farmers and pastoralists

After the ice receded, the steppes - unlike the European plains - remained primarily hunting grounds. Its human culture included the Kurgans, who were certainly an Indo-European race, and a number of other peoples whose history and environment were more or less similar. It was these, particularly once their lands began to dry out with a shift in the climate, who clashed so dramatically with the nascent proto-civilisation of Europe:

> The Old European and Kurgan cultures were the antithesis of one another. The Old Europeans were sedentary horticulturalists prone to live in large well-planned townships. The absence of fortifications and weapons attests [to] the peaceful co-existence of this egalitarian civilization that was probably matrilinear and matrilocal. The Kurgan system was composed of patrilineal, socially stratified herding units which lived in small villages or seasonal settlements while grazing their animals over vast areas.
>
> One economy based on farming, the other on stock breeding and grazing, produced two contrasting ideologies. The Old European belief system focused on the agricultural cycle of birth, death and regeneration, embodied in the feminine principle, a Mother Creatrix. The Kurgan ideology, as known from comparative Indo-European mythology, exalted virile, heroic warrior gods of the shining and thunderous sky. Weapons are non-existent in Old European imagery; whereas the dagger and the battle-axe are dominant symbols of the Kurgans, who like all historically known Indo-Europeans, glorified the lethal power of the sharp blade.[517]

Such is the passionately stated view of Marija Gimbutas and Riane Eisler; and no doubt it is broadly true. As Colin Tudge has pointed out, "In much of the world through most of history arablists and pastoralists have been in conflict, often mortal. After all, they practise very different kinds of activity which, except in highly controlled circumstances, are an 'either or'." [518] But even in circumstances that are not highly controlled, conflict does not have to be inevitable. As Bruce Chatwin observed, during a visit to Afghanistan in late summer:

> This is the time of year when the farmers and nomads, after a season of acrimony, are suddenly the best of friends. The harvest is in. The nomads buy grain for the winter. The villagers buy cheese and hides and meat. They welcome the sheep onto their fields: to break up the stubble and manure it for autumn planting.[519]

So it is possible for what Chatwin called "the twin arms of the so-called neolithic revolution" to live interdependent lives. 'Nomadic pastoralism', after all, does not mean simply wandering opportunistically across the landscape; it refers to a mobile lifestyle with portable houses (yurts), generally travelling within an ancestral range, often between a winter base camp and summer pastures. Nomads and farmers will often have lived in the same regions for millennia: serious conflict between them is likely to be a function of environmental resources becoming, for reasons outside their control, insufficient to support both. The causes of the current (2007) civil war in the Darfur region of Sudan, for example, have uncomfortable modern parallels with DeMeo's Saharasian model, as illuminated by Julian Borger in the *Guardian Weekly*:

> Less than a generation ago ... African farmers had allowed Arab herders to graze their camels and goats on the land, and the livestock had fertilised the soil. The coexistence was so natural, in fact, that the tribes of Darfur did not even think of themselves as Arab or African. It is only now, in light of the bloodshed of the past four years, that they look back and affix ethnic titles to the protagonists in their story, with all non-Arabs claiming the title African. Only a few years ago, it was just nomads and farmers. What changed, the evidence suggests, was the climate ...
>
> The real roots of the disaster stretch back to the mid-1980s when a ferocious drought and famine transformed Sudan and the whole Horn of Africa. It killed more than a million people and laid waste livestock herds. Whether they maintained their way of life or tried to take up settled cultivation, the pastoralists of Darfur clashed repeatedly with its farmers. A string of conflicts broke out as both sides armed themselves, and those conflicts created the template for today's disaster.[520]

But climate is not the only consideration in the conflict between arablists and pastoralists. Colin Tudge notes that "traditional pastoralists prefer to leave the wild vegetation as it is while arablists begin by getting rid of it; and since arablists must choose the most fertile spots the pastoralists are inevitably marginalized". Furthermore pastoralism can produce pleasant meadows that last indefinitely, whereas arable farming "tends to degrade the soil quite quickly - except in favoured circumstances, with plenty of added manure". In other words arable farming, the way of life favoured by the Old European goddess-worshippers, has the greatest negative environmental impact.[521] In this context it is also worth noting the biblical story of Cain and Abel:

> Abel was the 'keeper of sheep' while Cain was 'a tiller of the ground' (Genesis 4:2) ... In the post-hippy 1970s, many who were advocating vegetarianism were apt to offer Cain and Abel as a morality tale - but this obliged them to invert the story and so to suggest that Abel, the gentle victim, was the vegetarian while Cain, the bloody-handed murderer, was the archetypal carnivore ... If anyone had referred to the text they would have seen that Cain was the vegetarian ...
>
> Arable farming in Egypt as depicted in Exodus is literal slavery. When Jesus is born he is attended by shepherds; nobody brings any sheaves of wheat ... [In Biblical times] arable farming would have been considered far more 'aggressive' than pastoralism because it has a far greater immediate impact on the environment.[522]

However, none of this contradicts Eisler and Gimbutas' contention that the Old European Goddess culture was peaceful and egalitarian, and that it was progressively destroyed by invasions from the steppe-dwelling pastoralists. What Colin Tudge fails to note is that the negative and invasive aspects of farming are far more pronounced with plough-based agriculture, which followed the shift to patrism, than with horticulture. But let us not jump to any simplistic, black and white conclusions.

If the Kurgans and those like them created violence and chaos which ultimately spread across the world, it was not because they were inherently more inclined than the Europeans to foster violence and chaos.

It was because something specific had happened to change their essentially co-operative human nature, and there must have been particular reasons for that.

Climatic and environmental trauma

The Asian side of this equation is described in meticulous detail by James DeMeo, in *Saharasia.* As the title implies, the scope of his work includes north Africa and the Middle East, as well as central Asia. He describes an enormous area of land, the central portion of the inhabited world, large enough to support millions of people through a mixture of hunting, gathering, herding and agriculture. This region, 'Saharasia', is now largely arid, much of it desert, but in mesolithic and early neolithic times it was ideal for human habitation:

> While Northern Europe was covered in ice as far as the Harz, and the Alps and the Pyrenees were capped with glaciers, the Arctic high pressure deflected southwards the Atlantic rainstorms. The cyclones that today traverse Central Europe then passed over the Mediterranean basin and the Northern Sahara and continued, undrained by Lebanon, across Mesopotamia and Arabia to Persia and India. The parched Sahara enjoyed a regular rainfall, and further east the showers were not only more bountiful than today but were distributed over the whole year ... We should expect in North Africa, Arabia, Persia and the Indus Valley parklands and savannahs, such as flourish today north of the Mediterranean.[523]

Following the ice age, the climate had first become warm and relatively moist, optimum conditions for human habitation, before the rain belt gradually shifted back north. This view of "a vast procreant Eden, luxuriant with plant life ample to support a wide range of fauna" was widely held in the first half of the twentieth century. Its subsequent desiccation - particularly in the Middle East - was believed to have been the reason why people adopted farming, "the 'physical challenge' to which agricultural civilization was the response." By the 1970s, according to Julian Jaynes, "recent evidence shows that there was no such extensive desiccation, and that agriculture was not economically 'forced' on anyone." [524]

Such evidence was limited, however. Today there is plenty to show that north Africa, for instance, was at one time densely populated and that the Nile valley, once a gigantic swamp, only became habitable as the whole region dried out around 3000 BCE, prior to the establishment of the Egyptian kingdoms. DeMeo describes the widespread use of irrigation in areas peripheral to 'Saharasia' as the desiccation progressed; but gradually, both this and large-scale herding on abundant natural pastures became untenable.

By 4000-3000 BCE the landscape was becoming significantly arid, leading eventually to the creation of the 'dry belt' that now stretches from the Sahara through to the Gobi desert on the borders of China. This enormous area became steadily less hospitable. Nomadic herding, moving around the landscape in search of forage, became the only viable lifestyle:

> Nomadic herding may be seen as a survival adaptation to a low carrying capacity. It should be noted that in most of the central regions of Saharasia nomadic herding is a tenuous and risky business at best ... In its moist state, Saharasia was settled by various Neolithic groups who established small and large settlements based upon hunting, animal herding and limited agriculture; they traded with each other and lived peacefully. By c.4000-3500 BCE, however, the Saharasian environment began to dry up ... As drought and desertification intensified, famine, starvation, mass migrations and conflicts inevitably developed, intensified, and have continued ever since.[525]

DeMeo convincingly links Asian incursions into Europe, Mesopotamia, India and elsewhere to this process of desiccation and desertification:

> As Arabia began drying up after c.4000 BCE, various warrior-nomad semitic groups repeatedly irrupted and invaded territories with secure water supplies ... Central Asia also began drying out after c.4000 BCE, and various warrior-nomad Indo-Aryan groups (e.g. Kurgan, Battle-axe peoples) repeatedly irrupted from the region ... [and later] the Scythians, Sarmatians, Shang, Chou, Huns, Mongols and Turks.[526]

The desertification of large parts of Saharasia became an environmental condition so severe that people were unable to adapt. Arctic conditions had been met by the 'insurance' provided by extensive palaeolithic social networks; forestation, sea level rises and other post-glacial encroachments on available land had been overcome by the neolithic development of farming. This, at first, included arid conditions which were met by intricate irrigation schemes - but in the end there is no way that a large population can adapt to living in a desert.

Connection and separation

DeMeo's particular contribution is to establish that the migrations and incursions which resulted from this desertification, and the patristic social changes carried with them, were not the result of any innate human tendency towards violence and a desire for power. On the contrary, he spends considerable time describing the earliest human societies as 'matrist' - peaceful and co-operative, with a balance of power and responsibility between men and women.

'Patrist' societies - characterised by male dominance, suppression of females, a military caste, endemic warfare, social violence, and in many cases the institutionalised mistreatment of children - he describes as not just an aberration but pathological. Such behaviour has been followed, on a scale that has affected humanity across the globe, during the last 5,000 to 6,000 years.

In support of this thesis he provides an encyclopaedic review of archaeological evidence, and he presents an exhaustive (and exhausting!) catalogue of invasions, massacres, cruelties, oppressive practices and social destruction that have come about as a result. He uses little input from the work of Marija Gimbutas, and none at all from Riane Eisler's interpretation, but nevertheless his conclusions match theirs very well:

> Cultures which tended to inflict pain and trauma upon infants and young children, punish young people for sexual expression, manipulate them into arranged marriages, subordinate the female, and otherwise greatly restrict the freedoms of young people and older females to the iron will of males also tended to possess high levels of adult violence, with various social institutions designed for expression of pent-up sadistic aggression. Such cultures I call the *patrist* groups.

> It was found that, at various times in their past histories, all patrist cultures once possessed ... extremely authoritarian and cruel cultural expressions such as divine kingship, ritual widow murder, human sacrifice and sadistic ritual tortures of enemies, heretics, social rebels and criminals. These patrist groups contrast in almost every manner with the peaceful *matrist* cultures, where child treatment and sexual relationshps were of an entirely different character, being very gentle and pleasure oriented. Matrist cultures are also democratic, egalitarian, sex-positive, and possess very low levels of adult violence.[527]

In explaining the reasons for such a radical change in culture, and for such widespread pathological behaviour, DeMeo breaks new ground by examining the psychology of the historical process. This was explored more fully in the previous chapter, but to summarise briefly:

Based on the thinking of Wilhelm Reich, he argues that desertification created conditions in which the ancient (matrist) ways of social organisation broke down, life for huge numbers of people was reduced to a level of barest survival, and those who did survive (particularly the children) were so traumatised by the experience that they were unable to recover fully. Behaviour patterns brought about through the sustained experience of such conditions becomes endemic, and is passed on from one generation to the next.

These patterns of 'armored' (emotionally inhibited) behaviour are quite different from anything that could be described as natural. English psychologist and writer Steve Taylor describes human life during the past 6,000 years as having been infected by a 'collective psychosis' as a result, though he proposes that 'The Fall' was linked to an 'ego explosion', the acquisition of "a new intellectual power or awareness," [528] as a result of which "Saharasian peoples were the first human beings to develop a sharpened sense of ego ... [and] the intensification of the human sense of 'I' or individuality." [529]

However, the ego in itself is not the issue. The true nature of the change is stated clearly by Taylor nearly 200 pages later: "The real problem is not the sharpness of our sense of ego but its separateness." [530] And this separation, which is at root an emotional separation from each other and from the natural world, is certainly a key part of the 'armoring' that Reich and DeMeo highlight - part of the 'insanity' that Taylor acknowledges:

> Some colonists ... realised that they would never be able to fully 'civilise' the natives unless they developed their sense of 'self-ness'. Senator Henry Dawes put his finger on it when he wrote of the Cherokees in 1887, 'They have got as far as they can go ... because they hold their land in commmon. There is no selfishness, which is at bottom of civilisation.'[531]

Taylor lists examples of colonial powers making every effort to undermine and destroy this natural lack of selfishness, this sense of mutual connection; for without it, to put it bluntly, we are all forced to suffer the loss of an essential element of our humanity, and are thereby rendered vulnerable to capitalist economic exploitation. This, quite clearly, was the purpose of efforts at 'developing' the native peoples' 'sense of individuality'. Such efforts, however, have often been less than completely successful:

> Primal peoples seem to have a more acute sense of empathy than European-Americans. Our highly developed sense of self means that, to a greater or lesser degree, we are 'walled off' to the world, trapped inside ourselves with our own needs and desires. As a result, we often find it difficult to 'put ourselves in other peoples' shoes' and 'feel with' them.[532]

It is precisely this sense of empathy, this ability to see things from another's point of view, that was central to the development of human intelligence and consciousness in the first place. Its partial loss has, if anything, made us less human in this respect than our ancestors. We are still struggling to get beyond racist assumptions from the early twentieth century: "To the primitive's mind, the limits of the individual are variable and ill-defined"; and "native peoples' sense of identity is bound up with their community" rather than "existing as self-sufficient entities,"[533] as if this was a failing which our modern mind-set has overcome.

In fact, this is merely an ideological stance taken by patriarchal thinkers and writers. Evidence for care of the sick and disabled, individual burials, and also self-adornment and decoration - all in the very real context of a "sense of identity bound up with community" - go back thousands and thousands of years. There is no case for there once being "ill-defined limits of the individual."

If there has been some intellectual gain, in terms of our capacity for abstract and intellectual thought, then such a gain could just as well have been made *without* the loss of empathy and connectedness. However, historically this has not been the case. As Baring and Cashford point out in *The Myth of the Goddess*, it was only in the Bronze Age that "for the first time, we learn the names of individual men and women, what they say and do", since the emergence of the individual from the tribal group appears to have been an aspect of the separation from nature:

> The separation of heaven and earth is an image of the birth of consciousness in which humanity is set apart from nature ... Creation myths that show the division of the primal unity into two halves portray the human capacity to act reflectively rather than instinctively, which inevitably involves an initial dissociation from the instinctive life of nature. The new development of consciousness finds expression in the god who orders from beyond rather than the goddess who moves from within. The difficulty of this dissociation is the temptation to call the goddess (nature) 'lower' and the god (spirit) 'higher'.[534]

This last statement certainly characterises the new way of life that appeared out of central Asia from about 4000 BCE onwards.

Before 'Saharasia'

DeMeo's 'Saharasia' thesis is more than plausible, and is undoubtedly a major part of the story - but not perhaps the whole story. His assumption that wherever there was a process of desertification the automatic result was patristic behaviour patterns requires some modification. In particular, it does not explain why this has only happened during and since the neolithic, but not during earlier cycles of climate change within the human era: I would suggest that the development of technology, economics and human society had reached a particular stage in the neolithic and created the pre-conditions for the development of patrism. In earlier cycles, people had simply died out in regions where adverse conditions had become extreme.

Neither does DeMeo's thesis explain why patrism followed desertification, but not apparently floods, freezing, earthquakes or volcanoes. Flooding caused by post-glacial rises in sea level is a particular case highlighted by Colin Tudge; whilst the onset of the glacial maximum 15-20,000 years earlier - though it effectively created deserts just as inhospitable as anything brought about through heat and drought - had no such long-term effect on the human population.

There is a tradition from Central America - where DeMeo struggles to find a correlation between patrism and desertification - which says that often "wars were preceded by tremendous destruction wrought by earthquakes and volcanoes", leading in turn to the establishment by conquest of oppressive empires.[535]

What DeMeo actually describes in most regions of Saharasia is a gradual process of environmental desiccation, drawn out over periods of hundreds of years, to which people adapted more-or-less successfully by developing nomadic herding. The onset of desert on the scale of the Sahara or the Gobi took far longer than a generation or two. Such changes tend to happen in staccato fashion, with one particularly bad season making a dramatic change; though instances where populations were reduced to a few shell-shocked survivors must have been relatively rare.

Nevertheless, the combined effect of severe long-term drought and having to abandon ancestral homelands would certainly have been traumatic. For those whom Steve Taylor calls 'primal peoples', even without changes in climate, "being forced away from their land would be tantamount to death." [536] For those who survived, being forced to be almost constantly on the move in search of pastures, with no secure homeland, moving through landscape that was either parched or else inhabited by others who were likely to be hostile, would undoubtedly have been stressful to an extreme degree. Significantly, it was circumstances such as these that led to the practices of child swaddling and cranial deformation:

> Another major aspect of nomadism which would work to transform character structure towards violent, antifemale tendencies is that of infant cranial deformation, which appears to have originated among nomadic peoples of Central Asia. It is known that infant cranial deformation occurs when a baby is unmovingly secured against a cradle board, similar to those employed by the Asian nomads. The newborn baby's head might be tied against the cradle board, to prevent it from flopping about as the mother walked over irregular terrain. The child's arms and legs would be wrapped and also securely tied against the cradle board.
>
> Such children would spend great amounts of time in the cradle, particularly as migrations were under way; and the drier the environment, the longer the migration time. Not only would a child's movement be inhibited, frustrating its need to explore its world, but the pressure against the head would deform the skull, in a painful, often life-threatening manner ... Once raised in such a deforming manner, adults would not only carry the psychic trauma, with a hostile and anxious view of the maternal figure, but also a head with a biologically unnatural shape.[537]

This practice became extremely widespread, and the resulting deformities were often viewed as a 'special mark' of the tribe, a fearsome attribute of the warrior, and ultimately even as a mark of ruling class distinction. Nevertheless, with the pain and discomfort, and the disruption of the natural mother-child interaction, "the child's view of the maternal figure would likely become contaminated with anxiety and rage." [538]

This is important and relevant. However, nomadic herding - almost certainly including such treatment of children - pre-dates the desiccation of central Asia, probably by thousands of years. The Saharan rock art noted in Chapter 1, for instance, shows the influence of nomadic herders from central and southern Asia going back to around 5000 BCE, and the tradition of pastoral economies on the steppes began earlier still.[539] The patristic social structure which came with it also appears to pre-date serious desiccation, which DeMeo dates in central Asia as beginning around 3500 BCE.[540] According to Gimbutas, the Kurgan invasions began in 4300 BCE; by this time the warrior way of life must already have been firmly established, at least in the regions adjacent to Europe. Marija Gimbutas acknowledges Demeo's contribution, but points out that:

> Pastoral economy, growing herds of large animals, horse riding, and the need for male strength to control the animals must have contributed to the transition from matrism to armored patrism in southern Russia and beyond at the latest around 5000 BC. (Although the accurate date for this process as yet is difficult to establish, it certainly started much earlier than 4000 BC, the date used [by DeMeo] for the transition to patrism and violence in Saharasia caused by the pressures of severe desertification).[541]

DeMeo himself notes the apparent anomaly of Jericho, where "fortification walls, towers, and tombs for dead kings" were being constructed as early as 8000 BCE.[542]

The likelihood is, then, that the beginnings of herding in the sense of controlling wild herds - with male control of the principle means of production (Engels) and a degree of infant anxiety and rage towards the mother (DeMeo) - was roughly contemporary with the Goddess culture as exemplified by Catal Huyuk in Asia Minor. It was still several thousand years before the new, male-dominated, militaristic way of life came to systematically mistreat its women and children, invade its neighbours, take slaves, and institute rule by fear and coercion.

It is here worth recalling that both James DeMeo and Marija Gimbutas - both the Reichians and the feminists - stress that this mode of behaviour has been going on for *only* six thousand years or so. Although this is long enough for the loss of all but the flimsiest memory of a time when life was substantially different, nevertheless patrism is by no means natural or inevitable; and 6,000 years is not very long compared to the total span of human life on the planet.

It is also worth repeating Colin Tudge's contribution to our understanding of 'the real origins of farming': the first fully-fledged farming cultures may not have appeared until the neolithic, but the skills and social pre-conditions were already there, and can be traced well back into palaeolithic times. A variety of environmental factors acted as triggers for their integration into what we recognise as farming. Much the same could be said of patrism; or, at least, the emergence of male-defined social structures that - in particular circumstances - became 'patristic' in the psychological and moral sense described by DeMeo and Gimbutas.

Whilst desertification undoubtedly was a crucial factor in driving the change towards patrism, it remains unconvincing as the *single* cause of such a complex and sophisticated societal shift. There are other major environmental considerations, as well as economic factors arising from neolithic advances in technology. However much it later became overlaid, reinforced and given momentum by psychological distress - particularly as it came about through desertification - the overwhelming likelihood remains that the basic pattern first arose beforehand, somewhere else and for some other reason. Male-defined social structures began to appear considerably more than 6,000 years ago.

The patrilocal band

As mentioned above, the 'patrilocal band' is a form of society studied amongst some native American cultures and, according to Alexei Panshin, "appears where a culture is primarily dependent on male hunting for food and other resources and women's plant gathering makes a far more limited contribution." This appears to have been the case on the ice age steppes.

Such a society is not, however, in evidence amongst the Innuit, contemporary native American people living in conditions similar to those of the ice age steppes; and north America - believed by many to have been populated from east-central Asia after the end of the ice age - retained many of its matrilineal social systems right through to the nineteenth century. Nevertheless, there is increasing evidence that north America was first populated much earlier, whilst Panshin supports his contention that ice age steppe culture was patriarchal, patrilocal and patrilineal with reference to Indo-European linguistic evidence:

> This patrilocal structure is an exact match for the model of society deduced from the most ancient Indo-European kinship terms. For example, there were specialized words meaning 'son's wife', 'husband's father', 'husband's mother', 'husband's brother',

> 'husband's sister', and even 'husband's brother's wife.' But there were no equivalent terms for 'daughter's husband' or 'wife's father' or the rest. They were simply not needed.[543]

In this respect, Indo-European appears to have been widely at variance (in fact more or less opposite) to languages in the parts of the world which were the subject of Lewis Morgan's study in the nineteenth century (on which Engel's work was largely based). This suggests that the patrilocal band was a social form that matched extremely well the clan system as identified by Engels as once being universal - in fact, which surely had developed from it - but with matrilineality and the female position of power within the clan being replaced by the male. In all other respects the ordering of society appears to be precisely the same.

Panshin highlights "many purely technical innovations" as well as the development of "far more extended social groupings", both needed to help deal with the risks presented by life on the ice age steppes. He then looks at further possible cultural differences between the steppe hunters and other palaeolithic peoples, including innovations such as "a mutually advantageous partnership with the gray wolf", from which the domestic dog emerged somewhere in east Asia around 40,000 years ago; shamanism, "a canny shaman would have been every bit as crucial to the survival of the band as its pack of faithful wolf-dogs"; and, perhaps later, the heroic ideal.

> The hunting peoples of the north have long had a tendency to view themselves as noble warriors, engaged in mutually respectful battle with their prey - a self-image which is missing from the more pragmatic attitudes and philosophies of the south.[544]

None of this automatically results in a 'patrist' society as defined and documented by DeMeo, though it does call into question Steve Taylor's concept of an 'ego explosion' - the positive side of which he describes as the appearance of "our creativity, ingenuity, and technological and scientific prowess"[545] - about 20,000 years later. Human beings have always been creative and ingenious, and if the development of our ingenuity has in some phases been related to the development of male-defined society, then the patrilocal band is an example that goes back to before the last ice age. Panshin describes a variant of what we generally expect in hunter-gatherer societies, but it is the same in most of its essentials. In the patrilocal structure:

> The men of a particular band consider themselves to be descended from a common male ancestor, and even if the actual lines of descent cannot be traced, they still maintain this belief as a mythological truth. All the men relate to one another equally as brothers. There may be a headman, whose role is primarily religious and advisory, but there are no kings and no nobility. This simple egalitarianism is in line with both Gravettian archaeology - which shows occasional elaborate burials but no signs of a fixed class system - and Indo-European vocabulary.[546]

Again, what Panshin describes appears to be the clan system, as identified by Engels in north America and elsewhere, except that it has become patrilineal rather than matrilineal.

There are other indications of a protracted period of transition. For instance, amongst the bronze age Sarmatians of the Black Sea steppes, there were "matriarchal survivals" characterised by female warrior-priestesses.[547] The American researcher Jeannine Davis-Kimball has made a particular study of this phenomenon,[548] which is also mentioned in the earliest written records. In this case the ancient matrilineal structure remained, even with the development of a warrior culture.

Over a long period of time, cultural adaptations had come about that were to become the preconditions for a radical shift to patriarchy. As the ice age receded, with rising temperatures and initially lusher pasture land and larger herds of grazing animals, the resulting economic changes further tipped the balance.

The Overthrow of Mother-Right

Panshin's conjectures are based on his belief that the distinctive features of the patrilocal band "correlate well with the archaeological, genetic and linguistic evidence for the Gravettian culture" of palaeolithic Eurasia. The implication, in fact, is that two branches of Gravettian culture, whose divergence must have come about with the Gravettians' movement into Europe nearly 30,000 years ago, were ancestral to both of the radically different cultures that were to clash some 25,000 years later.

Panshin's model, of course, is based on research carried out in North America rather than Asia, and more recently than the widespread nineteenth century shift from matrilineal to patrilineal clan organisation that had been recorded by Lewis H. Morgan:

> How easily it is accomplished, can be seen in a whole series of American Indian tribes, where it has only recently [1884] taken place and is still taking place under the influence, partly of increasing wealth and a changed mode of life ... and partly of the moral pressure of civilisation and missionaries. Of eight Missouri tribes six observe the male line of descent and inheritance, two still observe the female. Among the Shawnees, Miamies and Delawares the custom has grown up of giving the children a gentile name of their father's gens [clan] in order to transfer them into it, thus enabling them to inherit from him.[549]

That a similar process had taken place in Asia is undoubtedly true. Whether this occurred as early as Panshin suggests is difficult to judge, but that it had occurred well before the population displacements and invasions prompted by the Saharasian desiccation from about 4000 BCE is more or less certain. The shift must have already taken place if the invasions by the Kurgans and similar groups had the character described by Gimbutas. Whether it was the result of the development of herding, or whether the patrilocal form of social organisation was already in place amongst pre-neolithic steppe hunters, cannot be said for certain.

The latter is perfectly likely; and as suggested above, the improved conditions for herding that followed the ice age would have increased men's economic importance relative to women, further tipping the balance. Either way, Gimbutas' evidence appears to show incursions by horse-riding warrior groups from a cattle-herding culture beginning several hundred years before DeMeo's estimate for the beginnings of desertification.

The economic importance of cattle and herding was particularly highlighted by Engels:

> In Asia they found animals which could be tamed and, when once tamed, bred. The wild buffalo-cow had to be hunted; the tame buffalo-cow gave a calf yearly and milk as well. A number of the most advanced tribes - the Aryans, Semites, perhaps already also the Turkanians - now made their chief work the taming of cattle.[550]

"But to whom'" he asks, "did this new wealth belong?" This is a key question, since amongst hunter-gatherers the hunting was carried out by the men and therefore "the instruments of labour necessary for the purpose" (i.e hunting equipment) belonged to them, and would be retained even if a husband and wife parted company. Similarly, the wife would keep her household gear. When either of them died, however, such property as they had owned was always inherited by their closest relatives within the clan - and the children of a deceased man did not belong to his clan, but to that of their mother. According to this ancient system the man was the owner of the new and increasingly substantial source of subsistence, the cattle, and later of the new "instruments of labour", the slaves; but his children could not inherit from him:

> As wealth increased, it made the man's position in the family more important than the woman's, and ... created an impulse to exploit this strengthened position in order to overthrow in favour of his children the traditional order of inheritance. This, however, was impossible so long as descent was reckoned according to mother-right. Mother-right, therefore, had to be overthrown.[551]

Morgan's examples from North America show that this could be accomplished by a simple decree. The same could have been true in Asia, where - according to Soviet thinking based on Engels' Marxism - by the Bronze Age "hunting had become unimportant and stock-rearing had become the main source of meat ... Successes in the sphere of material production and the development of social division of labour and barter led to changes in the social relationship between peoples. The old matriarchal clan with its equality of the fields was transformed into a new patriarchal clan."[552]

Nevertheless it took millennia for the old structures of tribe and clan to disappear completely. Control of the clan passed to the men, but this by no means implies the instant creation of the monogamous, patriarchal family. The basic unit of society remained the clan, which had evolved and had been constructed around female leadership, and in this context women could still hold considerable social status well into historical times. Most of the documentary evidence for this comes from Europe and the Middle East,[553] though it is a reasonable assumption that the same would have been true in the Asian heartlands.

Ancient clan structures which survived well into classical times included the law against marriage within the clan, and the basic mechanism whereby property remained within the clan, both of which remained until the eventual establishment of the nuclear family as the basic unit of patriarchal society. Economic control meant control of property and property rights - which would have meant male control of the clan. As a result in Athens, for instance, a special law was necessary to force rich heiresses to marry *only* within their clan, to prevent their property from going out of the clan through being inherited by their sons.[554]

The general rule was marriage outside the clan, so that the emergent family structure based around husband and wife belonged half to one clan and half to another. In ancient law the family was not recognised as a social unit at all. No doubt (as Engels said) it was insufficiently stable! The Roman term 'familia' referred originally to the master and his slaves; his wife and children were not legally part of it. Gradually, of course, they did effectively become so - and this was recognised in civil law as it developed. To this day, however, the family has no recognised role in constitutional law, whereas in ancient times the clan was absolutely central to the constitution of the tribe.

On the Asian steppes, as noted, there is a strong suggestion that the preconditions for the transition from matrism to patrism appeared very early on, with the development of the patrilocal band. Certainly by the time that the Kurgan invasions into Europe began during the fifth millennium BCE, patriarchal rule would have been the established pattern across wide tracts of territory.

We are getting closer to answering the question 'where did patriarchy begin?' In an attempt to narrow it down further than 'somewhere in Central Asia,' we shall next look at a particular area that has held special importance in folk memory and mythology - the Altai-Baikal region of eastern Siberia.

6 Asia (2): The Ancient 'Cultural Seedbed'

I have argued that the basic shift from a female-defined to a male-defined social structure first arose "somewhere else and for some other reason" than in the desertification of Central Asia - though the psychological distress caused by desertification must certainly have reinforced and given momentum to this change. The 'some other reason' I have sketched out in describing the patrilocal band, the egalitarian but neverthless male-defined hunting culture of the ice age steppes, which would have come about as a strategy for dealing with climatic conditions of extreme cold. The original place, the 'somewhere else', is strongly suggested by Geoffrey Ashe in *Dawn Behind the Dawn.*

Specifically, Ashe presents a detailed case for the existence of an ancient shamanic religion, which originally had only female shamans but which later became dominated by men. He locates this in the region of the Altai Mountains and Lake Baikal, towards the eastern end of the Asian steppes. There are two aspects to this proposition: first shamanism, as a spiritual system that became the forerunner for much of later religion and philosophy; and secondly the region itself, steeped in legend, which Ashe sees as the geographical context for an early 'cultural seedbed' with far-reaching significance.

The shamanic roots of religion

Alexei Panshin suggested that one of several important innovations marking out the early steppe hunters from other palaeolithic peoples "may have been shamanism". He goes on to say "although that word is used rather loosely these days to describe almost any magical practices involving trances and healing, shamanism in the strictest sense is exclusive to northern Eurasia and the Americas", with its focus not just on healing but also on "wilderness spirits, highly individualistic practitioners, weather magic, and control of game animals." [601] Geoffrey Ashe, writing of the same early inhabitants of Siberia, states clearly that shamanism is the quintessential key to understanding their culture.[602]

Steve Taylor, in looking at the origins of the goddess religion, noted that its earliest form would probably not have included the worship of any deities, male or female, in the sense that we understand religious activity in the modern world. Rather it would have been based on a sense of the sacredness of nature, which was "closely connected to both the hunter-gatherers' and simple horticultural peoples' life". He suggests that the religions of all such peoples were so similar that it is possible to use the general term 'primal religion' to cover all of them:

> There are two main aspects of 'primal religion' ... primal peoples' sense that the whole world - and everything in it - is pervaded with an animating force ... [and] the concept of spirits (in the plural). They are everywhere; every object and every phenomenon is either inhabited by or connected to a particular spirit.[603]

Rogan Taylor, who explores shamanism ancient and modern in *The Death and Resurrection Show*, goes a step further: for him *possession* by such spirits is the essence of religious experience, resulting in ecstatic states of mind in which we can "experience intensely the normal human condition" and touch upon that which is fundamental to being ourselves and to being human beings - "In such strange accounts we may recognise our very beginnings." [604] This was the essence of shamanism:

> The fact that shamanistic religion is so universally widespread, and so closely associated with the nomadic hunter-gatherer way of life, also clearly indicates its extreme age. So convincing has the evidence appeared that some scholars have associated shamanism with the origin of religion itself. Leonard Leh, who studied the shamanism of the North American Indians, came to the conclusion that 'Shamanism, in some form, seems to have been characteristic of practically every type of human society in its early stages.' There is also abundant evidence of the imprint of shamanistic ideas in ... such sophisticated religions as Buddhism, Hinduism, Islam and Judeo-Christianity.[605]

Nevertheless, he acknowledges that shamanism "is not easy to define quickly or clearly" and, being concerned primarily with the roots of western traditions, he focuses on "what is known about the nomads of the northern hemisphere ... The Siberian and Asiatic tribes (one of whom, the Tungus people, actually provided the word 'shaman'), the Eskimos and some of the North American Indians." [606]

In other words, precisely those whom Panshin and Ashe refer to as the heirs of 'shamanism in its strictest sense', as first practised by the steppe hunters of ice age Siberia. Rogan Taylor describes the universe that hunter-gatherers inhabited as "saturated with spirits", and the cosmos of shamanistic peoples as triple-layered: "The world of everyday was seen as a 'Middleworld', suspended between two other realms of experience" into which the shaman could descend and ascend so as to "mediate between the spirits who dwell there and the people ... that lies at the centre of the shaman's activities":

> The shaman is the fine tuner of the psyche of the tribe. It is the shaman's responsibility to ensure that what can be done is done. Like a prophet, he is called upon to see into the future, predict the weather and the behaviour of animals. Like a priest, he must make the proper sacrifices, conduct the spirits of the dead to their resting places, know the details of the ceremonies. Like a historian but without the aid of writing he must know the history of the tribe, their heritage, their tribal spirits, their myths and legends, and the origins of things and their functions. Like an all-purpose doctor, he must be able to diagnose physical and mental illnesses, heal the sick, prescribe herbal and other remedies. He is the ombudsman to the all-pervading spirit worlds. If people or objects are lost, he must locate them. If people experience bad luck in any area of life, he must console and help them.[607]

It begins to become clear just why a 'canny shaman' would have been so crucial to survival on the Asian steppes. This region had first been populated during the inter-glacial period by people migrating up the Indus valley and through Afghanistan. According to Alexei Panshin:

> As the climate grew warmer and moister after 45,000 BP, they were able to settle in the vast open steppes of Siberia, which had become well-watered grassland, full of big game. There they expanded rapidly to both east and west. By 40,000 BP, one group of Upper Palaeolithic people was living in the region of Lake Baikal in east-central Siberia. Another had reached as far as the River Don in southern Russia ... We don't know a lot about those Upper Palaeolithic hunters who first ventured out across the northern steppes, but it is clear that they were great pioneers, boldly going where no modern human had ever gone before.[608]

Whether or not 'true' shamanism first appeared on the glacial steppes, as something more developed and functional than the 'primal religion' of other palaeolithic peoples, is a question that cannot be answered in the normal way: no, in essence of course it cannot have been different; and yes, of course it was, for these pioneers were carving out a new way of life beyond the boundaries of previous human existence - and their shamans, no doubt, were leading the way.

Regarding these shamans, Geoffrey Ashe - who has spent his life studying esoteric subjects and relating them to accepted archaeological and scientific facts - has this to say:

> The shaman is a person deserving respect and qualified to exert influence. He is not a witch doctor in the worse sense, exploiting superstition, nor is he a holy lunatic, despite his often bizarre outfit, his dancing and drumming ... On receiving his vocation he undergoes a rigorous training, with gruelling initiatory ordeals. He comes through, if he does, as a person superior to his fellow tribesmen in wisdom, self-control, and strength of character, a guide, healer, and diviner for his community.[609]

Rogan Taylor goes even further:

> The full scope of shamanistic behaviour is truly astounding, for it appears to contain within it, as if waiting to flower, virtually every artistic discipline and a fair few of the sciences as well.[610]

This statement is particularly worth bearing in mind as we come to Geoffrey Ashe's suggestion that central Asian shamanism was the active ingredient in a 'cultural seedbed' whose germinations eventually came to flower as arts, sciences, religions and philosophies in India, the Middle East and south east Europe.

Altai-Baikal

The Altai mountains lie north of the Himalayas and the Tarim Basin, south and east of the Siberian steppes, and west of Mongolia. Not surprisingly, they are prominent in the folklore of peoples throughout those regions. Lake Baikal, somewhat further east, is the world's largest fresh water lake and has been a focus for populations of hunters and herders for at least 30,000 years. A wide plateau, known as the Dzhungarian Gate, provides a corridor between the Dzhungar-Alatan and Altai mountains, connecting the steppes of Kazakhstan, China and Mongolia. Rock drawings in the region, depicting wild horse and aurochs, are believed to be the oldest artistic monuments in northern Asia, dating back to the end of the last Ice Age.[611]

Ashe identifies cultural motifs in the mythology of India, Sumeria, Asia Minor and Greece, which all point to what he calls a common cultural seedbed in the region of the Altai mountains and Lake Baikal. The motifs he particularly notes are the number seven (as in seven planets, seven colours of the rainbow, seven days of the week, etc); the labyrinth (in most cases a seven-fold pattern); and also the constellations of the Pleiades (the 'seven sisters', universally recognised as seven stars although only six are generally visible) and Ursa Major (also consisting of seven stars). All these, Ashe suggests, were originally part of the shamanic cosmology of ancient Siberia.

The imagery is very interesting and will be explored further below. First, however, the 'seedbed' is associated with male-defined cultures and civilisations, although "to become a shaman it made no difference whether you were a man or woman, aged or youthful, great or small." [612] On the glacial steppes, the climate and landscape may well have heightened the importance of hunting relative to plant gathering, and therefore a social balance tending towards the male rather than the female; but what we already know about ancient societies strongly

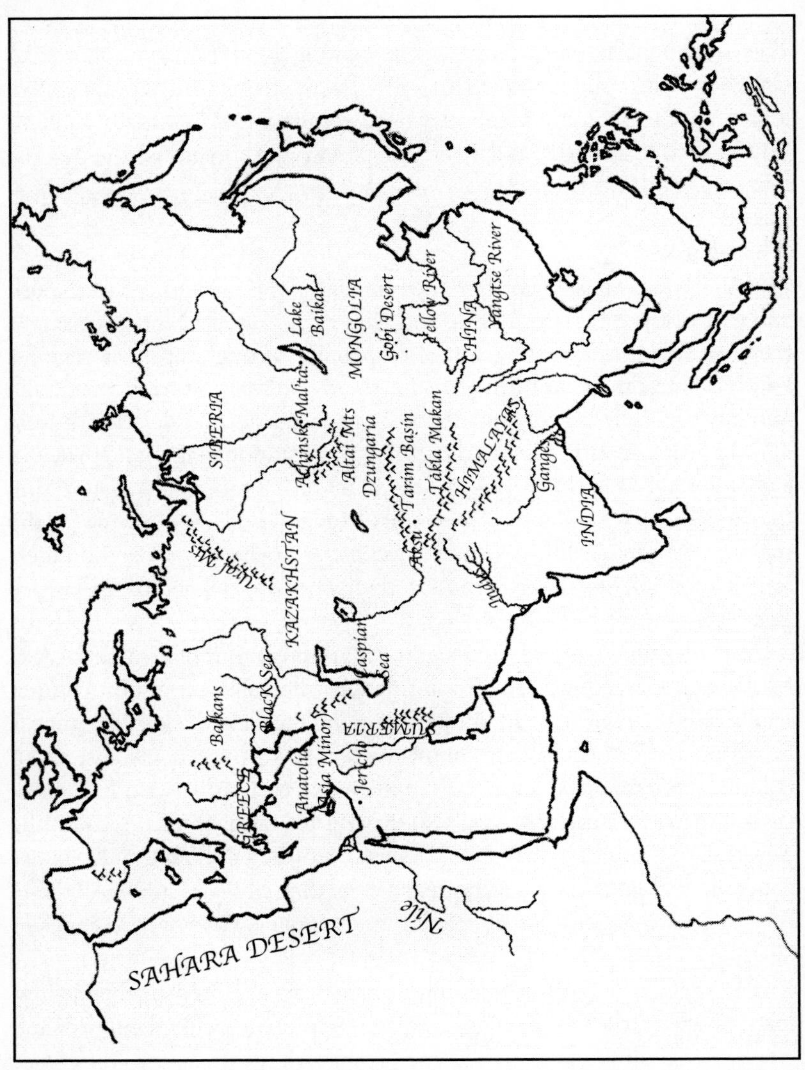

Pre-historic Eurasia, showing the steppe-lands as central to the palaeolithic world.
Based on the map from 'Dawn Before The Dawn', Geoffrey Ashe.

suggests that the first shamans, priestesses, would have been women. The suggestion, therefore, is that a change from female to male shamans came about in the Altai-Baikal, and this is a key point:

> Male shamans sometimes show a penchant for transvestitism and sex change, as if their nostalgia looked backward to an older feminine magic, with a notion that the true source of inspiration is female and that assumed feminity can set up a rapport with it ... Women can be shamans themselves, sometimes with an effectiveness that may help to explain the actions of sex-changed men. Shamanesses' performances have deeply impressed outside observers. A Tatar poem tells of a knowledge contest between two sages in which both were defeated by a woman who knew more words than either. Women's status may have been higher once because of this very command of magical arts. A more radical view, favoured by some Soviet anthropologists, is that female shamans were formerly the only ones, so that the nostalgia reflects historical fact.[613]

It seems more likely that any shamanic predilection for sexual ambiguity is to do with ambiguity itself being a shamanic tool, a way of avoiding any fixed ideas or assumptions that may be held by his people - rather than 'nostalgia'. Nevertheless, there is some kind of memory of a change from female to male shamans. For instance, several related languages in the Altai-Baikal region have very similar words for a female shaman (*utygan, udagan or udaghan*, "but never anything etymologically different"), though different tribes each have different names for a male shaman:

> The inference is that these tribes are descended from groups that were closer together, or in close touch, and then all shamans were women ... Male shamans appeared only after the separation, so the words for them were invented independently ... The female-shaman word *utygan* may have derived from the Mongol *Etugen*, or Earth Goddess.[614]

Such a religion was spread right across to Scandinavia and northern Europe - that is, into the areas where hunting remained the principal way of life after the ice sheets had receded. Archaeological evidence for it begins with rock carvings around 30,000 years ago, and then the celebrated 'goddess figurines', which date back to 28,000 years ago in Europe and to a similar time-frame in Siberia:

> Most of the older objects are in the Soviet Union, and some of the very oldest, dating from 24,000 BC or thereabouts, are also the farthest from Europe. Where the USSR meets Mongolia and China is the great curve of the Altai mountain chain, its peaks numinous to this day in Mongol eyes. Farther east is Lake Baikal, one of the world's largest bodies of fresh water ... The Altai-Baikal stretch of Siberia has yielded some of the richest and earliest Goddess hauls. At Mal'ta, fifty five miles northwest of Irkutsk, the figurines are among the best artistically.[615]

No date is suggested for the shift from female to male shamans. The 'richest and earliest Goddess hauls' are reliably dated to before the last glacial maximum (c 18,000 BCE). Richard Rudgley quotes the Russian researcher Vitaliy Larichev:

> The Upper Palaeolithic inhabitants of Siberia ... attained a not inconsiderable grasp of scientific principles ... He notes the symbolic artefacts from the central Siberian site of Mal'ta as recording - amongst other things - both the solar year and the phases of the moon, and believes that the calendars of the Upper Palaeolithic inhabitants of Mal'ta, some 24,000 years ago, were particularly made as a means to predict solar and lunar eclipses. He also believes that an object found at the even earlier site of Malaya Siya in western Siberia (about 34,000 BP) may be an extremely archaic but nevertheless rather complex astronomical instrument of the calendrical type, and that a mammoth ivory baton from the site of Achinsk, another early Upper Palaeolithic site, is engraved not for decorative purposes but as 'a numerical pictogram reflecting three years of a complex lunar-solar calendar system'.[616]

The earliest pottery remains so far discovered have been from eastern Siberia, dated to well before the neolithic era.[617] Otherwise we know remarkably little until, thousands of years later, invasions by warrior peoples from central Asia left their indelible mark in the archaeological records of India and many parts of the Middle East and Europe.

Ashe suggests that the supposed 'Indo-European race', after a brief contact with Shamanism, took on its most important and numinous aspects - elements of which then lasted for millennia.[618] This is unconvincing; he presents a package of ancient pre-historical religious motifs that appears to have been ingrained in the people over countless generations. It is not plausible that all this was absorbed during a brief contact. But it could be that the Altai mountains were considered sacred, and legends associated with them and their inhabitants were numinous, throughout a vast area of Siberia, Mongolia and Khazakhstan; and this could have been so for millennia.

Cultural dissemination

Whether the change from female to male shamans came before or after the conjectured Indo-European contact with shamanism, Ashe does not make clear. He does give us a very good account of the Indo-Aryan dispersal into India, parts of the Middle East and south east Europe; and although he talks in terms of 'cultural drift' rather than wholesale invasions, nevertheless his conclusions tie in well with those of James DeMeo's 'Saharasia' premise. DeMeo in turn has catalogued the incursions and invasions originating from central Asia from around 3000 BCE onwards, and affecting all the areas Ashe is looking at. As suggested, the original cultural shift - from a matrilineal to a patrilineal social order - would have occurred well before this. The evidence from Indo-European language analysis puts it back several thousands of years.

Ashe looks not so much at archaeology, more at documentary evidence. Tribal histories and folk memories from this huge span of time, oral traditions going back deep into the Aryans' ancestral memories, eventually became some of the first stories ever written down. As oral traditions, often passed on (we can assume) by specially trained bards who had spent years learning by rote the sacred culture of their tribe, they could be handed down without change through many centuries.

It was as written texts that such stories - notoriously - become subject to alteration as they were passed from generation to generation, whether through errors as they are copied from one manuscript to another, by political or theological interpretation, or artistic license. This difference may be counter-intuitive, but it is nevertheless true. Interpreting such texts becomes, therefore, the job of detection and intuition that is known as scholarship.

In this light, Ashe has looked at the Rig Veda and the Mahabarata from India, the Epic of Gilgamesh from Sumeria, Homer's Odyssey, and other Greek legends and traditions, particularly those relating to the god Apollo. All of these contain references to the seven motif (see above). In Indian mythology there is also 'the golden Mount Meru', which - like the Altai - exists beyond the Himalayas and other ranges, "central to Earth and the heavens;" [619] and in the Greek myths associated with the goddess Artemis he sees an ancient Earth goddess whose origins can be traced back, more or less plausibly, to central Asian shamanism.[620]

We are left with the question of why this has never been suggested before; and as Ashe points out, by the time these Indo-Aryan cultures were fully established their chroniclers were civilised, patriarchal and proud, as has been true until recently of most historians and scholars, so that:

> Ancient civilisations cannot have owed a debt, even a mythic debt, to the barbaric north. It must have been the other way around. A culture with proper credentials, in India or Mesopotamia, must have been the source, and any shamanic parallels are mere decadent borrowings. On this showing, an Altaic seedbed simply is impossible. Shamanism must always have been too primitive, and, in a sense, too trivial, to be an active ingredient in the mystiques and mythologies of more advanced peoples ... The plain truth is that there is no hard evidence for early transmission of any relevant motifs from India or Mesopotamia to shamanic country. A sceptic might retort that there is no hard evidence for early transmission from shamanic country to India or Mesopotamia ... But there is.[621]

Since Ashe was writing, new evidence has suggested that "a strong case can be made that the Indic-speaking composers of the *Rig Veda* (oldest parts composed about 1500-1300 BC) and the Iranian-speaking composers of the *Avesta* (oldest parts composed about 1200-1000 BC) probably were derived from steppe populations with a pastoral economy." Such evidence includes the archaeological discovery of "the remains of a mid-winter dog-centred ritual that corresponds in its details with ceremonies described in the *Rig Veda*." [622]

Ashe, however, focuses particularly on the number seven. He especially highlights the labyrinth (which was known amongst the north Americans and must therefore have originated in Asia and travelled before the closing of the Beringian land bridge around 6000 BCE); and the constellations of the Pleiades (associated with the 'seven Rishis' in India) and Ursa Major.

The number seven

These days, seven is the world's most popular sacred or 'magic' number. If this is a cultural and religious motif that originated in ice age Siberia, it would suggest some kind of understanding at a very early date of the seven-fold process of creation - as expressed in geometry by Pythagoras and others during classical times, and mythologically in the Bible's book of Genesis. It also reminds us that what came out of Asia was not entirely negative or destructive. Ashe describes the oldest example so far discovered of something based on "the peculiar mystique of the number seven":

> At Mal'ta ... retrieved from a cave burial, is an oblong panel of mammoth ivory dated about 24,000 BC ... [inscribed with] a design composed of lines of dots. They curve around to form seven spirals, six little ones framing a seventh that is much larger. In the large spiral the line goes around seven times, circling inward to a hole in the centre.[623]

> On one side of the panel are [the] spiral designs of dots, on the other are three serpents. The latter may doubtless be accepted as Goddess images ... The seven mystique of Altaic shamanism has an immensely long past and may descend from a time when, as some anthropologists maintain, women were the principal shamans or even the only ones. Moreover, the wide dispersal of the backtracking labyrinth spiral, which may be derived from the one exemplified on the panel, favours a belief that dissemination from this region did

> happen. It is found among the Hopi in Arizona, who call it the Mother Earth symbol, and this is evidence both for dissemination before 6000 BC and for the original Goddess character of the spiral.[624]

That the 'seven mystique' had its place in Siberian shamanism is confirmed by its widespread appearance in the mythology of the region. For instance, this Mongolian legend was recorded in the early twentieth century by Nicholas Roerich in Altai-Baikal:

> To Gessar-Bogdo-Khan were sent seven heads, cut off from seven black blacksmiths. And he boiled the seven heads in seven copper kettles. He fashioned out of them chalices, and inlaid these chalices with silver ... The wise Manzalgormo ... took the seven chalices fashioned from the seven heads of the blacksmiths and scattered them into the heavens, and the seven chalices formed the constellation Dolan-Obogod (the Great Bear).[625]

And drawing on the work of Mircea Eliade:

> Among the Ostyak, a man about to become a shaman cooks a squirrel, divides it into eight portions, discards one, and eats the other seven. After seven days, revisiting the spot, he receives the sign of his vocation. Among the Yurak-Samoyed, a man on the verge of the same step lies unconscious for seven days and nights passive to assailing spirits. An account of such a shaman's initiation tells of a trance experience in which he was taught the healing virtues of seven plants, found seven talking stones on a beach, and remained with them for seven days listening to secrets they taught him. A fully fledged shaman of the same tribal grouping wears a glove with seven fingers. Ostyak and Lapp shamans put themselves in a trance by eating a mushroom with seven spots. An Ugrian shaman has seven helping spirits.[626]

But why seven? Those things we think of as being counted in sevens have generally had this number imposed on nature by human consciousness.

They are not 'natural' in the way that two eyes, four limbs or five fingers are clearly natural. There are seven colours of the rainbow - but this depends on our human perception: there could just as well be six, or maybe eight or nine. A musical scale with seven notes is culturally defined, the result of aural conditioning, and has nothing inevitable about it. Seven days of the week seems at first sight to be a completely arbitrary idea, and in some ways quite inconvenient; "neither economic practicality nor calendric convenience" can be shown to have dictated it, "ever, anywhere." [627] So what is it about seven? Why does it appear to have become the most widely acknowledged sacred number in the world?

I offer this suggestion: if we close our eyes, ignore for a while the external wonders of nature, and focus our abstract thought, we can imagine a single point of consciousness. And this point can move - up, down, left, right, forward and back - in six basic directions. Of course, movement is possible in an infinite number of directions; but these six, plus the initial point of stillness, are what we need to describe, organise, and intellectually understand the business of movement and direction. "These are the axes X,Y and Z in geometry, and they are all that is needed to define a dimensional space. The sacredness of this six is emphasisied when you see how many ancient cultures use the six directions in their ceremonies." [628] Together with the point of origin, in fact, they create the basic mental framework with which we can relate to, and about, the outside world. This 'spatialisation' is "the first and most primitive aspect of [human] consciousness" described in chapter 4. So it is not surprising that we like sevens; that we have decided to have seven days in a week (including Sundays off), and that we apparently impose the number seven on nature - because for us it has become the 'natural' number to use for organisation and categorisation.

The point of origin, plus the six directions from it, are the basis of geometrical form - and in ancient times geometry was regarded as sacred science. The seven days of the week in turn are based on this - the seven days in Genesis correspond to a seven-stage geometrical construction that was used to describe, metaphorically, the entire cosmic process of creation.[629] I would conjecture that this, with its extensive ramifications, formed a major part of what was taught in the mystery schools of classical times.

It is possible to work through this geometrical construction - in two dimensions - using only a compass and straight edge. It was more likely undertaken as a purely abstract series of mental exercises - in three dimensions - using visualisation. The first exercise would begin with the single point of consciousness, extended in each of the six directions, then spun on its axes to form a sphere. From there, the student would one by one create a series of intersecting spheres, each adding to the complexity of the whole and defining a further range of angles, proportions and geometrical relationships (which are fascinating, but which there is not space to go into here). By the time he had seven spheres - one in the centre and six around it - there would be a sense of completeness and symmetry; he would now have the ability to start from scratch with a single point, and to create from there, step by step, a mathematical model of the universe.[630]

So this is far more than a matter of interesting architecture; it is the basic mental framework with which we can intellectually understand the outside world. It is fundamental to abstract thought and the mental processes distinctive to the human species. And at least 20,000 years ago this was understood, and expressed in the construction of the seven-fold labyrinth, as an interest in particular heavenly bodies, and so on. Perhaps not understood in exactly the philosophical terms as used here; but understood, in an abstract, mental way, and expressed as such.

This mode of understanding, this capacity for abstract, mathematical

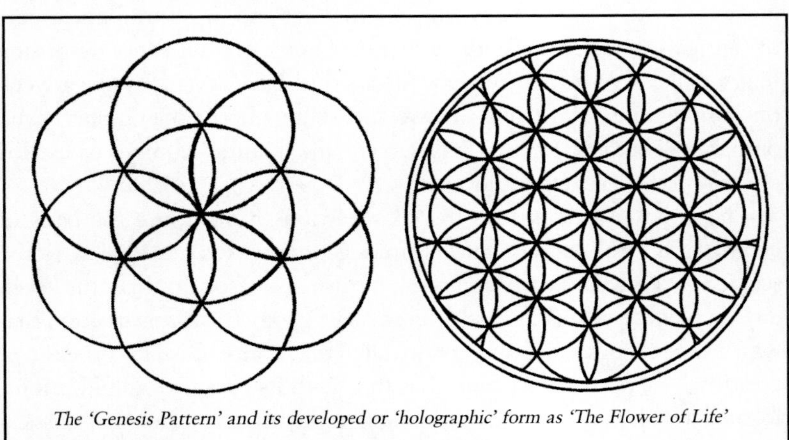

The 'Genesis Pattern' and its developed or 'holographic' form as 'The Flower of Life'

thought, this ability to organise and categorise, to plan and theorise, is what lies behind everything we can admire about civilisation. It is an innate ability, available to every human being; and yet - as presented by Geoffrey Ashe, as hinted at by the archaeology of the ancient steppes, as apparently recorded in the sacred literature passed down by cultures across a huge arc from India to Southern Europe - the evidence is that something about this basic understanding was crystallised, became clearer and more accessible, germinated like a seed in a seed-bed, somewhere in the Altai-Baikal region of eastern Siberia, probably more than 20,000 years ago.

Abstract thought and scientific enquiry

Alexei Panshin's work relating to Indo-Europeans was considered in the previous chapter; in particular his suggestion that the mode of social organisation that evolved on the ice age steppes was the patrilocal band - a pre-patrist but male-defined form of society. It is associated with important developments, including technological advances needed to deal with the extreme climatic conditions, as well as with shamanism.

Julian Jaynes, in *The Origins of Consciousness in the Breakdown of the Bicameral Mind*, identified two crucial elements in the evolution of human consciousness: metaphor, and the way we construct inner mental space.[631] The 'point of origin plus six directions' is clearly relevant here. The geometrical construction which follows on from this, described briefly above, can be further developed by an extension of the same method to become the 'Flower of Life' - intended as a representation of the pattern of Universal Creation. This is what Jaynes would call an 'analog' - in other words it is analogous to the process of creation, in the same way that a map is analogous to the geographical area it represents.

These two factors - technical advances enabling the successful adaptation to an extreme climate, and the importance of the number seven and its relevance to the construction of inner mental space - put together, suggest that what took place in the Altai-Baikal region around the time of the last ice age was a significant refinement in the human ability for abstract thought. It is this that represents the 'positive' side of the more male-defined social forms. The number seven appears to have become symbolic of this development, and a kind of cultural 'marker' by which the progress of the new way of thinking can be tracked.

This 'new way of thinking' was not a new human faculty, but a refinement of something that had always been there - something innately human. Inner mental space can be constructed by the same basic means but more simply, using just 'right, left and centre', 'in front, behind, and here' and 'above, below and level' - three threes.

Three, which is also 'past, present and future', has a satisfying sense of completeness to it, and it is not surprising to discover that it is the second most popular sacred number in the regions examined by Geoffrey Ashe. It is also the most popular in the Celtic west. However, in constructing inner mental space, the three threes are more cumbersome than the seven, and three could be seen as symbolic of the mode of abstract thought which was superceded by that symbolised by seven.

Meanwhile, in China, the most prominent sacred number is and was five - as in the five elements, the five senses; and the five directions. Indeed, Ashe observes that seven is remarkable for its absence in parts of the world that fall outside those he discusses. He also examines - and dismisses - the idea that seven is 'archetypal' in a Jungian sense; it is not universal:

> Even among Indo-Europeans, those who had it - the Indo-Aryans - were an untypical minority. With Indo-Europeans in general the sacred or magical number was three ... The seven mystique ... is formed culturally and is a product of regional influence rather than society in general, or psychology in general.[632]

Nevetheless, since classical times, seven has continued to spread and to gain currency. Life is now universally organised according to the seven-day week, which - with its recurrent rest day - differs from other quasi-weeks which have preceded it "in structure as well as length". Over the centuries, it has "imposed a rhythm of social behaviour as ancestrally right and wise, though neither its rightness nor its wisdom can stand up to scrutiny." [633] Today the number seven has become prominent throughout western popular culture - as in (for instance) *The Seven Samurai, The Magnificent Seven, Seven Brides for Seven Brothers* and so on.

This is something which has come about gradually; it is not in itself an innate quality of the human mind. "For thousands of years the seven mystique can be seen taking hold. It travels and grows more serious as a method of mental ordering." [634] Ashe arrives at this conclusion without looking at geometry: he points out that the seven planets of the astrologers and the seven metals of the alchemists, and specifically the requirement that there *should* be seven, led to the particular forms of scientific enquiry which created modern astronomy and chemistry. It is a fact, whether or not we give it significance, that these sciences did not arise from cultures that count in fives, or in nines; whilst "three is a triad rather than a number. Three objects are simply perceived as such, not counted":

> A mystique of three never could have inspired the counting that wove numerical patterns into nature and supernature. China's five gave more scope, but not enough. The heptad is the first set that is not, as a rule, directly perceived but has to be counted. Seven was the smallest number that, supposedly recurrent through earth and heaven, could produce counting as a habit beyond immediate need, a way of organising the world. Measurement and weighing could follow and could lead to science advancing without limits.[635]

The key thing, of course, was not some magical quality inherent in one number rather than another, but the refinement of humans' ability for abstract thought. This perhaps is what Steve Taylor has mistaken for an 'ego explosion'; increased 'self-awareness and self-assertion', a 'sharpened sense of ego', and a 'new kind of intellectual discrimination'.[636] It was not a new and acute awareness of the ego, the 'inner I'. Rather it was a better developed way of constructing the inner space that the sense of 'I' can inhabit. To achieve this it was not necessary for people to become egotistical, emotionally disconnected, or oppressive; and there is no reason to assume that, at first, this was the case.

Although such 'left brain' intellectual activity has come to be seen as typically 'male', it is not clear whether the reasons for this are dictated by culture, or whether culture has changed as a result of the development of this type of thinking. However, at some point the shamanic religion - once the natural preserve of women - did became male-dominated, with male gods and shamans.

Even where society later became entirely male-dominated and warlike, something of this sacred knowledge - or at least an appreciation of number and symmetry - was retained. Marija Gimbutas reports a series of rock carvings found in the Alps, dated to some time after the Kurgan invasions of Europe. She highlights the imagery of weapons; but the numerology must also have had significance:

> The god is represented by his weapons alone, or by weapons in combination with a belt, necklace, double-spiral pendant, and the divine animal - a horse or stag. In several of the compositions a sun or stag antlers occur in the place where the god's head should be. In others, the god's arms are represented as halberds or axes with long shafts. One, three, seven, or nine daggers are placed in the centre of the composition, most frequently above or below the belt.[637]

Riane Eisler argues passionately against the change represented by such imagery being regarded as 'adaptive' in evolutionary terms. She points out that "given our present high level of technological development, a 'dominator' model of social organisation is maladaptive."[638] Which indeed it is; but amongst hunters on the steppes during the ice age, a shift in that direction may well have been a useful adaptation - though also setting up the human race for cultural changes which, as the climate warmed, were to unfold as not just dramatic but traumatic.

This much, then, can rest on well-documented evidence and logical exploration: a shift in human thinking, which later would give rise to patriarchy, occurred somewhere in eastern Siberia, some time around the last ice age. By degrees, for reasons relating to culture and its adaptation to particular environmental conditions, to neolithic economic and technological developments, and finally to extreme climatic pressure, this way of being and thinking grew and gained in power. It shifted from being merely male-defined to being oppressively male-controlled, patriarchal.

Archaeology and scientific research may never come up with a more precise answer than that; but by now we have gathered sufficient clues to make it worth asking once again - where and when did patriarchy actually begin?

Aksu, in the Tarim Basin: 32,400 BCE

Ancient stories simply say that "He" came down "from the sky". Does this mean that a new kind of being had arrived from outer space - a 'horizontal gene implant' that changed the nature of our species? This is far-fetched; nevertheless there are a number of writers - enough that they almost constitute a *genre* of their own - who believe that the shift from 'primitive' to 'modern' human beings came about as the result of extra-terrestrial intervention. Such suggestions are a late twentieth-century phenomenon, and appear to be the successors to nineteenth-century ideas about 'primitive' man being crude and ape-like.

The extra-terrestrials are generally credited with introducing new genetic material to the planet, along with new life skills - and they usually arrive in time to initiate building the Egyptian pyramids, Stonehenge, or other monuments that in fact represent the architectural consummation of tens of thousands of years of stone age development. Such ideas may be bizarre and often ill-informed, but they nevertheless form part of the exploration into some kind of shift that did take place (though this shift would have come about before the great megalithic monuments were created). Geoffrey Ashe is interested, though not convinced, by the notion that:

> In some sort of paradisal past, humanity was taught arts and sciences and spiritual truths by superior beings: sages from lost Atlantis, or 'Hidden Masters', or visitors from distant worlds. While not greatly tempted by such fantasies, I found that my exploration turned up clues hinting at *something* unprovided for in offical prehistory.[639]

Richard Rudgley, in *Lost Civilisations of the Stone Age*, identifies this 'something' as being the result of a prejudice which prevents conventional historians of classical civilisations from acknowledging the deep prehistoric roots from which they developed:

> If mankind before the historical era was so primitive, how could civilisation have arisen from such poor cultural roots? ... [Consequently] it is argued that the astronomical knowledge and the advanced technology of the ancient world *obviously could not* have

> been inherited from Stone Age cultures and therefore can only be explained by recourse to Atlantis or to aliens.[640]

Rudgley presents a considerable body of evidence to show that, in every field, the beginnings of what became civilisation do go back to neolithic or even palaeolithic times. Humans were sufficiently advanced more than 50,000 years ago to plan and undertake the sea journey from south east Asia to Australia. There would have been no need for any genetic boost (many millennia later) to make our species more intelligent or capable.

Nevertheless some have assumed that the classical civilisations were degraded versions or surviving remnants of a more ancient 'golden age'; a perfect civilisation which existed, perhaps, on the lost continent of Atlantis. Such ideas are now losing currency, even in fringe circles, and with good reason; but were notably taken up in the 1970s by Elizabeth Gould Davis in *The First Sex.* She asserted that:

> In ancient times, indeed well into the historical era, woman had played a dominant role. The tradition shared by all early peoples, but glossed over by later historians and myth-interpreters, [is] that it was woman who had preserved the germ of the lost civilization and had brought it into its second flowering.[641]

It is the concept that our ante-deluvian forebears possessed 'civilisation' in the sense of an elaborate material culture that is now seen as unlikely; not the relative status of women in ancient society. The crucial shift was not from being 'primitive' to being 'advanced', but from being female-defined to being male-defined. Contemporary with the pyramids and Stonehenge is the equally impressive stone age civilisation on Crete; but this was different. It was not created as a means of dominating the landscape. Megalithic monuments were - and they may all have had their ancestry in the 'kurgans' of the Asian steppes. They certainly appear to be the work of male architects inspired by a male priesthood.

Amongst the 'extra-terrestrial' theorists, there is one book that does not contradict the known archaeological evidence, and that could perhaps cast some light on the subject. This is *The Only Planet of Choice,*[642] in which 'channelled' material presents the story of a being known as 'The Hawk' appearing at Aksu, in the Tarim Basin, east-central Asia. This puts a precise date on it: 32,400 BCE, when "the seed had evolved into a human being which was ready to receive new energies." [643] At first sight this may seem arbitrary and anachronistic; but for the purposes of the present investigation, this date will serve very well.

The book is couched in terms of macrocosmic drama, with humans on Earth being "seeded" genetically by beings from "more evolved civilisations" on other planets. The Hawk's mission was to bring the elements of civilisation to Earth from his galactic home - including the subtlety and poetry of language, but also such things as "the principle of one leader" and a moralistic attitude towards sex, so that ideally "mating would be utilised only for the highest purpose" (i.e. genetic improvement).[644] These, of course, are amongst precisely those attitudes cited by DeMeo as being indicative of humanity's pathological state.

This event, the coming of 'The Hawk', is presented as a great and positive step forward for humanity; not, as Riane Eisler would certainly see it, as part of our problem. According to *The Only Planet of Choice*, 'The Hawk' brought "enlightenment" and "knowledge and technology" - a curious counterpart, and contemporaneous, to the "first great flowering of human arts and culture" happening in Europe; and one that is described as appearing suddenly from the sky, rather than emerging over millennia from the landscape.

As channelled material, this needs to be considered alongside the mythological, and it does compare interestingly with the Adam and Eve story from the Bible. The Hawk did not arrive in the Garden of Eden; he arrived in a hostile environment which he set about mastering. And he did not have trouble with God for tasting the fruits of knowledge; he established the first centre of learning, and thereby eventually became a god himself (the Hawk is identified as the being remembered in folk memory who eventually became known as the Egyptian god Horus). He also introduced a distinctly male form of social organisation.

The Hawk is, perhaps, no more than an outmoded thoughtform from the latter part of the twentieth century; his existence is probably impossible to prove (or for that matter to disprove) through conventional science; and the publisher of his story did not intend for him to be held responsible for the psychological 'Fall' of the human race. If such ideas as this book suggests really had appeared in the world more than 30,000 years ago, they would have challenged humans' understanding of what it is to be human; they certainly would not have spread very quickly. Nevertheless, the story of 'The Hawk' is consistent with what archaeological pointers there are, and it is possible that just these attitudes could have arisen in just this time and place, and from there gradually spread to "what you now identify as China ... and out to other domains", eventually appearing on the central Asian plains around the time of the last ice age. After all, in answer to the question "where and when did patriarchy begin?" science and archaeology have nothing to offer so clear as "Aksu, in the Tarim Basin, 32,400 BCE".

The Tarim Basin is now exceptionally arid; it includes the Takla Makan, one of the world's largest sand deserts, and it is a barren, near-lifeless wasteland. It was once fertile, with an inland sea into which flowed the Tarim and several other rivers, fed by the copious glacial run-off from the surrounding mountains. In 1900 CE it was still known to the Chinese as *Han Hai*, 'the place of the dried-up sea'. It was home to the mysterious 'mummies of Urumchi', preserved by the dry desert sands since 2000 BCE and apparently European in origin; and to the enigmatic Indo-European language 'Tocharian', into which Buddhist texts were translated 1,000 years ago.

Around 4000 BCE, when Saharasian desiccation was just beginning, "a highly developed Neolithic culture was spread across North China" from the Tarim Basin to the Yellow and Yangtse river valleys.[645] Over an extensive period since then, "overgrazing, exten-sive use of shrubs and herbaceous vegetation for fuel, and plowing of over-grown sands for sowing, unaccompanied by the necessary soil preservation measures, have resulted in the mass destruction of natural vegetation." [646] Thus human activity has contributed greatly to its becoming desert. Ruins of villages on ancient shorelines still lie amongst the salt crusts and sand dunes, where the region was once "renowned for its library, its art, and its craft, as well as its might in war." [647]

An investigation into what effects 'The Hawk' may have had in China I leave to someone else. To the north and west of the Tarim Basin are the central Asian steppes, and it was here that ideas such as those presented in this material - wherever they originally came from - eventually found particularly fertile ground to grow in. Technological innovation was certainly important to the hunters on the ice age steppes; and cultural motifs that held significance for scientific understanding did spread from this region to many distant places. 'The Hawk' may be pure fiction, but his story provides a clue and a possibility, and an interesting tail-piece to this journey of investigation.

Reconciliation

By neolithic times there were two distinctly different ways of understanding and being in the world, which appear to have emerged separately at roughly the same time, in two different regions far apart. One is patriarchal and the other is matrist. Once the two cultures eventually came into contact - and conflict - then the mythologies of each would demonise each other's gods and goddesses; but it is unhelpful to say that one is 'wrong' and the other 'right'.

At the same time it is dangerous to assume or imply an equivalence between the patriarchy of the last few thousand years, and the social forms that preceded it. The Old European Goddess culture, towards the end, may not have succeeded in maintaining a comfortable balance between the sexes in the way we are assured it did by Riane Eisler and other feminists; but this in no way matches the wholesale slaughter and destruction that was to come about as the result of patrism. Accusations of pathological behaviour, or of threatening the destruction of the whole planet, have never been levelled at matrism.

Matrist society was the natural mode of human life, at least during its long period of formative evolution; patrism, at best, has been accepted reluctantly. It would be easy to assume that once the process of change had gained its violent momentum, the Goddess culture disappeared in just a few short centuries. In fact this is far from the truth. There is every reason to believe that people generally wanted to stay with the old, pre-patriarchal ways, and the patriarchy was imposed deliberately, often by force. The appearance that it represented the 'natural order of things' was created by the patriarchy itself: by hiding the truth about Minoan Crete, by presenting the illusion of male supremacy in Rome when in fact there was a huge and continuing power struggle, by creating the 'official' supremacy of the Christian church when - in Britain for instance -

paganism was alive and healthy enough to evolve the whole 'John Barleycorn' mythos during Christian times; and so on. In fact, the Kurgan invasions began in 4300 BCE and 6,000 years later the patriarchy was sufficiently insecure that it was still burning witches.

Matrist society may have been slow to deliver 'progress', but it provided sustainable and psychologically healthy human society for tens of thousands of years. The example of Minoan Crete shows that it could produce 'high' civilisation just as well as - and in many ways better than - patrism. Its replacement brought some benefits, but also war, cruelty, oppression, environmental destruction ... it becomes impossible to avoid the value judgements brought to this by feminists, marxists, environmentalists and even psychologists.

At the same time, there was some inevitability to female-defined society giving way to male-defined society. That is not to suggest that male-defined society is in some way an improvement on female-defined; rather that the patriarchal experiment has been a painful but necessary part of human development, a stage in a dialectical process. It has all been one process, the evolution of one species. However, fueled by Saharasian climate change, male-defined society became patristic - potentially derailing what might have been the smooth and natural evolution of a synthesis - and this in turn has resulted in the modern crisis that creates a moral imperative and a practical urgency to seek a change of direction.

There is an instructive story of a Canadian university graduate who 'dropped out' and went to live in a hut on a small Caribbean island, eking out a simple living by making goat-skin bags. The people on this island could not understand him: why should anyone with easy access to a university education, and the prosperity that it provides, come to live in a hut on their island? For them, the opportunity to gain a degree at a Canadian university was an unattainable dream. On the other hand - for those of us who have seen the pitfalls of our highly developed, materialist western culture - the attractions of a simple life in beautiful surroundings are easier to understand. But this understanding comes with having had the opportunities denied to the Caribbean islanders.

Human intelligence, in its natural form and without the restrictions caused by rigid cultural patterns and power structures based on the imposition of control, is capable of finding fresh, original answers to every question, an elegant solution to every problem. As noted above, it is dangerous to assume an equivalence between patriarchy and the matrist forms of society that preceded it. Such assumptions are bound to come from within the patriarchy - are themselves an example of patriarchal thinking, infected by rigid cultural patterns and structures of control - for they assume a change from one set of ('matriarchal') patterns to another, a reversal of the dominance of one sex over the other. In fact what took place was thewholesale creation of such patterns where before they had been the exception.

The issue of sexual politics - indeed, of sexism - is not the point. It is part of the confusion arising with and out of the patriarchy. To state the obvious: male and female should be complementary, not contradictory. This is not just hopeful idealism; it matters, because each is manifestly out of balance without the other.

> Balance is born from choice - in nature and in human design ... The loss of our Goddess Mother is a crippling blow that all of humanity is suffering from - physically, mentally, emotionally, socially and spiritually. Our Creatress Mother Goddess is the single most powerful symbol and fact of Life. When humanity respects and honors Sacred Life as our Creatress Mother Goddess, equal to the Creator, this one act will restore balance to our world.[648]

Once, people were humans first, male or female second, and everyone was equally and creatively a part of the whole. There may be no way to prove this conclusively, but to believe it of the past is surely helpful in creating it for the future.

Magic, music and art are as important as enlightenment, knowledge and technology. A society based on the "principal of one leader", where the prevailing virtues are strength, courage and obedient loyalty, is not a society in balance. But neither is one that is focused exclusively on motherhood, mystery and sensuality. Patriarchy has been the loss of that equality and balance.

7 Recap: 'The Past is the Key to our Future'

The story of modern human development (or of the development of modern human beings) is not one that has taken place only in Europe and Asia. Neither is it really one story - or even two, running in parallel, as I have described it. It is of course an endless number of interwoven stories, human life lived with all of its myriad plots and subplots, and with exceptions to every rule that could possibly be produced, deduced, or imposed on the huge rambling reality of prehistory.

There is no such thing as a definitive view of history, much less prehistory. Historians can and do come up with widely differing interpretations of events that took place only a generation ago, where there is ample documentary evidence and the buildings and landscapes in which the action took place are still largely intact. After all, human actions and motivations are thoroughly complex and often unclear, and no doubt always have been. The more I have researched, the more I have realised that the task which I have set myself is impossible.

Nevertheless it is still worth the effort; it is fascinating to draw out the major threads, to mark off the key events, and in particular to discover that the nearest approximation that I can find to 'the truth' is so different from the assumptions I grew up with. It is also important to make this effort, to understand as well as we can what we are as human beings, and how we became so. For, as Richard Leakey said so clearly in quoting his father Louis, "The past is the key to our future." Humanity has huge decisions to make, and the better we understand how we arrived at where we are, the better we shall be able to see clearly where we need to go. Here is my version of the narrative so far ...

The early prehistory of human culture

Human consciousness began with the ability to 'map' the environment in the way that has been best preserved in the 'songlines' of aboriginal

Australia. Similar ways of relating to the land in other parts of the world suggest that this ability, this intimate relationship between the human mind, the spiritual world and the physical landscape, was once universal: everything - animals, plants, the weather, and particularly prominent landmarks - was understood to be imbued with spirit, to have meaning for people, to have its counterpart in the inner landscape.

This understanding and mode of perception, objective consciousness based in the development of inner mental space, evolving along with language, is what made humans human. This process of evolution came about amongst humans in their 'natural' habitat, following what has been called the 'hunter-gatherer' way of life.

Human beings - including all members of the genus *homo*, principally *homo sapiens* and our ancestors *homo habilis* and *homo erectus* - have always been cultural creatures. This statement sounds straightforward, but in some circles it would be controversial, since many believe that culture - and indeed true humanity - are much more recent phenomena.

In fact, human culture is sufficiently ancient to have become embedded in our biology: humans' unique pattern of growth and maturation includes an extended childhood lasting into the early teens, by which time the brain has reached almost its full size and capacity, followed by a pause in physical growth before a growth spurt enables the body to catch up with the brain. This pattern maximises the potential for learning and cultural assimilation before we reach full maturity, and had already developed to a significant degree amongst *homo erectus* - in other words, nearly two million years ago.

Culture, at least in the context of prehistoric evolution, can be defined as the body of information held by the people in a given society that is useful in terms of their survival, and the form given to that information. There were several different inter-related elements to this, gradually developing from the earliest times until the Upper Palaeolithic (c 40,000 to 10,000 years ago) when 'culture' emerged in a concrete way which is clearly recognisable to the modern mind. The key elements during this enormously long period of development were: conscious thought, language, social skills and conventions, the hunter-gatherer lifestyle, and mythology and spiritual life. Although most of these have their roots in the pre-human animal world, humans have come to be seen as cultural beings par excellence, our humanity even being defined by our uniquely extensive capacity for culture.

'Human culture' is the collective name that we use to cover all these elements of distinctively human life; and though most of them originated with pre-human hominids, nevertheless it was with *homo erectus* that they all came together in genuinely human form. These were the people who first used fire, who developed skills to make tools with an element of technological and aesthetic design, and who could adapt to different environments and climatic conditions. They were the first to move into large tracts of new territory, and they were inhabiting most of Africa and Eurasia by about 750,000 years ago, perhaps earlier. Humanity, and human culture, are very ancient.

Human development to the upper palaeolithic

There is no real agreement concerning the number of different species or sub-species who subsequently evolved over this huge geographical area and during this enormous span of time. *Homo erectus* continued to inhabit some regions until relatively recently; whilst a number of different skeletons known generically as *archaic homo sapiens* have been discovered in different locations and dated to different times. They all used broadly similar technologies; in many cases anatomically different types of people using the same types of stone tools. It is reasonable to assume that they followed similar lifestyles.

In the relatively cold, northern climate of Europe, a particularly large-brained and strong-limbed type of people, whose remains were first discovered in the Neanderthal valley of Germany, are seen in the archaeological record from about 250,000 years ago. 'Anatomically modern' human beings (*homo sapiens sapiens*) first appeared in Africa, between 200,000 and 100,000 years ago.

Humans evolved as social, co-operative beings, free from the behaviour patterns that later led to violence, cruelty, domination of one group by another, and taboos regarding sex and other bodily functions. The natural mode of human relationships is co-operation and affection. When emotional hurts get in the way of this, there is a natural recovery process which can be effectively used to clear the distressing feelings and to 're-set' the emotions back to this natural mode.

Humans have an exceptionally long period of maturation, necessary for our development as highly intelligent cultural beings, but during which we are vulnerable to emotional pain and trauma beyond our capacity to cope with. We have therefore developed the unique ability to suppress painful emotional material, along with mechanisms to release or discharge it. Early forms of society included time and space for this discharge process to take place in the normal course of life. Only when this ceased to be the case did negative behaviour patterns become institutionalised and endemic.

The form of governance, though no doubt varying widely in its detail, was until about 6,000 years ago almost universally of a type that has been called 'matrist' - based on the nurturing model of the mother in the family. There was nevertheless a balance between the sexes. Men took the lead in hunting and other matters external to the group, defining the species in terms of its place in the environment; women took the lead in relation to the family and matters internal to the group, defining the species in terms of its social organisation.

100,000 years ago, modern humans had already populated most of Africa and were beginning to move into the rest of the world. By about 50,000 years ago they had spread through Asia and into Australia. They lived in groups of increasing size and complexity, evolving their social organisation so as to progressively eliminate in-breeding. This meant that the earliest forms of group marriage developed such that, first, parents did not take their own children as mates, and later a group of closely related women would collectively 'marry' a group of unrelated men. This was the forerunner of the 'clan', a kinship network within which marriages were not permitted. Two or more clans coalesced to form a 'tribe', which generally inhabited a given area of territory separate from other tribes. In the earliest times, the only genealogy to be measured was through the female line, and the clan became both the basic unit of social network and the basis of women's status in society. Men's status related more to the tribe. Over time, tribes grew and divided to form groups and alliances of related tribes, networks of kinship and trading relationships, often covering enormous areas.

This pattern appears to have been so similar, right across the world, that the simplest and most basic form of the clan must have come about very early. By 40,000 years ago, during the interglacial period when people first moved into the wildest regions of central Asia and northern Europe, the sophisticated and widespread mutual social support provided by the developed tribal system was already in place. At this time, Europe and parts of Asia were still the home of neanderthals, whose social networks were, perhaps, less sophisticated and more localised, though nevertheless completely functional. It was at least another 5,000 or 10,000 years before neanderthals were completely displaced by the moderns. The reasons for their gradual displacement are taken to be the moderns' greater social and technological sophistication; but the change was certainly not abrupt, and was unlikely to have been violent. On the contrary, their interaction with modern human beings must have been considerable, and appears to have contributed to the major developments in human culture that followed.

These developments are signalled in the archaeological record by the appearance of representative art. Beginning about 35,000 years ago, this remarkable era for the visual arts coincided with far more efficient technologies in the production of stone tools; with 'campsites' first becoming what we could describe as villages; with the beginnings of 'proto-agriculture'; and with greater longevity - such that it was now normal for children to grow up with living grandparents. It is this time that conventional archaeologists look back to for the beginnings of 'human culture' in its modern sense, and also the time that radical goddess-worshippers see as containing the origins of their tradition. There is growing evidence that the neanderthals contributed significantly to this 'first great flowering' of the human arts, whether through social interaction or genetic cross-breeding. This, the 'neanderthal factor', in turn provides one possible reason for the subsequent radical differences between human society in Europe and its counterpart in Asia.

Early shifts from female-defined to male-defined social forms

What evidence there is supports the growing assumption that ancient spirituality, like ancient methods of tracing lineage and observation of the process of creation throughout the natural world, was focused on the female. This does not mean that palaeolithic society was matriarchal. It was, however, the antithesis of patriarchy. It was a society without rigid power structures, and with a balance between male and female roles and status. Nevetherless, creation comes about through the female, and society's cohesion is derived from the role of the mother. This would have been the basis of the social principles described as 'matrifocal' or 'matristic' - a society ordered so as to derive maximum enjoyment of life's pleasures, with an absence of warfare or widespread social violence.

Of course there were acts of violence and oppression, but the clans provided both mutual protection for their members and checks and balances within and between tribes. Basic social stability was maintained, without the need for any coercive agencies. Nevertheless the reality of political history since classical times, and the threat to our planet posed by major current problems such as nuclear weapons and environmental destruction, strongly suggest that something has since gone wrong. Certainly a huge change in basic human outlook took place, at some time before the era of classical civilisation.

Precisely where and when this change first came about is the elusive subject of this book - which concludes that there is no one simple reason for it, though several have been suggested. Geographically, pointers lead to the eastern end of the vast central Asian plains, once perhaps the richest hunting grounds in the world. The first steps in this shift may not have been anything we should describe as 'going wrong'; the subsequent spread of 'patrist' values and practice has been accompanied, for instance, by an appreciation of sacred numbers and geometry, and a study of the stars, such as we associate with the Pythagoreans of Greece or the mystery schools of ancient Egypt. These are very valuable components of human culture. Their antiquity may be far greater than we have imagined, going back to palaeolithic times, even to the last ice age or before.

The reason for the shift from female-defined to male-defined society is less simple than some have suggested. The Marxist view of Friedrich Engels, for instance, attrubutes it entirely to economic changes during the neolithic; James DeMeo, the Reichian analyst, identifies the cause as mass trauma caused by desertification; and Steve Taylor, the new age thinker, pins the blame on his novel concept of an 'ego explosion'.

In fact, the social preconditions were laid down well before the neolithic, when the Asian steppes appear to have been the first location in which male shamans took precedence over priestesses. Initially there may have been no other major difference, though this change is associated with technological and social innovations, arising from a significant refinement in the human ability for abstract thought. The technological developments and economic changes of the neolithic made the process inevitable; and 'Saharasian' climate change ensured that this was not just a dialectical progression from female-defined to male-defined society, but the onset of a pathological shift from the essentially benign human nature which our species had evolved with, to militant patriarchy.

Europe and Asia

Nearly 40,000 years ago the 'Gravettian' culture originated in Asia, with both technological and social developments that enabled people to live successfully in the extreme conditions of peri-glacial Eurasia. One branch of this culture moved as pioneers into the uninhabited eastern steppe-lands, the other into the region around the river Don and eventually into Europe.

As the climate moved towards the last glacial maximum, these two branches dealt with the challenges they faced in two different ways. In the east, they lived in mobile groups and subsisted largely by hunting rather than gathering, so that the social emphasis shifted towards the men. In the west, they started to develop homesteads and focussed more on domestic technologies - so that the social emphasis shifted more towards the women. The latter also had extensive interaction with the indigenous neanderthals, who had evolved in the prevailing cold climate, and whose different ways of thinking would have been an added element to the overall human picture.

Later, with the ending of the ice age, and whilst 'proto-farming' and 'the first true villages' were appearing in Europe, in Asia the first taming of horses took place, alongside the first 'proto-herding' (in the sense of following the natural migrations of herd animals). With this would have come a further shift in thinking, because the traditionally male role in hunter-gatherer life would have been given greater emphasis. The opposite, increased emphasis on the female, would have been true where horticulture began to become important and where life first became less mobile.

This was the time when property first became significant. Until then, possessions amounted to little, and would have been an encumberance to a hunter-gatherer's life. With the establishment of farmsteads on the one hand, and herding on the other, this was no longer so and property (the farms and the herds) became an important factor.

It was fundamental to the clan system that there was no marriage within the clan, and that the clans were matrilineal. In the ancient hunter-gatherers' world, tools and personal effects would be passed from mother to daughter, and from elder man to younger - though kept within the clan. Paternity was not a factor in inheritance. Farming and herding were, respectively, developments of gathering and of hunting - of the female and the male roles in palaeolithic society.

So in Europe, hunting was no longer central to people's lives and property accrued to the women; in Asia, gathering foodstuffs was no longer of critical importance and property was in the hands of the men. Whether through fathers' desire to pass on their property to their sons, or as the result of an earlier change that now had additional impetus to spread, Mother-right was ended amongst peoples of the Asian steppes. In Europe and in Asia, in these two opposite ways, the ancient balance between the sexes was now threatened.

Both farming and herding had resulted from the ingenuity of modern humans, faced with dramatic changes in climate and ecology. Modern people were differently (and far better) equipped to meet such challenges than people had been in earlier cycles of glaciation and warming. They were better able to control their environment - and, in different regions, in different environmental conditions, they dealt with the challenges in different ways.

The changes in climate and ecology were indeed dramatic. Post-glacial rises in sea level, for instance, resulted in a gradual disappearance of land under the water, over millennia, with occasional sudden events when major ice sheets slid massively into the oceans. As hospitable coastal regions were lost under the sea, higher population density, particularly in the Middle East, provided the impetus for grain cultivation. In northern latitudes, the retreat of the ice sheets allowed hunting to spread northwards.

In central Europe, however, warmer and wetter conditions resulted in the spread of forests across what had once been open plains, so that hunting became far less viable and at first the human population was reduced. In time, forest clearance and what became a predominantly agricultural way of life meant that humans could successfully adapt to the conditions in larger numbers than had ever existed there before. They developed what has been plausibly described, by Marija Gimbutas and others, as the earliest example of a genuine civilisation.

This lifestyle began to spread into central Asia, where it was incompatable with hunting and its development into herding; in some places, increasing desiccation was at first countered by irrigation, but ultimately only herding was possible as huge areas of formerly well-watered land became progressively more arid.

Climate change and psychological distress

In this context of people in different regions having to adapt to different environmental challenges, Europe and Asia produced different types of neolithic culture, which ultimately clashed: the agrarian, goddess-centred culture of Europe - particularly south east Europe - and the pastoral, warrior culture emerging from central Asia.

Around 6,000 to 5,000 years ago, the ongoing changes in world climate that followed on from the last ice age reached a critical stage. The belt of perennial rainfall that had watered north Africa, the Middle East and central Asia shifted north. Huge areas, which for millennia had been fertile hunting grounds carrying large human populations, began to dry out. By 4000 BCE the progressive desiccation of central Asia (and later north Africa) was beginning to mean the complete abandonment of ancestral homelands, accompanied by psychological distress on a scale that had not previously been experienced.

Once this desiccation had gained momentum, it was not merely a change in environmental conditions requiring fresh human adaptations. It was, across a vast and central region of the inhabited world, the end of continuity, of security, of the basic and intimate relationship between the human mind and its environment that had been crucial in the evolution of human consciousness itself. In reducing life - temporarily or permanently - to a desperate process of mere survival, it would also have disrupted the relationship between mothers and their children.

The significance of psychological distress is a novel concept in the study of history and pre-history. The use of 'Palaeopsychology' as a chapter title was somewhat tongue-in-cheek, but it is a subject that will become increasingly important if we are to understand more fully the evolution of our species. The primary contention is that patriarchal or patrist societies and their values, far from being based on 'human nature', are a distortion of our nature and actually less than fully human.

The paradox, of course, is that these values arose along with the development of human culture into being 'fully human' in a way that is recognisable in the modern world. People had achieved a level of technical expertise that enabled them to survive, and even flourish, in their changing environment; but this was at the cost of a deleterious effect, both widespread and long-term, on the quality of human life.

There has always been human psychological distress; but before this change, mechanisms built into society allowed it to be dealt with effectively and constructively. Eventually, these mechanisms were largely lost, and the scale of the problem became ever greater. Distressed, anxiety-ridden states of mind were passed from one generation to the next and became embedded in society as 'traditions'. A whole range of attitudes and practices which are cruel, oppressive and irrational became enshrined as 'normal', even laudable behaviour, necessary for the existence of civilisation. This is 'patrist' society.

Prior to about 4000 BCE, there is virtually no archaeological evidence for fortifications or warfare anywhere in the world, nor for any kind of social stratification or warrior class. After 4000 BCE migrations, invasions and warfare were what came to characterise human events. It was at this time that the Goddess culture of ancient Europe began to come under pressure. Gradually the violent displacement of peoples became widespread; the establishment of kings and kingdoms, of hierarchical, oppressive societies based on slavery, became more and more the norm.

The old social patterns based on the matrilineal clans were steadily broken down, with the growth in importance of new economic and military structures all based on the patriarchal ideal. The classical civilisations of the Mediterranean all followed this pattern - the only exception being Minoan Crete, which (even as a major and cosmopolitan trading power) maintained its essentially matrist society right through until 1500 BCE. After its eventual collapse, the nature of its culture was suppressed by the imperial Romans. Its rediscovery in the last hundred years has astonished archaeologists and inspired a generation of feminists and others. It has given us an indication of what might have been possible. The fruits of human ingenuity could have been so much more delightful.

Sexual dialectics or the miracle of paradox

For all its achievements, the matrifocal society of Old Europe meant the gradual decline of hunting as the primary male role, and did not give adequate expression to male power. Eventually - partly in response to the external threat of invasion from the East - that power found its own expression, and things swung to the opposite extreme. This was the end of a tradition that stretched back perhaps 25,000 years.

A feeling of inevitability about its demise leads to the conclusion that the Old European Goddess culture was not an ideal to look back to, but a phase of human development that included many lessons for today, many elements that now need to be reclaimed, but that had the seeds of its own destruction sown within it. Certainly it did not survive the challenges that arose from about 4000 BCE onwards.

It is here that my narrative ends. 'History' and 'civilisation' have followed; and there is a tendency to see the last 6,000 years as the only part of the human story that counts, though it is but a small portion of the time that people have been on the planet. It has been the 'patriarchal phase'; now, at the beginning of the twenty-first century, it is becoming clear that the seeds of its own destruction are also sown within it - and indeed they are starting to sprout. Its ways no longer work - which is something that men, in particular, are having enormous difficulties in coming to terms with.

At the same time it is worth noting that in modern society, for the first time ever, women no longer have to spend their entire reproductive lives bearing children, and this can be seen as a change as great as the end of the primal hunting role was for men.[701]

In looking for the origins of patriarchy, I have characterised the story of the past few tens of thousands of years as a process based on the interaction of male and female elements in society. A natural balance had always been maintained between the two, but through most of the historical period this balance has been lost and the female has been suppressed. This process is now entering a new phase, a period of transformation. It must, or we shall surely destroy ourselves.

It is scarcely acknowledged, and perhaps mostly overlooked or denied entirely, that patriarchy is as oppressive to most men as it is to most women. On average, men in our society die younger, spend more time in prisons and more time in mental institutions. It is predominantly men who are coerced into military 'service' to fight wars. At home, men are more likely to suffer industrial injury, to have drug- or alcohol-related problems, and generally to feel overburdened with work and responsibility.

If most people in our culture are 'armored' or, in Steve Taylor's words, 'walled off' from one another, this tends to be more true for men than for women - which in turn is the underlying reason for the litany of symptoms listed above. Yes, patriarchy and sexism mean the oppression of women; they do not mean real power and freedom for men, only an unfortunate means of passing on the fears and frustrations arising from their own oppression. Nobody actually wins at all.

Men and women are natural allies in our mutual struggle against this oppression, which is perpetrated and perpetuated by the irrational nature of society itself rather than by any gender, class or conspiratorial clique. When we see clearly, we soon understand that those who have power and property - those who perhaps are envied by the great majority - are as fearful, dissatisfied and unfulfilled as everyone else. If the goal of society is to enable people to realise and achieve their potential as creative, loving human beings, then it fails more or less everyone.

Those who do achieve some measure of fulfilment often do so in spite of the culture's prevailing values and value-systems, rather than being supported and encouraged by them. Seen as a means of enhancing our humanity, modern society simply doesn't work.

One hallmark of patriarchy is the assumption, usually competitive, that one half of any dichotomy is right and the other wrong - and this attitude is fraught with destructiveness. As the Jungian writer Robert A. Johnson puts it, when faced with pairs of opposites - of any sort - we tend to focus on their opposition, rather than accept "the miracle" of paradox.[702] In other words, when faced with two choices which seem to be mutually exclusive, rather than fretting over which is right we have the option of sitting with both and trusting that a fresh answer will emerge. Like counterpoint in music, two contrasting realities can form one whole that is greater than either.

Once, before the great cultural advances of 35,000 years ago, before the technological developments which made life possible through the last ice age, before the beginnings of farming, before the neolithic 'revolution' which included all these things and made from them new ways of life, before the first towns, before the first cities, there was one basic reality to human life. And afterwards there was the farmer and the herder, the European and the Asiatic, the 'matrist' and the 'patrist', the hunter-gatherer and modern civilisation. We cannot escape from these dichotomies, nor arrive at some compromise that somehow successfully caters for them all. What we can do - taking a 'large leap in evolution' - is to transfer our energy, from opposition to paradox.

This is surely what we need, to usher in a genuine period of transformation: a shift in attitude, so as to be always looking for the elegant solution rather than imposing one point of view over another.

Synthesis and transformation

Transformation is the stuff of life. It is growth, and therefore the dynamics of life itself. It is not quiet and even, like a clock ticking away on an undisturbed mantlepiece; it is something that forms patterns, with highs and lows, and dramatic times of great change. It is the coming together of different elements to form something new, something more than just the elements combined. It is an ongoing process marked by critical points of growth.

We can talk of physical, mental or spiritual transformation; of personal transformation, of social and cultural transformation, of global transformation. On every level the essential process is the same - though manifested in infinite ways. And, though we may be able to name the elements and describe their interaction, in every case the spirit of transformation that infuses them and creates that 'something new' is always mysterious and magical, indefinable, paradoxical. We can only trace its progress and note the effects, hoping that its nature can be read between the lines.

The particular paradox which we humans have presented ourselves with is that modern life is more 'advanced', sophisticated and technically accomplished than anything that has ever gone before, and yet in a real sense it is less rewarding, and less secure. A real understanding of the limits placed on our material consumption by environmental realities is desperately needed. And, in an important sense, the way people relate to the environment is mirrored in the way men relate to women.

One hopeful fact is that, in spite of such horrific episodes as the Inquisition, patriarchy has never completely succeeded in stamping out humanity's aspirations for a non-patriarchal world. It is patriarchy that has brought us to our current precarious situation, but all of human evolution has contributed, and every phase has its lessons to be remembered and its hopeful possibilities to be tried again in a new context. Perhaps we are soon to enter another period about which future palaeontologists will say, "This is when hominids first became real human beings." Let us not forget, for instance, that though we are beset by enormous problems such as climate change, in the past it has often been climate change that has driven evolution. And, as Steve Taylor has pointed out:

> There's an important difference between human beings and other forms of life ... In human beings the process of evolution has, in the biologist Julian Huxley's famous phrase, 'become conscious of itself'. For us evolution doesn't have to be just an unfolding natural process. If we're actually aware of the process of evolution it's possible for us, if we so desire, to consciously aid or direct the process.[703]

This is very hopeful. Taylor echoes Huxley and also other pioneering thinkers such as Viktor Schauberger [704] in suggesting that "by consciously working on ourselves, by practising meditation and other 'first-wave' methods of intensifying consciousness-energy, we can push the evolutionary process forward ... and in the process help our species as a whole to do the same." [705]

Such 'conscious working on ourselves' will have to involve the painful reality of pushing through our resistance. It means stepping outside the apparent comfort of our own psychological patterns and irrationalities, facing up to our inner demons, taking on our addictions and neuroses, and accepting full responsibility for our individual contribution to humanity's collective pathology and psychosis. This may prove to be a little more challenging than 'practising meditation' or 'intensifying our consciousness'; but if the intention is there, then yes, we really can become active participants in a new evolutionary shift. And as Bruce Lipton concluded in *The Biology of Belief*:

> Most human violence is neither necessary nor is it inherent ...
> Survival of the Most Loving is the only ethic that will ensure not only a healthy personal life but also a healthy planet. [706]

There is plenty of evidence to show that political hierarchy and economic inequality are harmful to health, both physical and psychological,[707] so that bringing them to an end is, after all, the rational option. In looking forwards, we can only wonder about the ultimate effect that current changes will have, for instance, on family and social structures. It is a time for experiment, and models from palaeolithic and neolithic times are worth exploring afresh for clues as to how we might conduct ourselves in the future.

Bruce Lipton goes further, drawing parallels between our present situation and that facing single cell organisms when, after three and a half billion years of evolution, they faced a crisis of over-population. "Those pressures led to a new and glorious era in evolution," in which single cells joined together to form the first multi-cellular organisms. "The end result [eventually] was humans ..." [708]

Which brings us back to the socialist ideals of the nineteenth century. "What will there be new?" asked Engels more than a hundred years ago, and responded to his own question by highlighting the issue of patriarchy. He looked forward to "a new generation" for whom life and love was free from economic oppression, and "When these people are in the world, they will care precious little what anybody today thinks they ought to do; they will make their own practice." [709]

Such recovery is still possible, however traumatised and pathological human behaviour may have become, however much cruelty and destruction may have been meted out. Indeed, one of the most remarkable things about human beings is our ability to come through the most appalling situations and still lead functional, creative lives. This is true both individually and collectively. As a result, the prevailing patriarchal values are now being challenged, tools for psychological recovery are now becoming available, dealing with environmental degradation is now finding its way onto the political agenda.

Of course there is still the increased power of weaponry, the growing momentum of inappropriate development and economic exploitation, the extinction of cultures, species and habitats ... There is a very big choice to be made, over the next few years. Generations already alive must make that choice. My hope is that this book will help to clarify what the choice is, how it can be made, and its place in the overall context of the human story. In many ways our species has been the most successful ever. It is also in danger of becoming one of the most short-lived. The question is whether we can fully activate our extraordinary intelligence, make use of the information already available to us, and adapt to meet the challenges that are already fast arriving.

Bibliography

Geoffrey Ashe, 'Dawn Behind the Dawn', Henry Holt & Co (USA) 1992.

Anne Baring and Jules Cashford, 'The Myth of the Goddess', Arkana/Penguin Books 1993.

Hugh Brody, 'The Other Side of Eden - hunter-gatherers, farmers and the shaping of the world', Douglas & McIntyre (Canada) 2000; English edition Faber & Faber 2001.

Bruce Chatwin, 'The Songlines', Jonathan Cape 1987.

Barry Cunliffe (ed), 'The Oxford Illustrated Prehistory of Europe', Oxford University Press 1994.

Elizabeth Gould Davis, 'The First Sex', G.P.Putnam (USA) 1971/ Penguin Books 1972.

James DeMeo, 'Saharasia', Orgone Biophysical Research Lab (USA) 1998.

Margaret Ehrenberg, 'Women in Prehistory', British Museum Press 1989.

Riane Eisler, 'The Chalice and the Blade - our history, our future', Harper Collins (USA)1988.

Friedrich Engels, 'The Origins of the Family, Private Property and The State' (4th edition) 1891; English edition Camelot Press 1940.

Clive Gamble, 'Timewalkers - the prehistory of global colonization', Alex Sutton (USA) 1993.

Marija Gimbutas, 'The Civilization of the Goddess - the world of Old Europe', Harper San Francisco (USA) 1991.

Harvey Jackins, 'The List', Rational Island Publishers (USA), (2nd edition) 1997.

Julian Jaynes, 'The Origin of Consciousness in the Breakdown of the Bicameral Mind', Houghton Mifflin (USA) 1976.

Kenny Klein, 'The Flowering Rod - Men, sex, and spirituality' , Delphi Press (USA) 1993.

Marek Kohn, 'As We Know It - coming to terms with an evolved mind' , Granta Publications 1999.

Richard Leakey and Roger Lewin, 'Origins Reconsidered - in search of what makes us human', Little, Brown & Co 1982.

Bruce Lipton, 'The Biology of Belief', Elite Books (USA) 2005; English edition Cygnus Books 2005.

Nicholas R. Mann, 'His Story - masculinity in the post-patriarchal world', Llewellyn Publications (USA) 1995.
Alexei Panshin, 'The Paleolithic Indo-Europeans', published on-line at www.enter.net/~torve/trogholm/wonder/indoeuropean, 2004.
Richard Rudgley, 'Lost Civilisations of the Stone Age'1999; US edition Touchstone Books, 2000.
Mary Jane Sherfey, 'The Nature and Evolution of Female Sexuality', Random House (USA), 1966/1972.
Malidoma Patrice Somé, 'Ritual - power, healing & community', Swan Raven & Co (USA) 1993; English edition Gateway Books 1996.
Hyemeyohsts Storm, 'Lightningbolt', Ballantine Books (USA) 1994.
Christopher Stringer and Clive Gamble, 'In Search of the Neanderthals - solving the puzzle of human origins', Thames and Hudson 1993.
Rogan P. Taylor, 'The Death and Resurrection Show - from Shaman to Superstar', Anthony Blond 1985.
Steve Taylor, 'The Fall', O Books 2005.
Colin Tudge, 'Neanderthals Bandits and Farmers - how agriculture really began', Weidenfield & Nicolson 1998.

Notes & References

References to books included in the bibliography are here referred to only by author and title. Publishing details are in the bibliography.

1 'The World Defeat of the Female Sex'

101 Riane Eisler, 'The Chalice and the Blade', see page 3.

102 Richard Leakey, 'Origins Reconsidered' page xvii.

103 Steve Taylor, 'The Fall' page 32.

104 Richard Rudgley, 'Lost Civilisations of the Stone Age' page 34.

105 Riane Eisler, 'The Chalice and the Blade' page 21.

106 Anne Baring and Jules Cashford, 'The Myth of the Goddess' page xii.

107 Germaine Greer, 'Worlds Apart', The Guardian, Tuesday 3 July 2007.

108 Marek Kohn, 'As We Know It' page 283.

109 Margaret Ehrenberg, 'Women in Prehistory' page 43.

110 Ditto, see page 49.

111 Friedrich Engels, 'The Origins of the Family, Private Property and The State' page 49.

112 Hugh Brody, 'The Other Side of Eden' page 5.

113 Malidoma Patrice Somé, 'Ritual - power, healing & community'.

114 Steve Taylor, 'The Fall' page iii.

115 James DeMeo, 'Saharasia' pages 11-12.

116 Ditto, pages 225-228.

117 Paul Mellars, 'The Upper Palaeolithic Revolution', in 'The Oxford Illustrated Prehistory of Europe' page 76.

118 Ljilja Cvekic, 'Prehistoric Women had Passion for Fashion', Reuters 12 November 2007.

119 Riane Eisler, 'The Chalice and the Blade' page13, quoting Marija Gimbutas.

120 Richard Rudgley, 'Lost Civilisations of the Stone Age', see chapters 4 and 5. For Marija Gimbutas' theory concerning the Old European sacred script, see 'The Civilization of the Goddess' chapter 8.

121 Andrew Sharratt, in 'The Oxford Illustrated Prehistory of Europe' page 175.

122 Lewis H. Morgan, 'Ancient Society' , 1877. His work was drawn on extensively by Friedrich Engels in writing 'The Origins of the Family, Private Property and The State'.

123 Friedrich Engels, 'The Origins of the Family, Private Property and The State', see chapter 2

124 Harvey Jackins notes that to some extent this system persisted into the twentieth century: "Polynesians from various parts of the Pacific ... [have] told me how marvellous it was not to 'belong' to their 'natural parents' as we seemed to in Western cultures, but to have every adult in the village available as a 'parent'. Whenever they chose, they moved from one house to another, knowing that their 'original' parents had no particular claim on them and that they would be welcomed just for being themselves in every household into which they moved." Harvey Jackins, 'The Longer View', Rational Island Publishers 1987, page 26.

125 Friedrich Engels, 'The Origins of the Family, Private Property and The State', see pages 26-28.

126 Ditto, see pages 38-41.

127 Ditto, see chapter 2.

128 Ditto, see pages 93-96.

129 Hyemeyohsts Storm, 'Lightningbolt', see pages 409-423.

130 Friedrich Engels, 'The Origins of the Family, Private Property and The State', see chapters 5 and 6; also (e.g.) Elizabeth Gould Davis, 'The First Sex' chapters 11 and 12.

131 Friedrich Engels, 'The Origins of the Family, Private Property and The State' page 23.

132 Ditto, page 57.

133 See, for instance, 'Early hominids dug food from the ground', New Scientist, 12 December 1985.

134 Friedrich Engels, 'The Origins of the Family, Private Property and The State' page 158.

135 See Marija Gimbutas, 'The Civilization of the Goddess' page 394: "Cattle (pecus) were the main possession that had the meaning of our word money. Hence, the Latin word for money, pecunia".

136 Friedrich Engels, 'The Origins of the Family, Private Property and The State' pages183-184.

137 Richard Leakey, 'Human Origins' (Hamish Hamilton 1982) page 78.

138 For a very good summary of Dart's discoveries and interpretations, and their subsequent refutation, see Bruce Chatwin, 'The Songlines' pages 235-238.

139 Nick Cater, 'Why Competition is the Final Frontier', Mendip Messenger 21 May 2008.

140 See, for instance, Colin Tudge, 'Neanderthals Bandits and Farmers' page 26. He quotes Clive Gamble and Matt Ridley in support of his contention that 'human beings are innately co-operative creatures'.

141 Riane Eisler, 'The Chalice and the Blade' page xvii.

142 Ballantine, New York. See Riane Eisler, 'The Chalice and the Blade' pages 138-139.

143 Riane Eisler, 'The Chalice and the Blade' page 38.

144 James DeMeo, 'Saharasia' page 107, note to 'The World Behaviour Map'.

145 Steve Taylor, 'The Fall' page 249.

2 Europe (1): Neanderthals, Hunter-Gatherers and Farmers

201 Alexei Panshin, 'The Paleolithic Indo-Europeans' page 7, based on Stephen Oppenheimer, 'The Real Eve'.

202 Stringer & Gamble, 'In Search of the Neanderthals' page 179.

203 Alexei Panshin, 'The Paleolithic Indo-Europeans' page 6.

204 Ditto, page 10.

205 Ditto, page 11.

206 Sarah Bunney, 'Mammoth killers could have done it with stone', New Scientist February 3 1990. Tests carried out by George Firson of the University of Wyoming on elephant carcasses show that palaeolithic weapons would have been quite capable of killing a mammoth.

207 Colin Tudge, 'Neanderthals Bandits and Farmers' pages 21-22. 'Pleistocene' refers to the most recently completed geological epoch (1.8 million to 12,000 years ago), characterised as 'the age of mammals' including giant mammals or 'megafauna', and also humans.

208 Clive Gamble, 'Timewalkers' page 216.

209 Stringer & Gamble, 'In Search of the Neanderthals', see pages 211-212.

210 Clive Gamble, 'Timewalkers' page 120.

211 Stringer & Gamble, 'In Search of the Neanderthals', see pages 212-213.

212 Ezra Zubrow, quoted in Stringer & Gamble, 'In Search of the Neanderthals' page 194. See also Richard Leakey, 'Origins Reconsidered' pages 234-235.

213 The discovery in Slovenia of a 45,000-year-old Neanderthal flute which could have produced "a wide range of pentatonic melodies" was reported in 'The Independent on Sunday', 25 February 1996.

214 *Richard Leakey, 'Origins Reconsidered' page 232.*

215 *Marek Kohn, 'As We Know It', see page 180.*

216 *Stringer & Gamble, 'In Search of the Neanderthals' page193. Paul Graves quote from 'Current Anthropology' 1991.*

217 *Stringer & Gamble, 'In Search of the Neanderthals', see pages 91-93.*

218 *As reported in 'The Week' February 28 2009, page 17.*

219 *Dan Jones, 'The Neanderthal Within', New Scientist 3 March 2007; quoting Bruce Lahn (Proceedings of the National Academy of Sciences, vol 103 page 18178).*

220 *Colin Tudge, 'Neanderthals Bandits and Farmers' page 15.*

221 *Stringer & Gamble, 'In Search of the Neanderthals' pages 174-175.*

222 *Ditto, page 208.*

223 *Ditto, page 204.*

224 *Marek Kohn, 'As We Know It' page 180.*

225 *Richard Leakey, 'Origins Reconsidered' page 228.*

226 *Marek Kohn, 'As We Know It' page 181.*

227 *Ditto, quoting Jared Diamond. Others have used similar epithets.*

228 *Jared Diamond, 'The Great Leap forward - Dawn of the Human Race' in 'Discover - the World of Science' May 1989; quoted in 'The Only Planet of Choice' (see below, chapter 5) page 162.*

229 *See Richard Leakey, 'Origins Reconsidered' chapter 10.*

230 *See, for instance, 'Human jaw hints at African trek', Sarah Bunney, in 'Science' 30 October 1993, page 15; and 'Butchered bodies: food or fad?', New Scientist 26 March 1987, page 29.*

231 *Bruce Chatwin, 'The Songlines' pages 248-249.*

232 *Erik Trinkaus, quoted in 'How our hominid ancestors caught their dinners', New Scientist 14 February 1985, page 25.*

233 *See for instance Richard Leakey, 'Origins Reconsidered', pages 177-199.*

234 *Hugh Brody, 'The Other Side of Eden' page 7.*

235 *Ditto, page 87.*

236 *Ditto*

237 *Bruce Chatwin, 'The Songlines' page 249.*

238 *Hyemeyohsts Storm, 'Lightningbolt' pages 164-166.*

239 *Hugh Brody, 'The Other Side of Eden', see pages 87-89.*

240 *Clive Gamble, 'Timewalkers' page 226, quoting John Mulvaney and*

Isabel McBryde. ('The Chain of Connection', D.J.Mulvaney, in 'Tribes and Boundaries in Australia' ed. N.Peterson, A.I.A.S., Canberra 1976, pages 72-94; 'Goods from Another Country', I.McBryde, in 'Archaeology to 1788' ed. J.Mulvaney and P.White, Waddon Associates, Sydney 1988, pages 253-273).

241 *Bruce Chatwin, 'The Songlines' page 280.*

242 *Nicholas R. Mann, 'His Story' page 30.*

243 *Clive Gamble, 'Timewalkers' pages 1-3.*

244 *There is growing evidence that Homo Erectus could have populated southern Asia considerably earlier; for instance, 'New Scientist' reported in 1994 that fossils from Java had been re-dated to more than 1.6 million years old (Roger Lewin, 'Damburst of humans flooded from Africa', New Scientist 5 March 1994, page 14). Other more tentative datings are earlier still.*

245 *Clive Gamble, 'Timewalkers' pages 116-120.*

246 *Richard Leakey, 'Origins Reconsidered' page 29.*

247 *Clive Gamble, 'Timewalkers' page 182.*

248 *Marek Kohn, 'As We Know It' page 43.*

249 *Richard Rudgley, 'Lost Civilisations of the Stone Age' page 245.*

250 *Clive Gamble, 'Timewalkers' pages 246-247. My emphasis.*

251 *Ditto, see pages 10-11.*

252 *Novelist Elizabeth Marshall Thomas in an appendix to 'Reindeer Moon', William Collins Sons & Co Ltd 1987, based on the work of Russian researcher N.K.Vereshchagin.*

253 *Alexei Panshin, 'The Paleolithic Indo-Europeans' pages 6-7.*

254 *Clive Gamble, 'Timewalkers' page 244.*

255 *Ditto, see page 209.*

256 *Ditto, page 246.*

257 *A.L.Mongait, 'Archaeology in the U.S.S.R.', Moscow (1955); extracts translated and edited by M.W.Thompson (1961) published on-line at rbedrosian.com/Classic/Mongait1.htm, chapter 2.*
This description relates specifically to southern regions of the former USSR (The Crimea, Caucasus and Central Asia), but would not have been dissimilar in other regions where there was "an appreciable growth in the [palaeolithic] population".

3 Europe (2): Goddesses, Gods and the Holy Grail

301 *Geoffrey Ashe, 'Dawn Behind the Dawn' page 12. For Marija Gimbutas' 'build-up of Goddess artifacts and imagery' see 'The Civilization of the Goddess' chapter 7.*

302 *Steve Taylor, 'The Fall' page 47.*

303 *Ditto, page 204.*

304 *Ditto, page 47.*

305 *Riane Eisler, 'The Chalice and the Blade' page 23.*

306 *Ditto, page xvi.*

307 *Ditto, pages 2-6, quoting Edwin James, 'The Cult of the Mother Goddess' (Thames & Hudson 1959).*

308 *Anne Baring and Jules Cashford, 'The Myth of the Goddess' page xi.*

309 *Marija Gimbutas, 'The Civilization of the Goddess' pages 222-223.*

310 *Anne Baring and Jules Cashford, 'The Myth of the Goddess' page 147.*

311 *Ditto, page 8, quoting James Mellaart, 'Catal Huyuk' (McGraw-Hill 1967).*

312 *Alexei Panshin, 'The Paleolithic Indo-Europeans' pages 15-16.*

313 *Richard Rudgley, 'Lost Civilisations of the Stone Age', see pages 26-28.*

314 *Riane Eisler, 'The Chalice and the Blade' page 8, quoting James Mellaart.*

315 *Elizabeth Gould Davis, 'The First Sex' pages 79-80, quoting the work of J.J.Bachofen and U. Bahador Alkin.*

316 *Anne Baring and Jules Cashford, 'The Myth of the Goddess' page xi. See also page 54, quoting Marija Gimbutas, 'The Goddesses and Gods of Old Europe' and 'The Language of the Goddess'.*

317 *See Steven J. Mithen's essay on 'The Mesolithic Age' in 'The Oxford Illustrated Prehistory of Europe'.*

318 *Colin Tudge, 'Neanderthals Bandits and Farmers' page 3.*

319 *Ditto, page 3.*

320 *Richard Rudgley, 'Lost Civilisations of the Stone Age' page 8.*

321 *'Skeletons reveal prehistoric industrial diseases', New Scientist 9 September 1989, page 39.*

322 *Richard Rudgley, 'Lost Civilisations of the Stone Age' pages 36-37.*

323 *Wild grains suitable for cultivation were not restricted to the middle east. Marija Gimbutas points out that "to this day wild wheat, both einkorn and emmer, is found between Greece and Afghanistan, and wild barley still grows between the Aegean basin and Baluchistan". 'The Civilization of the Goddess' page 2.*

324 Ditto, page 43.

325 Margaret Ehrenberg, 'Women in Prehistory', see Chapter 3, pages 77-107.

326 Ditto, page 83.

327 Hugh Brody, 'The Other Side of Eden' page 88.

328 Ditto, page 89.

329 Colin Tudge, 'Neanderthals Bandits and Farmers' page 35.

330 Marija Gimbutas, 'The Civilization of the Goddess' page xi. See also map depicting the spread of farming in Europe, page 6.
Note that the cultivation of crops spread more readily east and west than north and south, due to the need for plants to adapt to differences in climate, seasonal variation and day length which occur with changes in latitude (see Jared Diamond, 'Guns, Germs and Steel', Vintage 1998, chapter 10).

331 See Alasdair Whittle, 'The First Farmers', in 'The Oxford Illustrated Prehistory of Europe', pages 136-166.

332 Often referred to as 'Linearbandkeramik' or LBK. Marija Gimbutas points out that "linear bands do not accurately describe this pottery since its design includes spirals, snakes, meanders, rectangles, concentric squares, triangles, V's, chevrons, two lines, three lines, M's, X's, a.o." 'The Civilization of the Goddess' page 37.

333 Ditto, page 334.

334 Margaret Ehrenberg, 'Women in Prehistory' page 96.

335 Ditto, page 94. For details of LBK longhouse plan and construction see Marija Gimbutas, 'The Civilization of the Goddess' pages 40-41.

336 Margaret Ehrenberg, 'Women in Prehistory' page 98.

337 James DeMeo, 'Saharasia' pages 143-144.

338 Lewis H. Morgan, quoted in Friedrich Engels, 'The Origins of the Family, Private Property and The State' page 50.

339 Riane Eisler, 'The Chalice and the Blade' page 13, quoting Marija Gimbutas, 'Goddesses and Gods of Old Europe' (University of California Press 1982).

340 Friedrich Engels, 'The Origins of the Family, Private Property and The State' page 101.

341 Ditto, page 165.

342 Ronald Hutton, 'The pagan religions of the ancient British isles: their nature and legacy', Basil Blackwell Ltd 1991, page 14.

343 Nicholas R. Mann, 'His Story' page 25. See also Marija Gimbutas, 'The Civilization of the Goddess' pages ix-x.

344 Marija Gimbutas provides an extensive description of the social structure of Old Europe as can be derived from archaeology and linguistics. This does not go into the detail of tribe/clan organisation, but generally supports the description provided by Engels. See 'The Civilization of the Goddess' pages 334-335 and 347.

345 Friedrich Engels, 'The Origins of the Family, Private Property and The State' page 94.

346 Ditto, page 95.

347 See, for instance, Nicholas R. Mann's description of the nature of Celtic warfare as ritual display, during which actual bloodshed was minimal and "If there was a death, then blood-guilt would have been a severe burden for the slayer, requiring assuagement through ritual and economic reparation". Nicholas R. Mann, 'His Story' pages 34-36.

348 Friedrich Engels, 'The Origins of the Family, Private Property and The State' page 106.

349 Riane Eisler, 'The Chalice and the Blade' page 30, quoting Nicolas Platon, 'Crete' (Nagel Publishers 1966).

350 Julian Jaynes, 'The Origin of Consciousness in the Breakdown of the Bicameral Mind' page 209.

351 Riane Eisler, 'The Chalice and the Blade', draft title to chapter 3 (as circulated by Fraser Clark, 'Parallel Youniversity' 2007).

352 This passage relies heavily on Riane Eisler, 'The Chalice and the Blade' chapter 3; quoting Nicolas Platon, 'Crete'.

353 Starhawk, 'The Spiral Dance' (20th Anniversary Edition, Harper Collins 1999) page 27.

354 Marija Gimbutas, 'The Civilization of the Goddess' pages 249-251.

355 Kenny Klein, 'The Flowering Rod' pages 10-11.

356 Anne Baring and Jules Cashford, 'The Myth of the Goddess' page 84, quoting James Mellaart, 'Catal Huyuk' (page 176).

357 Riane Eisler, 'The Chalice and the Blade' page 25.

358 Ditto, page 35.

359 Mary Jane Sherfey, 'The Nature and Evolution of Female Sexuality' page 87

360 Nicholas R. Mann, 'His Story' page 56.

361 Anne Baring and Jules Cashford, 'The Myth of the Goddess' page 156, quoting Gertrude Levy, 'The Gate of Horn' (page 169).

362 Robert A. Johnson, 'He' (Harper Row, revised edition 1989), page 16.

363 Anne Baring and Jules Cashford, 'The Myth of the Goddess' page 163.

364 Ditto, page 164.

365 For Marija Gimbutas' detailed description of this, based on the archaeology of the period 4,300-2,500 BCE, see 'The Civilization of the Goddess' chapter 10.

366 Anne Baring and Jules Cashford, 'The Myth of the Goddess' page 157.

367 Kenny Klein, 'The Flowering Rod' pages 42-47.

368 Landscape monuments were not a new phenomenon, though the megalithic structures of western Europe date back to before 4000 BCE and represent a culture which was essentially egalitarian, whilst "the megalithic tombs ... continue to speak of the permanent association of the kin groups with their ancestral lands and ancestors": Marija Gimbutas, 'The Civilization of the Goddess' page 184.
The kurgan mounds were the first to be constructed primarily to enclose high-ranking burials, and may have been the precursors of bronze age round barrows - which in the west represented a shift to patriarchal culture. See Nicholas R. Mann, 'His Story' pages 64ff.

369 Andrew Sharratt, in 'The Oxford Illustrated Prehistory of Europe', see page 175.

370 Riane Eisler, 'The Chalice and the Blade' pages 43-44, quoting James Mellaart, 'The Neolithic of the Near East' (Scribner 1975).

371 Marija Gimbutas, 'The Civilization of the Goddess' page 43.

372 Ditto, page 371.

373 Friedrich Engels, 'The Origins of the Family, Private Property and The State', see chapter 4

374 Elizabeth Gould Davis, 'The First Sex' page 195.

375 Friedrich Engels, 'The Origins of the Family, Private Property and The State' page 59.

376 Ditto, see chapter 5.

377 Steve Taylor, 'The Fall' page 207.

378 For a detailed account of this process see 'The Jesus Mysteries', Timothy Freke and Peter Gandy (Thorsons/Harper Collins,1999).

4 Palaeopsychology

401 *Re-evaluation Counselling ('RC'), i.e. Co-counselling. This estimate appeared in Harvey Jackins, 'The Human Side of Human Beings' (Rational Island Publishers 1963), page 59.*

402 *Riane Eisler, 'The Chalice and the Blade' page 39.*

403 *James DeMeo, 'Saharasia' page 24.*

404 *Mary Jane Sherfey, 'The Nature and Evolution of Female Sexuality' page 112.*

405 *Ditto, page 52, my emphasis.*

406 *Ditto, pages 112-113.*

407 *Ditto, page 139 (footnote).*

408 *Ditto, page 139.*

409 *James DeMeo, 'Saharasia' page 24, quoting Sigmund Freud.*

410 *Stuart Wavell, 'A Brush with Human History', Sunday Times, 31 December 1995.*

411 *James DeMeo, 'Saharasia' pages 399-400.*

412 *Ditto, page 47.*

413 *Ditto, pages 44-45.*

414 *Ditto, pages 6-7.*

415 *'Did Neanderthal babies have bigger brains than ours?', Sarah Bunney in New Scientist 29 May 1986, page 28.*

416 *Richard Leakey, 'Origins Reconsidered' page 145.*

417 *James DeMeo, 'Saharasia' page 48, quoting Wilhelm Reich.*

418 *Harvey Jackins, 'The Postulates of Co-Counselling' (Nos 10-13); included as an appendix to 'The List'.*

419 *Malidoma Patrice Somé, 'Ritual - power, healing & community' page 97.*

420 *Rogan Taylor, 'The Death & Resurrection Show' page 21.*

421 *See, for example, Bruce Lipton, 'The Biology of Belief' page 150: "The processing of information in the forebrain, the centre of executive reasoning and logic, is significantly slower than the reflex activity controlled by the hindbrain. In an emergency, the faster the information processing, the more likely the organism will survive ... [but] while it is necessary that stress signals repress the slower processing conscious mind to enhance survival, it comes at a cost ... diminished conscious awareness and reduced intelligence".*

422 Harvey Jackins, from a talk quoted by Micheline Mason in 'Inclusion: The Intentional Rebuilding of Communities', Present Time April 1999.

423 Ditto.

424 See Tim Jackins, 'Ending War', published on-line at www.rc.org/irp/index.html, 19 June 2006.

425 Julian Jaynes,'The Origin of Consciousness in the Breakdown of the Bicameral Mind' pages 46-47.

426 Harvey Jackins, 'The Postulates of Co-Counselling' (Nos 1-3); included as an appendix to 'The List'.

427 Richard Leakey, 'Origins Reconsidered' page 280.

428 Ditto, page 296, quoting Thomas Hobbes.

429 Ditto, page 297.

430 Ditto, page 285, quoting Cambridge psychologist Nicholas Humphrey.

431 Ditto, page 293.

432 Ditto, page 258.

433 Ditto, page 67.

434 Rogan Taylor, 'The Death & Resurrection Show' page 14.

435 Richard Leakey, 'Origins Reconsidered' pages 306-307.

436 Anne Baring and Jules Cashford, 'The Myth of the Goddess' page 8.

437 Nicholas R. Mann, 'His Story' page 32.

438 Richard Rudgley, 'Lost Civilisations of the Stone Age' pages 157-158.

439 Elizabeth Fisher, 'Women's Creation', (McGraw-Hill 1975). Quoted by Ursula K. le Guin (below).

440 Ursula K. le Guin, in an essay 'The Carrier Bag Theory of Fiction', 1986.

441 Margaret Ehrenberg, 'Women in Prehistory' pages 46-48.

442 Julian Jaynes,'The Origin of Consciousness in the Breakdown of the Bicameral Mind' page 53.

443 This is not to say that the more egotistical a person is, the more conscious they are; egotism is one result of distress patterns, as discussed earlier in this chapter. Human consciousness arises from the 'inner I' and the mental space which it inhabits - and like our other attributes such as intelligence, physical strength or athletic ability, the use to which it is put can be either positive or negative.

444 Robert A.Johnson, 'Inner Work', Harper & Row (USA) 1986, page 8.

445 Ditto, page 6.

446 Julian Jaynes,'The Origin of Consciousness in the Breakdown of the Bicameral Mind' page 49.

447 Ditto, page 54.

448 Ditto, page 55.

449 John McCrone, 'Inner Voices, Distant Memories', New Scientist 29 January 1994.

5 Asia (1): The Indo-European Question

501 Natalia I. Shishlina, 'Early Herders of the Eurasian Steppe', published on-line at www.penn.museum/documents/publications/expedition/PDFs/43-1/Early%20Herders.pdf

502 Riane Eisler, 'The Chalice and the Blade' page 48.

503 Alexei Panshin, 'The Paleolithic Indo-Europeans' pages 1-2.

504 Ditto, page 20.

505 Marija Gimbutas, 'The Civilization of the Goddess' pages 354-355.

506 Geoffrey Ashe, 'Dawn Behind the Dawn' page 21.

507 See Colin Renfrew's 'Archaeology and Language' (Jonathan Cape 1987), and Marija Gimbutas' own undestanding that there was "considerable knowledge of agricultural terminology in the European branch of the Indo-Europeans": 'The Civilization of the Goddess' page 395.

508 Riane Eisler, 'The Chalice and the Blade' page 43.

509 Ditto, see page xxii.

510 See, for instance, David W. Anthony and Dorcas R.Brown, 'Samara Valley Project', published on-line at
www.users.hartwick.edu/anthonyd/introduction.html
"Western archaeologists' understanding of Bronze Age subsistence economies in the steppes is improving with the increasing number of international projects. In the past, Western attempts to integrate steppe economic prehistory with the prehistories of neighbouring regions in Europe and the Near East have suffered from five problems: 1. the essential publications are in Russian and Ukranian; 2. most Soviet and post-Soviet excavations have not systematically collected palaeo-botanical data so we have little information on prehistoric agriculture; 3. theories of culture change in Soviet and post-Soviet archaeology depend too much on simplistic mechanisms of climate change and migration, neglecting

internal political, social and economic factors; 4. a linear model of evolutionary economic stages has been imposed on steppe prehistory, obscuring the rich variety of steppe economic adaptations; and finally 5. steppe archaeology has focused on individual sites, primarily cemeteries, rather than considering whole landscapes".

511 *Alexei Panshin, 'The Paleolithic Indo-Europeans' pages 2-3.*

512 *Ditto, page 5.*

513 *Ditto, page 4.*

514 *Ditto, page 14.*

515 *Ditto, page 12.*

516 *Ditto, page 8.*

517 *Riane Eisler, 'The Chalice and the Blade' page 48; quoting Marija Gimbutas, 'The First Wave of Kurgan Steppe Pastoralists' (The Journal of Indo-European Studies, winter 1977)*

518 *Colin Tudge, 'Neanderthals Bandits and Farmers' page 8.*

519 *Bruce Chatwin, 'The Songlines' page 191.*

520 *Julian Borger, 'Scorched Earth Policy', Guardian Weekly 18 May 2007.*

521 *Colin Tudge, 'Neanderthals Bandits and Farmers' pages 8-10.*

522 *Ditto, page 9.*

523 *V. Gordon Childe, quoted in James DeMeo, 'Saharasia' page 210.*

524 *Julian Jaynes, 'The Origin of Consciousness in the Breakdown of the Bicameral Mind', see pages 137-138.*

525 *James DeMeo, 'Saharasia' pages 102-103.*

526 *Ditto, page 103.*

527 *Ditto, page 4.*

528 *Steve Taylor, 'The Fall' page 108.*

529 *Ditto, pages 114-115.*

530 *Ditto, page 303.*

531 *Ditto, page 111.*

532 *Ditto, page 112.*

533 *Ditto, page 109, quoting anthropologist Lucien Levy-Bruhl.*

534 *Anne Baring and Jules Cashford, 'The Myth of the Goddess', page 154.*

535 *Hyemeyohsts Storm, 'Lightningbolt' page 298.*

536 *Steve Taylor, 'Transcending the Madness of the Ego' in Kindred Spirit, January/February 2009, page 77.*

537 *James DeMeo, 'Saharasia' page 86.*

538 Ditto, page 86.

539 See David W. Anthony, 'The Horse, the Wheel and Language', Princeton University Press, quoted in David W.Anthony and Dorcas R. Brown, 'Samara Valley Project', published on-line at www.users.hartwick.edu/anthonyd/introduction.html

540 James DeMeo, 'Saharasia' pages 317, 319.

541 Marija Gimbutas, 'The Civilization of the Goddess' page 352.

542 James DeMeo, 'Saharasia' page 259.

543 Alexei Panshin, 'The Paleolithic Indo-Europeans' page 12.

544 Ditto, pages 9-10.

545 Steve Taylor, 'The Fall' page 28.

546 Alexei Panshin, 'The Paleolithic Indo-Europeans' page 12.

547 A.L.Mongait, 'Archaeology in the U.S.S.R.', Moscow (1955); extracts translated and edited by M.W.Thompson (1961) published on-line at rbedrosian.com/Classic/Mongait1.htm, chapter 5.

548 Jeannine Davis-Kimball, 'Ancient nomads, female warriors and priestesses', published on-line at www.popgen.well.ox.ac.uk/eurasia/htdocs/davis.html

549 Friedrich Engels, 'The Origins of the Family, Private Property and The State' pages 58-59.

550 Ditto, page 181.

551 Ditto, pages 57-58.

552 A.L.Mongait, 'Archaeology in the U.S.S.R.', Moscow (1955); extracts translated and edited by M.W.Thompson (1961) published on-line at rbedrosian.com/Classic/Mongait1.htm, chapter 3.

553 See, for instance, Elizabeth Gould Davis' review of 'The Women of Greece and Italy' in 'The First Sex' chapter 12.

554 Friedrich Engels, 'The Origins of the Family, Private Property and The State' page 109.

6 Asia (2): The Ancient Cultural Seedbed

601 Alexei Panshin, 'The Paleolithic Indo-Europeans' page 9.

602 Geoffrey Ashe, 'Dawn Behind the Dawn', see chapter 2.

603 Steve Taylor, 'The Fall' page 202.

604 Rogan Taylor, 'The Death and Resurrection Show' page 15.

605 Ditto, page 16.

606 Ditto, page 17.
607 Ditto, page 18.
608 Alexei Panshin, 'The Paleolithic Indo-Europeans' pages 8-9.
609 Geoffrey Ashe, 'Dawn Behind the Dawn' page 28.
610 Rogan Taylor, 'The Death and Resurrection Show' page 17.
611 A.L.Mongait, 'Archaeology in the U.S.S.R.', Moscow (1955); extracts translated and edited by M.W.Thompson (1961) published on-line at rbedrosian.com/Classic/ Mongait1.htm, chapter 2.
612 Rogan Taylor, 'The Death and Resurrection Show' page 18.
613 Geoffrey Ashe, 'Dawn Behind the Dawn' page 28.
614 Ditto, pages 29-30.
615 Ditto, page 13.
616 Richard Rudgley, 'Lost Civilisations of the Stone Age', see page 100.
617 Ditto, page 29.
618 Geoffrey Ashe, 'Dawn Behind the Dawn', see pages 22-23.
619 Ditto, page 55.
620 Ditto, see chapter 13.
621 Ditto, page 52.
622 David W.Anthony and Dorcas R. Brown, 'Samara Valley Project', published on-line at www.users.hartwick.edu/anthonyd/introduction.html
623 Geoffrey Ashe, 'Dawn Behind the Dawn' page 16.
624 Ditto, page 213.
625 Ditto, page 36, quoting Nicholas Roerich.
626 Ditto, page 37, quoting Mircea Eliade.
627 Ditto, page 73.
628 Ros Winstanley, workshop notes entitled 'Sacred Geometry - Blueprint for Creation', Part 1 ('Before the Beginning') page 8.
629 Ditto, see Part 3 ('The Seed of Life').
630 Ditto, see Parts 1-3.
631 Julian Jaynes, 'The Origin of Consciousness in the Breakdown of the Bicameral Mind', see pages 59-61.
632 Geoffrey Ashe, 'Dawn Behind the Dawn' pages 68-69.
633 Ditto, pages 73-74.
634 Ditto, page 195.
635 Ditto, page 201.

636 *Steve Taylor, 'The Fall', see page 108.*

637 *Riane Eisler, 'The Chalice and the Blade' page 49; quoting Marija Gimbutas, 'The Beginning of the Bronze Age in Europe' (in the Journal of Indo-European Studies, 1973).*

638 *Ditto, page xx.*

639 *Geoffrey Ashe, 'Dawn Behind the Dawn', p vii.*

640 *Richard Rudgley, 'Lost Civilisations of the Stone Age' page 12.*

641 *Elizabeth Gould Davis, 'The First Sex' page 15. Riane Eisler notes "Like books by other women trying to reclaim their past with no institutions or learned colleagues for support, Davis's book has been criticised for veering into strange, if not downright esoteric, flights of fancy. But despite their flaws - and perhaps precisely because they did not conform to accepted scholarly traditions - books like this intuitively foreshadow a study of history in which the status of women and so-called feminine values would become central." (Riane Eisler, 'The Chalice and the Blade' page 149).*

642 *Palden Jenkins (ed), 'The Only Planet of Choice', Gateway Books 1993.*

643 *'The Only Planet of Choice' page 165. The questioner was asking for channelled information about "evolved civilisations on this planet millions of years ago". He didn't get it; the answer was that people this long ago were not technologically advanced, but they had human souls nonetheless. "... 20 million years ago there were beings with soul on this planet." 20 million years is a very long time ago. Science currently puts the evolutionary split with chimpanzees at only 5-10 million years ago; but archaeological finds are consistently extending the chronology of human evolution backwards, and this material is not necessarily at serious variance with archaeology.*

644 *Ditto, pages 170-181.*

645 *James DeMeo, 'Saharasia' page 346.*

646 *Ditto, page 317, quoting M.P.Petrov.*

647 *Ditto, page 357, quoting E.F.Huntingdon, 'The Pulse of Asia' (Houghton-Mifflin NY, 1907).*

648 *Hyemeyohsts Storm, 'Lightningbolt' page 407, quoting the native American teacher Estcheemah.*

7 Recap: 'The Past is the Key to our Future'

701 *Tom Graves, author of 'The Way of Wyrd', in a talk given at the Glastonbury Assembly Rooms, 17 October 1996.*

702 *Robert A. Johnson, 'Owning Your Own Shadow' (Harper Collins 1991), pages 85-86:*
"To transfer our energy from opposition to paradox is a very large leap in evolution. To engage in opposition is to be ground to bits by the insolubility of life's problems and events ... To transform opposition into paradox is to allow both sides of an issue, both pairs of opposites, to exist in equal dignity and worth ... If I can stay with my conflicting impulses long enough, the two opposing forces will teach each other something and produce an insight that serves them both".

703 *Steve Taylor, 'The Fall', page 305.*

704 *Schauberger was an Austrian scientist and inventor in the first half of the twentieth century, who pointed out that there is a natural process central to all life whereby "cyclical changes in temperature create the conditions suitable for the evolution of new life forms or the renewal of existing ones". He believed that nature has an evolutionary 'purpose' - "to facilitate the emergence of higher life forms, to promote greater complexity of inter-relationships and to raise the level of consciousness". Whether or not this is a 'purpose' in any conscious sense, he was certainly right to state that "highly ordered systems lose their stability when their environment suffers deterioration". He predicted that "a decrease in biodiversity in Nature would bring an increase in violence and a degradation of spiritual qualities in the human community". See Alick Bartholomew, 'Hiddden Nature - the startling insights of Viktor Schauberger' (Floris Books 2003) pages 34-35.*

705 *Steve Taylor, 'The Fall' page 305.*

706 *Bruce Lipton, 'The Biology of Belief' pages 201-202.*

707 *Marek Kohn, 'As We Know It', see pages 284-288.*

708 *Bruce Lipton, 'The Biology of Belief' page 199.*

709 *Friedrich Engels, 'The Origins of the Family, Private Property and The State' pages 89-90.*

Index